Prayer Book Studies
Volume Seven

Trial-use Prayers and Christian Initiation
Revisited, Issues 25-26s

Edited by
Derek A. Olsen

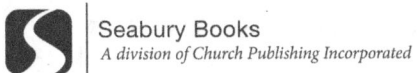
Seabury Books
A division of Church Publishing Incorporated

Copyright © 2026 The Domestic and Foreign Missionary Society of the Protestant Episcopal Church in the United States of America

The English text of the liturgies presented in this book is in the public domain and is freely available for quotation without restriction.

Unless otherwise noted, Scripture quotations are from The New Revised Standard Version Bible, copyright © 1989 National Council of the Churches of Christ in the United States of America. Used by permission. All rights reserved worldwide.

Seabury Books
19 East 34th Street
New York, NY 10016
www.churchpublishing.org

Seabury Books is an imprint of Church Publishing Incorporated.

Cover design by Newgen
Typeset by Integra Software Services Pvt. Ltd.

ISBN 978-1-64065-939-1 (paperback)
ISBN 978-1-64065-940-7 (hardback)
ISBN 978-1-64065-941-4 (eBook)

Library of Congress Control Number: 2025945265

CONTENTS

Introduction vii

Prayer Book Studies 25: Prayers, Thanksgivings, and Litanies

Introduction 3
  Scope of the Collection 3
  The Nature of Common Prayer 4
  The Announcing of Prayers 4
  The Meaning of Intercessory Prayer 5
  Style 8
  Arrangement 11
  The Litany and Other Prayers 12
  General Intercessions from The Holy Eucharist 1970 13
  A History of Intercessory Prayer 13
  The Drafting Committee 13

In Contemporary Language 14
  Concerning the use of Occasional Prayers 14
  Index of Titles 14
  Prayers for the World 18
  Prayers for the Church 20
  Prayers for the State 25
  Prayers for the Social Order 28
  Prayers for the Natural Order 32
  Prayers for Family and Personal Life 34
  Other Prayers 41
  Thanksgivings 46
  Litanies 51

In Traditional Language 65
  Prayers 65
  Thanksgivings 77

The Litany and other Prayers from the Prayer Book of 1928 78

General Intercessions from the Holy Eucharist 1970 84

A History of Intercessory Prayer in Christian Worship 97

Appendices ... 102
A Selected Bibliography ... 102
Key to Abbreviations ... 104
Index of Sources ... 104
Disposition of the Prayers, Thanksgivings, and Litanies
of the 1928 Prayer Book ... 111
Acknowledgments ... 115
General Index ... 116

Prayer Book Studies 26: Holy Baptism

Preface ... 129

Historical Background ... 129

Statement of Agreed Positions ... 130
A. Concerning Baptism ... 130
B. Concerning a post-baptismal Affirmation of Vows ... 131

The Structure of the Rites ... 132
Concerning the Service ... 132

Holy Baptism ... 133
Presentation of the Candidates ... 134
Presentation of Adults and Older Children ... 134
Presentation of Infants ... 134
Profession of Faith and Commitment ... 135
Blessing of the Water ... 137
Blessing of the Chrism ... 138
The Baptism ... 139
Affirmation of Baptismal Vows ... 140
Alternative Ending ... 140
Conditional Baptism ... 140
Emergency Baptism ... 140
Additional Directions and Suggestions ... 141

A Form for Confirmation or the Laying-On of Hands by the Bishop with the Affirmation of Baptismal Vows ... 143
Concerning the Service ... 143
A Form for Confirmation or the Laying-On of Hands by the
Bishop with the Affirmation of Baptismal Vows ... 143
Profession of Faith and Commitment ... 144
Dedication to Mission ... 145
Alternative Ending ... 146

Supplement to Prayer Book Studies 26: Holy Baptism

Foreword 149
Author's Preface 150
Introductory 151

   Some Basic Theological Meanings 152

   A Sketch of Historical Development 154
      A. The New Testament 154
      B. The Early Church 155
      C. Adaptation I: The Delegation of Ministries ... 158
      D. Adaptation II: The Division of the Rite 160
      E. The Churches of the Reformation 163
      F. Anglicanism 164

   The Situation Now: The Breakdown of "Christendom" 166

   Where Questions are Being Felt: (1) Infant Baptism 168

   Where Questions are Being Felt: (2) Confirmation 173
      A. The Inherent Instability of the Anglican Pattern 174
      B. Theological Confusion 180
      C. Pastoral Problems 184

   Where Questions are Being Felt: (3) First Communion ... 187

   The Dynamics of Becoming 191
      A. The Dynamism of Western Culture 191
      B. The Prophetic Christian Message 192
      C. The Generations and Rites of Passage 193

   The Proposed Rite: Some Principles 194
   The Shape of the Proposed Rite 196
   Baptism as the One Rite of Initiation 196
   Being and Becoming 197

   The Proposed Rite: A Commentary 199
      A. Holy Baptism 201
      B. Affirmation of Baptismal Vows 206

Bibliography 209

INTRODUCTION

The Series as a Whole

The *Prayer Book Studies* (PBS) series documents the 26-year process of study and conversation that led to the adoption of the American 1979 Book of Common Prayer. It falls broadly into two parts, distinguished by the use of Roman numerals and Arabic numerals. PBS I-XVII were published by the members of the Standing Liturgical Commission between 1950 and 1966 to communicate research and draft liturgies leading toward a revision process; PBS 18-29 were published by the various drafting committees between 1970 and 1976 once the revision process was formally begun and the earlier drafts were being transformed into new usable liturgies leading up to the adoption of the new prayer book in 1979. Finally, PBS 30 and its commentary were added in 1989 to discuss inclusive and expansive language for God for further liturgical efforts.

Context of these Studies

These studies belong to the second series of *Prayer Book Studies*, those using Arabic numerals for their numbering (PBS 18-29), and that followed the kick-off of a formal revision process with the 1967 General Convention. Within these eleven studies, the first seven (PBS 18-24), containing the most critical materials for public worship and pastoral use, were all published in 1970. The rites within these studies, shorn of their exposition, would be printed as *Services for Trial Use*, also known as "the Green Book." The next four (with two supplements) were published in 1973. These would be collected with the preceding materials into *Authorized Services 1973*, also known as "the Zebra Book" for its striped cover. The final study in this Second Series (PBS 29) is the sole publication in 1976 introducing the complete set of new rites to The Episcopal Church.

In contrast with the first series, a wide range of voices are brought into the conversation as both drafters and readers. The preface to the first of the new studies, PBS 18, describes the processes followed by the Standing Liturgical Commission, the drafting committees, reader-consultants, and the Editorial Committee, and should be consulted for full details.

At the same time, the timeline for completing these studies and their liturgies was greatly compressed. While some work on the First Series had been ongoing since the publication of the 1928 Book of Common Prayer, all of the work here—building on and informed by the work of the First Series—had to occur at lightning speed.

One telltale sign of the haste and subsequent disorganization present within this period is the wide range of formatting choices between the studies issued in this period. The choices of fonts for text and headings, the formatting of headings, and the presence or absence of color are entirely inconsistent between studies, leading to an impression of speed and chaos across the material.

Finally—and contributing even more to the pressure on the committees—all of the rites appear in contemporary language (now known as Rite II) rather than the Elizabethan/Jacobean idiom that had been used for all of the preceding liturgical work. Several rites, of course, appear in both (Rites I and II).

These Studies

PBS 25

The first study in this volume contains the proposed Prayers, Thanksgivings, and Litanies. The text edited here is that of the hardbound volume from 1973 rather than the pamphlet of 1970; this later edition contains some further additions, not included in the earlier work. A chief feature of this study is the painstaking care taken to document the sources of these prayers—and identifying prayers left out as well. An examination of these sources clarifies the continuing role of the liturgical heritage of the church even in the midst of revision. These are not simply *ad hoc* compositions, but rest upon a deep familiarity with and respect for liturgical works that had come before.

PBS 26

The second study in this volume is—like the study on the Eucharist before—a third attempt to engage the complexity of Christian initiation and the diversity of opinions across the church on its theological and sacramental weight. The unified rite of PBS 18 prompted a special session of the House of Bishops in 1972, followed by a joint meeting with the Standing Liturgical Commission that resulted in three agreed statements on baptism and six agreed statements on post-baptismal affirmation of vows. The rites included in the study do present a unified rite as normative, but a separate confirmation rite is also included.

PBS 26 Supplement

The first supplement appearing within either series, this document—six times longer than the study that it supplements—explains the perspective and intention of the new rites in the face of opposition. It was drafted by three members of the committee but appears under the name of its principal author, the Rev. Dr. Daniel B. Stevick. This very act indicates the diversity of opinions within both the committee and the church, as it allows the other participants to distance themselves from its contents. For any students of the prayer book who wish to understand how Christian initiation was understood and the forces shaping the argument at this point in time, this supplement is an invaluable resource.

PRAYER BOOK STUDIES 25: PRAYERS, THANKSGIVINGS, AND LITANIES

1973

INTRODUCTION

The following collection of prayers has grown out of the work of the Standing Liturgical Commission over a period of more than ten years. Three different drafting committees have been involved, and the opinions of a score of consultants have been embodied in this work. Already even the newest prayers in the collection have been subjected to the beginning of that process of loving wear which makes them common prayer. The publication of this Study invites the process to continue on a wider scale. If some of the new prayers in this anthology are finally included in a future Book of Common Prayer, they should be well broken in.

Scope of the Collection

A brief glance will show that this collection has as its nucleus the Prayers and Thanksgivings of the 1928 American Book of Common Prayer. Not all of the prayers of that book have been included. Those which have been retained appear in two versions. In one version slight emendations have been made by removing archaisms (e.g., vouchsafe, arrogancy, nigh) and phrases which are no longer felt as necessary for sense or rhythm (e.g., most of the interpolated phrases, "we beseech thee"). In the other version of the prayers retained from the 1928 book, a more drastic revision has put them into contemporary language and thought forms. This translation is, of course, a delicate operation. If there are infelicities in what is presented here, it is hoped that they will be revealed by use and corrected in subsequent editions of these prayers. It is perhaps worth reporting that in general the older the prayer, the more recasting was found to be necessary. Prayers which were new in 1928 could almost always be adapted by simply changing pronouns. The vocabulary and thought did not need much alteration.[1] Prayers from earlier centuries often required more radical treatment. In some of these cases, it is better to regard the result as a different prayer on the same subject.

A complete tabulation of the disposition of the prayers of the 1928 Prayer Book appears on page 111.

New prayers have been added: prayers for our enemies, for the family of man, for those who live in cities, for the church in a changing world, for the

---

[1]. Conversely, if it should be desired to change one of the new prayers in this collection from contemporary language into 'thou' style, it can usually be done simply by changing the pertinent pronouns and the corresponding verbs: 'you' to 'thou' and (for example) 'make' to 'makest.'

conservation of natural resources, and many others. These prayers grow out of concerns which press hard upon Christians in the 1970's, and almost certainly will continue to do so in the foreseeable future. We have tapped a number of rich resources for the new prayers, as will be seen from the Index of Sources, page 105.

The Nature of Common Prayer

Like the Boston lady who, when asked where she bought her hats, replied that she already "had her hats," those who regularly pray with a collection of written prayers may be said to "have their prayers." The task of adding to and subtracting from a collection which has served the church as well as that of the 1928 Prayer Book is not to be undertaken lightly. We have dropped only the prayers which in our judgment have in fact disappeared from general use. The nearly unanimous agreement of our consultants on these omissions confirms our decisions.

We have been under pressure to add even more prayers than we finally did. Some of those suggested to us seemed ephemeral. Some were worthy, but the topics are capable of being included under more general prayers. Others, which represented a considerable departure from Prayer Book models, we have deferred to a later projected Study on new ways of worship.

Common prayer is prayer on matters general enough to endure for decades at least: it prefers centuries; it is partisan only on an eternal scale; its language should be rich enough to stand up under frequent use and pointed enough to live in our hearts and minds between the times we hear it. Not all prayer is common prayer in this sense, even when it is good. With these criteria in mind, we have tried to be highly critical and selective in our choice of new material.

The Announcing of Prayers

To be sure, common prayer can be and often must be timely. The Commission desires to encourage those who lead public worship to focus the common prayers of this collection on matters of immediate concern by the thoughtful use of introductions, or invitations to pray. The titles to the prayers have been chosen with this use in mind. On many occasions, the titles may be used without any change to introduce or "bid" the prayers. But one should feel no hesitation about using considerable freedom and imagination in making such introductions. One might, for example, pray for a current session of the General Assembly of the United Nations by using one of the Prayers for the Peace of the World: "Let us pray for the General Assembly of the United Nations now in session." One might pray about unrest on college campuses by using the prayer for Schools and Colleges, or for a retreat of Church School teachers with the prayer for Christian Education. By being focused in new ways, good common prayers continually reveal new facets of meaning.

Whether the introduction points to some new and urgent situation or simply calls attention to a continuing need, it unites the congregation in a common concern before the prayer begins, and so aids participation in a significant way. In public worship, these prayers are intended to be introduced by some bidding.

The Meaning of Intercessory Prayer

Most of the prayers in this collection are intercessions. They express our concern for other persons in particular situations. In them, for example, we ask God to restore health to a person we love, or to bring peace into the arena of international affairs. Many thoughtful and sincere people question whether it is meaningful to think of God as acting in such ways. Before we comment further on the specific features of this collection of prayers, we should address ourselves to this radical criticism.

Prayer as man's relation to God

Most deeply considered, prayer is our relation to God. Particular prayers give expression to this relationship. The words may be spontaneous and free, or they may be refined and weighted by centuries of common use; but in either case they relate us to the infinite and holy God. They express our thoughts and feelings, our desires and hopes, when we approach him.

When a person finds it hard to pray, the difficulty often lies in his conception of God, or of God's action in the world. The questions we ask about intercessory prayer, for example, sometimes come from unreflective literalism. In our prayers — certainly in these prayers — God is regularly addressed as a person. "Father," "Lord," "Savior," we say. One seems to be asking a finite, limited being located at a point of space and time to interfere at another point of space and time to do what we want.

To be sure, such a notion has only to be mentioned to be repudiated. Anthropomorphic address, though unavoidable, is symbolic. It refers to a God who is not confined to the limits of our world, although he does manifest himself there.

Another set of difficulties with intercessory prayer arises from the opposite kind of considerations, when God is conceived only as transcendent, as being beyond our world, and so unable or unwilling to involve himself in our affairs, "our petty and mundane affairs," as we sometimes say.

This view of God, exalted and splendid though it may be, in fact falls short of Christian belief that "God was in Christ . . ." and that he can be known in his splendor only if he is at the same time known in humble particularity, at a specific place and time on the Cross, or on the road to Emmaus, or beside a Galilean lake, or in the answers to the prayers of hundreds and thousands of people, or on countless altars, or in the endless searching of the scriptures from that day to this.

How is the infinite and holy God known to be such? How do we recognize him? At least in the Biblical tradition on which our prayers are based, the experience which evokes the divine Name, the event which summons from the depths of man's being the acknowledgment of the presence of God, is an experience of power—of liberating power exercised on behalf of men far beyond what they expect or deserve. Such was the experience of the Hebrew tribes at the Red Sea. Those who participated in the Exodus were freed from an overpowering enemy. They interpreted that outcome as a disclosure of ultimate reality. At the Red Sea, God showed himself to be gracious. The Hebrew people understood their lives in the light of this revelation of the Ultimate, in this perspective; and they succeeded in convincing the generations which came after them of the validity of this understanding. Such also was the Resurrection of Christ. Those who participated in the first Easter wore grasped in a new way by the power of the divine, the infinite and holy God; they were freed from the power of death, the "last" overwhelming enemy. By the power of the Resurrection, God showed himself to be indeed a God of grace and love. The power which underlies all events, they believed, surfaced decisively in that event.

We for whom this collection of prayers is intended understand ourselves to be part of the ongoing community of faith which interprets its life from the point of view of Exodus and Resurrection. We believe that God works for good in every situation. And the God who showed his hand in those events and is present in all events, is in particular working to accomplish his will in those matters which concern us at any given time. Of course, God respects human freedom. He works through the wills of men, which often resist his will and obscure his presence. So it is not out of place, it is in fact supremely appropriate, to pray that some of us will freely open ourselves in love to accept his will as our own, that we will offer ourselves for the fulfillment of his purposes, and lent his saving presence will be disclosed in the circumstances which we hold before him in prayer.

Levels of meaning in intercessory prayer

What then is the significance of intercessory prayer? We can trace it on several levels.

1. *Intercessory prayer is an exercise in self-expression.* To pray for another is a significant part of expressing our thoughts and feelings in the presence of God. A deep life of prayer requires as much honesty and subtlety as we can muster in bringing the full range of our concerns into self-awareness. Our hearts are to be tried in their involvement with other persons as much as in their selfish desires. Those whom we truly love we will not forget in our prayers. Like the importunate widow of the parable (Luke 18:1-8), we will not cease expressing our concern for one who is incurably sick or for our nation in a

crisis. Sometimes we question the effectiveness of prayer because we give up too easily; we do not let our prayers disclose the true depth of our feeling.

2. *Intercessory prayer is an exercise in illumination.* To pray for another is to place him—in our thought— within the area of God's liberating action. To pray for a sick person is to see his sickness in the perspective of a faith which includes belief in the victory over sickness and death by God's act in Christ. We can endure his sickness with him, and hope for his health if not in this life, then in the eternal life he shares with God. To pray for peace among the nations is to see the world's present disorder in the perspective of God's coming kingdom. Experienced disruptions are included within our defining perspective on life. We can endure them, and hope for the coming of peace—if not in this world, then in the kingdom of God when it is fully realized.

3. *Intercessory prayer is an exercise in commitment.* To pray for another is to commit one's self to him in a sober and solemn way. To pray for him and to fail to do everything in one's power for him is to make a mockery of prayer, and does not deserve the name. The one who truly prays will offer himself to act in the situation he prays for He puts himself into God's hands as an instrument for the accomplishment of God's purpose in this case, and holds himself ready to obey God's will as he comes to understand it

4. *Self-expression, illumination, and commitment can all be understood* without attributing any transcendent reference to prayer. They are all values in their own right. But there is a fourth aspect to intercession. Prayer, finally, does what nothing else will do. If it is true that the liberating power of God—the power manifested in those crucial events which establish us in faith—under-lies all events, it is not meaningless to pray that that same power should be made manifest in this particular case. It is indeed impossible to know what difference a person's prayer may make in the hidden life of God; but one would be bold indeed to deny that our prayers have some effect. Our Lord prayed for others,[2] and he commanded his disciples to follow his example.[3] Careful studies of prayer in the New Testament reveal that one of the characteristics which distinguish it from prayer in the surrounding Graeco-Roman and Jewish communities was its certainty of being heard.[4] God is always accessible to one who prays. And Christians in every succeeding generation have found that God keeps his faith with his people.

---

2. Lk 22:32; Lk 23:34; cf. Jn 17:9ff.

3. Mk 9:29; Lk 18:1ff.

4. Greeven, Heinrich, *euchomai*, in *The Theological Dictionary of the New Testament*, ed. G. Kittel, tr. G. Bromily, Eerdmans, 1964. Vol. 2, p. 803. Also Smith, Charles W. F., *Prayer*, in *The Interpreter's Dictionary of the Bible*, Abingdon Press, 1962. Vol. 3, pp. 857-867.

So if one prays on these first three levels we have described — expressing his true feelings, seeing the situation in the light of the Cross and Resurrection of Christ, and committing himself to action to the limits of his ability—he has still not done all that he could do unless he also commends the matter in hope and trust to the care of a merciful God. And as in the case of the sacraments, though God is not tied to our prayers, we are.[5]

Style

We turn now to discuss certain features of the present collection of prayers and thanksgivings.

Thou or you?

One obvious question is whether we will address God as "thou" or as "you."[6] In this Study, we have retained both styles of address. Prayers taken over from the 1928 Prayer Book, and a few from other sources, appear both ways. All new prayers address God as "you."

A word must be said about the way "thou" has been used at various times in the history of the English language. Despite all that has been written recently, the matter is still not well understood.

Before 1100 A.D. in Old English, *thou* was used as the second person singular pronoun in ordinary speech. In Middle English (1100 —1500), however, *thou* was gradually superseded by the plural *ye* and *you* in addressing a superior and (later) an equal, but for a long time *thou* was retained in addressing inferiors, as well as intimates and God. This usage for the most part was Shakespeare's as it was Cranmer's. In *The Merchant of Venice*, for example, Launcelot and his father Gobbo, both servants, meet Bassanio, a gentleman. The following lines appear in the course of their dialogue: (Act II, Scene 2)

Gobbo:	I have here a dish of doves that I would bestow upon **your** worship; and my suit is…	(superior)
Launcelot:	In very brief, the suit is impertinent to myself, as **your** worship shall know by this honest old man, and, though I say it, though old man, yet poor man, my father.	(superior)

---

5. *Deus non alligatur sacramentis, sed nos.* (God is not tied to the sacraments, but we are.) The root of this axiom of sacramental theology is in Peter Lombard, *Libri Sententiarum* IV, 1, 4, *de triplici genere exercitiationis*.

6. This Study, like other Prayer Book Studies, follows the long-standing practice of the Books of Common Prayer and the King James Bible in not capitalizing pronouns which refer to God and Christ.

Bassanio:	One speak for both. What would **you**?	(plural)
Launcelot:	Serve **you**, sir.	(superior)
Gobbo:	That is the very defect of the matter, sir.	
Bassanio:	I know **thee** well; **thou** has obtained **thy** suit.	(inferior)

By the mid-twentieth century, *thou* had virtually disappeared in conversation except among Quakers and in certain dialects; but it was still commonly retained in address to God or in other elevated discourse.[7]

In the light of the foregoing review, it is clear that Cranmer had at his disposal no special grammatical form to address God, a form which would have been thought to carry automatically an aura of reverence. Quite the reverse. In 1549, *thou* was used to address knaves and fools as well as deity. But it is also clear that Archbishop Cranmer, following the normal usage of his time, did not simply address God in the same way he would have spoken to *anyone*. In those days, one had to *choose* how to address another; and the choice lay between what we might call a "plural of distance" or a "plural of respect" on the one hand, and on the other a singular which expressed either intimacy or condescension. The choice to address God as *thou*, was, of course, a decision for intimacy not condescension. It was left to the hearer to distinguish which was meant. He presumably had little trouble.

In our day, the second person "plural of respect" has captured the field. It expresses both intimacy and condescension as well as social superiority and equality. In every case except the religious one, *thou* seems simply antique or high-flown. And since *you* is now the language of love, there is widespread feeling that *you* should also become the language of prayer. A number of English-speaking churches have published liturgical texts and service books in "you" style, and many books of private devotion have appeared in contemporary language.[8]

---

7. "*Thou*: . . . Thou and its cases *thee, thine, thy*, were in OE used in ordinary speech; in ME they were gradually superseded by the plural *ye, you, your, yours*, in addressing a superior and (later) an equal, but were long retained in addressing an Inferior. Long retained by Quakers in addressing a single person, though now less general; still in various dialects used by parents to children, and, familiarly between equals, esp. intimates; in other cases considered as rude. In general English used in addressing God or Christ, also in homiletic language, and in poetry, apostrophe, and elevated prose." (Oxford English Dictionary, *ad loc.*)

8. In addition to *Services for Trial Use* for the Episcopal Church in the United States, note among others *The Australian Experimental Liturgy* and *The New Zealand Experimental Liturgy*, (Buchanan, Colin O., *Modern Anglican Liturgies*, Oxford. 1968); also *The Book of Catholic Worship*, The Liturgical Conference, Washington, D.C., 1966; *The Book of Common Worship, Provisional Services*, Westminster Press, 1966 (Presbyterian); *Contemporary Worship Services No 2, The Holy Communion*, Board of Publications, The Lutheran Church in America, Philadelphia, 1970.

Among books of private devotion, one thinks of Boyd, Malcolm, *Are You Running With Me, Jesus?*, Holt, Rinehart and Winston, 1965; Haven, Robert Marshall, *Look At Us, Lord*, Abingdon, 1969; Oosterhuis, Huub, *Your Word Is Near*, Newman, 1968; Quoist, Michel, *Prayers*, Sheed and Ward, 1963.

But there is another point which must be recognized and discussed. *Thou* is sometimes advocated not as a matter of better literary form but as a matter of theological precision. God, on this showing, is not a person. He is not one among equals. He is invisible, "without body, parts, or passions."[9] He is as much unlike a person as he is like a person. It is therefore not inappropriate that he should be addressed as "thou", a word which is at once personal, intimate, and numinous. Since it has been discarded in ordinary speech, "thou" has a numinous weight in modern usage which it never had before. It communicates far better than "you" who God is Martin Buber's title, *I and Thou*, is scarcely to be rendered *I and You*, or more gramatically, *You and I*.

This argument has force. Added to the weight of sentiment and long familiarity, it leads us to accept and provide for both styles. Both will doubtless be heard in our churches for some time to come. The gathering force of ecumenical liturgical practice, however, is altogether behind the move to address God as you, and it is our considered expectation that this usage will prevail in the long run.

We recognize with sympathy the difficulty which many people have with this shift in usage when they have prayed all their lives with the Prayer Book. Members of the Commission have difficulty too. But the foregoing considerations make it seem wise to prepare for this change. Reverence, after all, is not a matter of pronouns. It is a matter of intention. We believe that it is possible to express reverence in twentieth-century English. We hope that the new prayers embodied in this collection display it. We know from our own experience that it takes some time as much as a year or even more tune one's ears to hear it. We request that everyone who uses these prayers will use the prayers in *you* style long enough and regularly enough to get over the hurdle of unfamiliarity, and put himself in a position to judge them on their merits.

The existence of both styles side by side may seem awkward. It will be helpful to remember that our prayer books have long included several styles. Cranmer's Communion Service, Jeremy Taylor's great prayer to be used at the Visitation of the Sick, and Family Morning and Evening Prayer differ greatly in English style, though we have grown used to them all. The majesty of sixteenth-century prose, the opulence of seventeenth-century prose, and the elegance of eighteenth-century prose have all been permitted to make their contributions to our life of prayer. The twentieth century must now be allowed to add its particular eloquence—direct, taut, vivid—to the treasury of the ages.[10]

---

9. *The Articles of Religion*, Article I, Book of Common Prayer, p. 603.

10. Other liturgical arts also embrace many styles from many periods. We learn to love them all and use them all even, after a period of initial discomfort, the newest. We like Romanesque architecture, as well as Gothic and American Colonial; and we are learning to see the glory of structures like Coventry Cathedral.

The music of the church has equal range: Merbecke, Bach, Vaughn Williams, for example; and many worshipers are stirred by Geoffrey Shaw's 1925 setting of "Father eternal, Ruler of creation."

Relative Clauses

When God is addressed as *you*, the construction of the relative clause which frequently follows the address in prayers becomes a problem. "Almighty God, who declarest thy power . . ." presents no difficulties. But what shall we do when the second person singular form, *declarest*, is no longer available? Strict grammar and a mechanical translation require us to say, "Almighty God, who declare your power . . ." It is awkward on our tongues. We expect a relative clause to be in the third person.

Other solutions seem no better. One might be tempted to try, "Almighty God, you who declare your power . . ." But the sequence, *you who*, is both ugly and ridiculous when spoken. Rephrasing sometimes works: "Almighty God, whose power is . ." And, to be sure, the problem can be eliminated by eliminating these clauses altogether. But the ingenuity required by the former solution flirts with preciosity; and there is so much good theology in those relative clauses that to eliminate them, or even a large number of them, would impoverish our prayers.

In this collection, we have usually resolved the matter by making two sentences where there was one before. Thus, "Almighty God, you declare your power . . . Grant us . . ." In this form the prayer may be faulted because it "tells God something." But a moment's reflection will show that these two sentences constitute a natural turn of speech when we ask a favor of a friend, "John," we say, "you know this community. Help us with the Every Member Canvass." The first sentence does not presume to tell John something which he did not know before. It expresses our confidence in him. So in our prayers.

We believe that this solution is faithful to the collect form, and adequately translates it into contemporary English.[i]

Arrangement

Inspection of this Study will show that we have brought together in one place material which in the 1928 Prayer Book is scattered in a number of different sections. It contains not only what in 1928 appears in the section of Prayers and Thanksgivings and in the Additional Prayers at the end of the book, but also

---

Hymn texts also display a variety of styles. One thinks of Charles Wesley, John Keble and Walter Russell Bowie. Jan Struthers' hymn, "Lord of all hopefulness," (No. 363 in *The Hymnal 1940*) addresses God as 'you.' ("Give us, we pray, Your bliss in our hearts, Lord, at the break of the day.") We scarcely notice it.

[i] [Ed. Note: Classically, a collect has been understood as a prayer consisting of a single sentence, albeit with a variety of clauses. Whether English prayers must be bound by conventions originally pertaining to Latin prayers (which permits longer sentences than English) is an open question, and one clearly being answered here in the negative.]

the prayers which are placed at the end of Morning and Evening Prayer and the Visitation of the Sick. It is hoped that this new arrangement will prove more convenient.

The sequence—Prayers, Thanksgivings, and Litanies—obviously corresponds to the order of the 1928 book, where Prayers and Thanksgivings are followed by the Litany.

The order of the intercessions themselves has been considerably altered. In earlier books, there were, first, prayers for the state and its officers, then for the church, then for the people, then for the sick and those in special need. This order can be observed in the Prayer for the Whole State of Christ's Church, the Litany, and the intercessions at the end of Morning and Evening Prayer. This same ordering has obviously influenced the arrangement of Prayers and Thanksgivings in the 1928 book.

The traditional order seemed natural enough when the church was established and Christendom a reality. In today's pluralistic society, it is hard to justify. Where, then, we have asked ourselves, should a Christian begin his prayer? This collection suggests that prayer should begin with the world — with prayers for joy in the whole creation, for the family of man and for the peace of the world. Next for the Church, since the Church, in Christian hope (though not always, alas, in present experience), transcends the natural barriers which divide men. Then the state, the social order, the natural order, and family and personal life.

The prayers have been numbered and a Table of Contents and Indices have been provided, so that prayers may be readily located.

The Litany and Other Prayers

We have also included in this Study the Great Litany of 1544, in the version prepared for Prayer Book Studies V,[11] slightly altered. It is our belief on the one hand that no Anglican Book of Common Prayer would be complete without it, and on the other that it is almost a period piece—that in style, length, and mood it would not lend itself to effective modernization.

We have also put into this section a few other prayers from the 1928 Prayer Book with only those changes which it is hoped will encourage more frequent use. Some of these prayers, like the separate prayers for the Army and the Navy, have historic value. The language of others, like the Collect for Peace in the Prayer Book service of Morning Prayer, is so happily married to content that they should be preserved intact. In either case they should not be forgotten.

---

11. Prayer Book Studies V: "The Litany." The Standing Liturgical Commission, The Church Pension Fund, New York, 1953, pp. 41-47. Cf. pp. 140-145 of this Book.

The scope of this part of the collection will doubtless be questioned. It can be expanded or contracted on the basis of the Church's experience.

General Intercessions from The Holy Eucharist 1970

A number of new intercessions were included in Prayer Book Studies 21, The Holy Eucharist. They also appear, of course, in *Services for Trial Use*, and have already proved to be a welcome addition to available devotional material. We have reprinted them in this collection with a few editorial modifications, both for the sake of making them more accessible, and for the convenience of those who desire to use them outside the Eucharist.

A History of Intercessory Prayer

The last section of this Study[12] is a history of intercessory prayer in the Eucharist and of the growth of the collection of occasional prayers in English and American Prayer Books. It deals with a range of historical and technical matters not pursued in this introduction.

The Drafting Committee

The Drafting Committee chiefly responsible for the shape and content of this Study comprised the Reverend Canon James G. Birney, the Reverend J. Robert Zimmerman, Mrs. Lawrence Rose, and the Reverend Charles P. Price, Chairman. The Right Reverend Arthur Lichtenberger was a member until his death in 1968. His wisdom gave substance to this work in the beginning, and his loss has immeasurably impoverished it.

Mention was made of previous committees at work on Prayers and Thanksgivings. The present Study is built on the thought and work of the Reverend Charles W. F. Smith and the Reverend John Wallace Suter, Jr. What merit it possesses is due in no small part to them.

**The Standing Liturgical Commission
of the Episcopal Church**

---

12. This article was prepared for Prayer Book Studies 25 by the Rev. Charles W. F. Smith, Professor of New Testament at the Episcopal Theological School in Cambridge, Mass., and a member of the Standing Liturgical Commission.

In Contemporary Language

Concerning the use of Occasional Prayers

In public worship, these prayers are normally to be introduced in language based on the titles. The introduction may call attention to the special reason for using the prayer on a given occasion.

At the public services of the Church for which no other provisions are made, intercessions are normally offered for the Church and its mission, the State, those in special need, and those for whom there is particular concern.

Index of Titles

Prayers

For the World

1. For Joy in God's Creation, Traditional
2. For All Sorts and Conditions of Men, Traditional
3. For the Human Family
4. For Peace
5. For Peace Among the Nations, Traditional
6. For Those Who Work for Peace
7. For Our Enemies

For the Church

8. For the Church, Traditional
9. For the Mission of the Church, Traditional
10. For Clergy and People, Traditional
11. For the Diocese
12. For the Parish
13. For a Church Convention or Meeting
14. For the Election of a Bishop or Rector
15. For the Presiding Bishop, the Executive Council and its Staff
16. For the Unity of the Church, Traditional
17. For the Church in a Changing World
18. For the Ordained Ministry, Traditional
19. For the Supply of Candidates for the Ordained Ministry
20. For Christian Education, Traditional

21. For Monastic Orders and Vocations
22. For a Retreat
23. For Those About to be Baptized
24. For Those About to Receive the Laying on of Hands, Traditional

For the State

25. For Our Country, Traditional
26. For the President of the United States and All in Civil Authority, Traditional
27. For Congress or a State Legislature, Traditional
28. For Courts of Justice, Traditional
29. For Sound Government
30. For Local Government
31. For an Election
32. For Those in the Armed Forces of Our Country
33. For Those Who Suffer for Conscience' Sake
34. For Fellow-Citizens Abroad

For the Social Order

35. For Social Justice, Traditional
36. In Struggles for Social Justice
37. For Our Daily Work, Traditional
38. For Agriculture, Traditional
39. For Industry
40. For Those Whose Work is Difficult
41. For the Unemployed
42. For Schools and Colleges, Traditional
43. For the Good Use of Leisure Time
44. For Cities
45. For the Poor and Neglected, Traditional
46. For the Oppressed in the Land
47. For Prisons and Prisoners
48. For Christian Service, Traditional
49. For a Right Attitude Toward Our Work
50. For the Right Use of God's Gifts, Traditional
51. For the Responsible Use of Money
52. For Those Who Influence Public Opinion

For the Natural Order

53. For Knowledge of God's Creation
54. For the Harvest of Lands and Waters, Traditional
55. For the Conservation of Natural Resources
56. For the Exploration of Space
57. For the Responsible Use of Inventions and Discoveries
58. For the Future of Mankind
59. For Animals

For Family and Personal Life

60. For Families, Traditional
61. For Living in Families When There is Conflict
62. For Children
63. For the Care of Children, Traditional
64. For Young Persons
65. For Married Couples
66. For the Aged
67. For a Birthday
68. For the Absent, Traditional
69. For Those We Love, Traditional
70. For Travelers
71. For Sick Persons, Traditional
72. For One Critically Ill, Traditional
73. For a Sick Child, Traditional
74. For One About to Undergo an Operation, Traditional
75. For the Mentally Ill, Traditional
76. For Those Who Are Addicted
77. For Hospitals and Healing Ministries
78. For a Person in Trouble or Bereavement, Traditional
79. For Those Who Mourn, Traditional
80. For Dying in Faith, Traditional
81. For the Dead, Traditional
82. On Memorial Days, Traditional
83. For Guidance, Traditional
84. For Quiet Confidence, Traditional

85. For Trustfulness, Traditional
86. Prayers of Self-Dedication, Traditional
87. For Self-Mastery
88. For Self-Acceptance
89. A Prayer of Love (Attributed to St. Francis)

Other Prayers

90. On Sunday, Traditional
91. In the Morning, Traditional
92. In the Evening, Traditional
93. Before Worship, Traditional
94. Before Sermons
95. Before Receiving Communion
96. After Receiving Communion
97. For the Answering of Prayer, Traditional
98. After Worship, Traditional
99. Grace at Meals, Traditional
100. Blessings, Traditional

Thanksgivings

General

1. The General Thanksgiving, Traditional
2. A General Thanksgiving

For the Church

3. For the Mission of the Church
4. For the Saints and Faithful Departed

For National Life

5. For the Nation
6. For Heroic Service
7. For Negotiating Peace
8. For the Restoration of Peace
9. For the Restoration of Domestic Peace

For the Social Order

10. For the Diversity of Races and Cultures
11. For the Widening Vision of Social Justice
12. For Peacemakers

For the Natural Order

13. For the Creation
14. For the Harvest, Traditional

In Family and Personal Life

15. For the Birth of a Child
16. For the Gift of a Child
17. For the Restoration of Health, Traditional
18. For Safe Travel

Litanies

All these litanies are in the contemporary language section, p. 18ff. The Great Litany is on page 78ff., and the General Intercessions from The Holy Eucharist are on p. 84ff.

I. A Bidding Litany, Traditional
II. A Litany of Thanksgiving
III. A Litany for the Mission of the Church
IV. A Litany for the Ministry
V. A Litany for Personal Life - The Southwell Litany
VI. A Litany for Healing
VII. A Litany for the Dying or the Dead

Prayers for the World

1. *For Joy in God's Creation* [Traditional]
Father, you have filled the world with beauty: Open our eyes to see your hand at work in everything. Teach us to rejoice in your whole creation and to serve you with gladness; for the sake of your Son, through whom all things were made, Jesus Christ our Lord. *Amen.*

2. For All Sorts and Conditions of Men [Traditional]

Almighty God, Creator and Preserver of all mankind, we humbly pray for all sorts and conditions of men. Make your ways known to them and your healing power to all nations. We pray especially for the universal Church. So guide and govern it by your good Spirit, that all who profess and call themselves Christians may be led into the way of truth, and hold the faith in the unity of the Spirit, in the bond of peace, and in righteousness of life. We commend to your fatherly goodness those who are in any way afflicted or distressed, in mind, body, or estate; [especially those for whom our prayers have been asked]. Comfort and relieve them all according to their special needs, giving them patience in their sufferings and deliverance from their afflictions. All this we ask for Jesus Christ's sake. *Amen.*

3. For The Human Family

O God, you made us in your own image and redeemed us through Jesus your Son: Look with compassion on the whole human family. Take away the arrogance and hatred which infect our hearts. Break down the walls that separate us. Unite us in bonds of love. Work through our struggle and confusion to accomplish your purposes on earth, that in your good time, all nations and races may serve you in harmony around your heavenly throne; through Jesus Christ our Lord. *Amen.*

4. For Peace (1)

Almighty God, whose will it is to hold both heaven and earth in the peace of your kingdom: Give peace to your Church, peace among nations, peace in our homes, and peace in our hearts; through your Son, our Savior, Jesus Christ. *Amen.*

For Peace (2)

Eternal God, in whose perfect kingdom no sword is drawn but the sword of righteousness, no strength known but the strength of love: So mightily spread abroad your Spirit, that all peoples may be gathered under the banner of the Prince of Peace, as children of one Father; to whom be dominion and glory now and for ever. *Amen.*

5. For Peace Among the Nations [Traditional]

Almighty God, our heavenly Father, guide the nations of the world into the way of justice and truth, and establish among them that peace which is the fruit of righteousness, that they may become the kingdom of our Lord and Savior Jesus Christ. *Amen.*

6. *For Those Who Work for Peace*

Another form of this prayer appears in Services for Trial Use p. 631.[ii]

Almighty God, kindle in the hearts of all men the true love of peace, and guide with your peaceable wisdom those who take counsel for the nations of the earth, [especially in . . .]; that your kingdom may increase until the earth is filled with the knowledge of your love; through Jesus Christ our Lord. *Amen.*

7. *For Our Enemies*
O God, the Father of all mankind,
whose Son commands us to love those who hate us:
Hear our prayer for our enemies.
Lead them and us from prejudice to truth.
Deliver them and us from deeds beneath the dignityof man.
Turn us all from our evil ways.
Take from our hearts every trace of cruelty, hatred, andlust for revenge.
And in your good time enable us all to stand reconciled before you
as friends of our Lord and Savior Jesus Christ.
Amen.

Prayers for the Church

8. *For the Church* [Traditional]
Gracious Father, we pray to you for your holy Catholic Church. Fill it with your truth. Keep it in your peace. Where it is corrupt, reform it. Where it is in error, correct it. Where it is right, defend it. Where it is in want, provide for it. Where it is divided, reunite it; for the sake of your Son, our Savior Jesus Christ. *Amen.*

[ii] [Ed. Note: The collects referred to are these from Special Occasion 16. For Peace:

Almighty God from whom all thoughts of truth and peace proceed: Kindle in the hearts of all men the true love of peace; and guide with your pure and peaceable wisdom those who take counsel for the nations of the earth, that in tranquility your kingdom may go forward, until the earth is filled with the knowledge of your love; through Jesus Christ our Lord, who lives and reigns with you in the unity of the Holy Spirit, one God, now and ever. *Amen.*

Almighty God, from whom all thoughts of truth and peace proceed: Kindle, we pray thee, in the hearts of all men the true love of peace; and guide with thy pure and peaceable wisdom those who take counsel for the nations of the earth, that in tranquility thy kingdom may go forward, until the earth is filled with the knowledge of thy love; through Jesus Christ our Lord, who liveth and reigneth with thee in the unity of the Holy Spirit, one God, now and ever. *Amen.*]

9. *For the Mission of the Church* (1) [Traditional]

Another form of this prayer appears in Services for Trial Use, p. 628.[iii]

Lord, you have made all races and nations of men to be one family, and you sent your Son Jesus Christ to preach peace to them all, both far and near: Lead men everywhere to seek you and find you. Bring the nations of the world into your fellowship, pour out your Spirit on all mankind, and hasten your kingdom; through Jesus Christ our Lord. *Amen.*

For the Mission of the Church (2)
Ever-loving God, whose will it is that all men shall come to the knowledge of your Son Jesus Christ, and the power of his forgiveness, and the hope of his resurrection: Grant that in our witness to him we may make worthy use of the means you have given us; and prosper our efforts to share this glad news throughout the world; to the honor of your Name. *Amen.*

10. *For Clergy and People* [Traditional]
Almighty and everliving God, the Giver of every good and perfect gift: Grant to our Bishops and other clergy, and to the congregations committed to their charge, the abundant grace of your Holy Spirit; and that they may be truly pleasing in your sight, give them a continual sense of your presence. Grant this, O Father, for the sake of our Advocate and Mediator, Jesus Christ. *Amen.*

11. *For the Diocese*
O God, by your grace you have called us in this Diocese to a goodly fellowship of faith: Remember all the members of your Church who live within its borders. Bless its Bishop(s) *N.* [and *N.*], its clergy, and the people of its parishes. Grant that your Word may be truly preached in this place and truly heard, your Sacraments faithfully administered and faithfully received. By your good Spirit, fashion our lives according to the example of our Savior Jesus Christ, that we may show the power of your love to all the people among whom we live; through Jesus Christ our Lord. *Amen.*

[iii] [Ed. Note: The collects referred to are these from Special Occasion 14. For the Mission of the Church I:

O God, who made of one blood all nations of men to dwell on the face of the whole earth, and sent your blessed Son to preach peace to those who are far and to those who are near: Grant that all men everywhere may seek after you and find you; bring the nations into your fold, pour out your Spirit upon all mankind, and hasten your kingdom; through Jesus Christ your Son our Lord, who lives and reigns with you and the Holy Spirit, one God, now and for ever. *Amen.*

O God, who hast made of one blood all nations of men to dwell on the face of the whole earth, and didst send thy blessed Son to preach peace to those who are far off and to those who are nigh: Grant that all men everywhere may seek after thee and find thee; bring the nations into thy fold, pour out thy Spirit upon all mankind, and hasten thy kingdom; through Jesus Christ thy Son our Lord, who liveth and reigneth with thee and the Holy Spirit, one God, now and for ever. *Amen.*]

12. *For the Parish*
Almighty and everliving God, ruler of all things in heaven and earth: Hear our prayers for this parish family. Strengthen and confirm the faithful, arouse the careless, restore the penitent, convert the evil. Grant us all things necessary for our common life, and bring us all to be of one heart and mind within your holy Church; through Jesus Christ our Lord. *Amen.*

13. *For a Church Convention or Meeting*
Almighty and everliving God, Source of all wisdom and understanding: Be present with those who take counsel [in . . .] for the renewal and mission of your Church. Teach us in all things to seek first your honor and glory; guide us to perceive what is right; and grant us both the courage to pursue it and the grace to accomplish it; through Jesus Christ our Lord. *Amen.*

See also the prayer for General or Diocesan Conventions, p. 83.

14. *For the Election of a Bishop or Rector*
Almighty God, giver of every good gift: Look graciously on your Church, and so guide the minds of those who shall choose a Bishop for this Diocese (or, Rector for this Parish), that we may receive a faithful pastor, who will care for your people and equip us for our ministries; through Jesus Christ our Lord. *Amen.*

15. *For the Presiding Bishop, the Executive Council, and its Staff*
Almighty God, giver of wisdom, you never fail to answer the prayers of those who seek you: Bless *N.*, our Presiding Bishop, the Executive Council, and the staff who assist them in their work. Enlighten their minds, grant them patience and insight, and fill them with faith and obedience to your will; that, through your Spirit, they may enable this Church to carry out its mission in the world; through Jesus Christ our Lord. *Amen.*

16. *For the Unity of the Church* (1) [Traditional]
O God, the Father of our Lord Jesus Christ, our only Savior, the Prince of Peace: Give us grace seriously to take to heart the great dangers we are in by our unhappy divisions. Take away all hatred and prejudice, and whatever else may hinder us from godly union and concord. As there is but one Body and one Spirit, and one hope of our calling, one Lord, one Faith, one Baptism, one God and Father of us all; so we may be all of one heart and of one soul, united in one holy bond of truth and peace, of faith and love, and may with one mind and one mouth declare your glory; through Jesus Christ our Lord. *Amen.*

For the Unity of the Church (2)
Lord Jesus Christ, you said to your Apostles, "Peace I give to you; my own peace I leave with you": Regard not our sins, but the faith of your Church; and give to us the peace and unity of that heavenly City where, with the Father and the Holy Spirit, you live and reign now and for ever. *Amen.*

Prayers, Thanksgivings, and Litanies 23

17. *For the Church in a Changing World*
O God, sustain your Church as we face new tasks in the confusions of this changing world. By your Holy Spirit give us good judgment and the strength to persevere, so that we may boldly bear witness to the coming of your kingdom; through Jesus Christ our Lord. *Amen.*

> See also the Collect for the Fifth Sunday in Lent, formerly the Collect for the Fourth Sunday after Easter, Services for Trial Use, p. 503.[iv]

18. *For the Ordained Ministry* [Traditional]
Almighty God, the giver of all good gifts, who of your divine providence appointed various Orders in your Church: Give your grace, we humbly pray, to all who are [now] called to any office and ministration for your people; and so replenish them with the truth of your doctrine, and endue them with holiness of life, that they may faithfully serve before you to the glory of your great Name, and to the benefit of your holy Church; through Jesus Christ our Lord, who lives and reigns with you in the unity of the Holy Spirit, one God, now and ever. *Amen.*

> See also Services for Trial Use pp. 624-627.

19. *For the Supply of Candidates for the Ordained Ministry*
O God, you led your holy Apostles to ordain fellow-ministers in every place: Grant that your Church, under the guidance of the Holy Spirit, may choose suitable persons for the Ministry of Word and Sacrament, and may uphold them in their work for the extension of your kingdom, so that your Name may be glorified in all the world; through him who is the chief Shepherd and Bishop of our souls, Jesus Christ our Lord. *Amen.*

20. *For Christian Education* [Traditional]

> Another form of this prayer appears in Services for Trial Use, p. 623.[v]

[iv] [Ed. Note: These are the collects for the Fifth Sunday in Lent:

O Almighty God, who alone canst order the unruly wills and affections of sinful men: Grant unto thy people, that they may love the thing which thou commandest, and desire that which thou dost promise; that so, among the sundry and manifold chaanges of the world, our hearts may surely there be fixed, where true joys are to be found; through Jesus Christ our Lord. *Amen.*

Fun fact--my reference copy (the Church Publishing Office Copy) entirely lacks the section where this prayer is printed; pages 119-150 are in place of pages 487-518.]

[v] [Ed. Note: The collects referred to are these from Special Occasion 12. For Education:

Almighty God, the fountain of all wisdom: Enlighten by your Holy Spirit those who teach and those who learn, that, rejoicing in the knowledge of your truth, they may worship and serve you from generation to generation; through Jesus Christ our Lord, who lives and reigns with you in the unity of the holy Spirit, one God, now and for ever. *Amen.*

Almighty God, our heavenly Father, you have committed to your holy Church the care and nurture of your children: Enlighten with your wisdom those who teach and those who learn, that, rejoicing together in the knowledge of your truth, we may worship and serve you from generation to generation; through Jesus Christ our Lord. *Amen.*

21. *For Monastic Orders and Vocations*
O Lord, you became poor for our sake,
that we might be made rich through your poverty;
Guide and sanctify, we pray,
those whom you call to follow you,
under the vows of poverty, chastity, and obedience;
that by their prayer and service, they may enrich your Church,
and by their life and worship may glorify your Name;
for you reign with the Father and the Holy Spirit, one God, now and for ever. *Amen.*

22. *For a Retreat*
O Lord Jesus Christ, who went apart to pray with your disciples: Grant to your servants in *this* retreat (*or*, in the retreat for . . . in . . .) that *we* may rest a while with you and know that you have found us long before. Let the words that shall be spoken here not fall on barren ground, but, enriched by prayer and silence, bear good fruit in our lives to the glory of your holy Name. *Amen.*

23. *For Those About to be Baptized*

> *For use especially on days which precede public services of Holy Baptism, and at other times at the discretion of the Minister.*

Lord Jesus Christ, you desire that everyone who follows you shall be born again by water and the Spirit:

Remember your servants (here they may be named) who are soon to be baptized in your Name.

By their names, Lord:
> Grant that you will know them, and call them to a life of service. *Amen.*
> Grant that they may become the persons you created them to be. *Amen.*
> Grant that they may be written for ever in your Book of Life. *Amen.*

Almighty God, the fountain of all wisdom: Enlightenby thy Holy Spirit those who teach and those who learn, that, rejoicing in the knowledge of thy truth, they may worship and serve thee from generation to generation; through Jesus Christ our Lord who liveth and reigneth with thee in the unity of the same Spirit, one God, now and for ever. *Amen.*]

Through the water of their baptism, Lord:
> Grant that they may be united with you in your death. *Amen.*
> Grant that they may receive forgiveness for all their sins. *Amen.*
> Grant that they may have power to endure, and strength to have victory in the battle of life. *Amen.*

As members of your Church, Lord:
> Grant that they may rise to a new life in the fellowship of those who love you. *Amen.*
> Grant that they may suffer when another suffers, and when another rejoices, rejoice. *Amen.*
> Grant that they may be your faithful soldiers and servants until their life's end. *Amen.*

Through the abiding presence of your Spirit, Lord:
> Grant that they may lead the rest of their lives according to this beginning. *Amen.*
> Grant that when they pass through the dark waters of death, you will be with them. *Amen.*
> Grant that they may inherit the kingdom of glory prepared for them from the foundation of the world. *Amen.*

See also the Litany from the Baptismal Office, Services for Trial Use, p. 26.

24. *For Those About to Receive the Laying on of Hands* [Traditional]
O God, you prepared your disciples for the coming of the Spirit through the teaching of your Son, Jesus Christ: Make the hearts and minds of your servants ready to receive the blessing of the Holy Spirit through the laying on of hands, that they may be filled with the strength of his presence; through the same Jesus Christ our Lord. *Amen.*

Prayers for the State

25. *For Our Country* [Traditional]
Almighty God, we humbly thank you for this good land which you have given us for our inheritance. We pray that we may always prove to be a people mindful of your favor and glad to do your will. Bless this land with honest labor, clear thinking, and mutual regard. Save us from violence, discord, and confusion; from pride and arrogance, and from every evil way. Preserve and increase our liberties, and fashion into one united nation this people of many races and tongues. Fill with the spirit of wisdom those to whom we entrust the authority of government, that they may seek justice and peace, and that, through obedience to your will, we may show forth your praise among the nations of the earth. In time of prosperity, fill our hearts with thankfulness, and in time of trouble, do not allow our trust in you to fail. All this we ask through Jesus Christ our Lord. *Amen.*

26. *For the President of the United States and All in Civil Authority* [Traditional]
O Lord our Governor, the whole world is filled with your glory: We commend this nation to your merciful care, that we may follow your guidance and live in your peace. Give to the President of the United States, the Governor of this State (or Commonwealth), and to all in authority, wisdom and strength to know and to do your will. Fill them with the love of truth and righteousness; and make them always remember that they are called to serve this nation in the fear of your righteous judgments; through Jesus Christ our Lord, who lives and governs with you and the Holy Spirit, one God, now and for ever. *Amen.*

See also the prayer for Sound Government, below.

27. *For Congress or a State Legislature*
O God, the source of wisdom, whose statutes are good and gracious, and whose law is truth: Guide and support our Senators and Representatives in Congress assembled (*or*, in the Legislature of this State or Commonwealth), that by just and prudent laws, they may promote the well-being of all our people; through Jesus Christ our Lord. *Amen.*

See also the prayer for Sound Government, below.

28. *For Courts of Justice* [Traditional]
Almighty God, whose ways are just and whose judgments are true: Guide with your never-failing wisdom the Supreme Court and other courts of justice in our land; Give to our judges and those who assist them, patience, integrity, and compassion; that, remembering that the people they serve are yours, they may discern the truth and impartially administer justice; through Jesus Christ our Lord. *Amen.*

See also the prayer for Sound Government, below.

29. *For Sound Government*

The responses in italics may be omitted.

O Lord our Governor, bless the leaders of our land that we may be a people at peace among ourselves and a blessing to other nations of the earth.
Lord, keep this nation under your care.
To the President and Members of his Cabinet, to Governors of States, Mayors of cities, and to all in executive authority, grant such a measure of wisdom and grace in the exercise of their duties as will be equal to the challenges of our times.
Give grace to your servants, O Lord.
To Senators and Representatives, and those who make our laws in states and cities, give courage, wisdom, and foresight to provide for the needs of all our people, and to fulfill our obligations in the community of nations.
Give grace to your servants, O Lord.

To the Judges of our courts and administrators of our systems of correction, give understanding and integrity, that human rights may be safeguarded and justice served.
Give grace to your servants, O Lord.
And finally, teach all our people to rely on your strength and to accept their responsibilities to their fellow-citizens, that they may elect trustworthy leaders and make wise decisions for the well-being of our society; so that we may serve you faithfully in our generation and honor your holy Name.
For yours is the kingdom, O Lord, and you are exalted as head above all. Amen.

30. *For Local Government*
Almighty God, our heavenly Father, send down upon those who hold office in this State (Commonwealth, City, County, Town, . . .) the spirit of wisdom, charity, and justice; so that with steadfast purpose they may faithfully serve in their offices to advance the well-being of all people; through Jesus Christ our Lord. *Amen.*

31. *For an Election*
Almighty God, we must account to you for all our powers and privileges: Guide the people of these United States (*or*, of this Community) in the election of their officers and representatives; that by faithful administration and wise laws the rights of all may be protected and our nation enabled to fulfill your purposes; through Jesus Christ our Lord. *Amen.*

32. *For Those in the Armed Forces of our Country*
Lord of Hosts, we commend to your gracious care and keeping all the men and women of our armed forces at home and abroad. Defend them day by day with your heavenly grace; strengthen them in their trials and temptations; give them courage to face the perils that beset them; and grant them your abiding presence wherever they may be; through Jesus Christ our Lord. *Amen.*

33. *For Those Who Suffer for Conscience's Sake*
O God our Father,
whose Son forgave his enemies while he suffered shame and death:
Strengthen those who suffer for conscience' sake.
If they are accused, save them from speaking in anger;
If they are rejected, save them from bitterness;
If they are imprisoned, save them from despair.
Give us grace also to respect their witness,
and help us to discern the truth,
so that our society may be cleansed and strengthened for your service.
This we ask for the sake of Jesus Christ, our merciful and righteous Judge.
Amen.

34. *For Fellow-Citizens Abroad*
Watch over our fellow-citizens, O Lord, who live and travel in other lands. Open them to the values of different cultures, and make them worthy representatives of our own, that by their courtesy and good judgment they may strengthen the bonds of friendship and peace; through Jesus Christ our Lord. *Amen.*

Prayers for the Social Order

35. *For Social Justice* (1) [Traditional]

Another form of this prayer appears in Services for Trial Use, p. 636.[vi]

Almighty God, you have created man in your own image: Grant us courage fearlessly to contend against evil, and to make no peace with oppression; and, that we may rightly use our freedom, help us to employ it in the struggle for justice among men and nations, to the glory of your holy Name; through Jesus Christ our Lord. *Amen.*

For Social Justice (2)
Grant, O God, that your holy and life-giving Spirit may so move in every human heart, and among the people of this land, that barriers which divide us may crumble, suspicions disappear, and hatreds cease; that being healed of our divisions we may live in justice and peace; through Jesus Christ our Lord. *Amen.*

36. *In Struggles for Social Justice*
O God, you have bound us together in a common life: In all our struggles for justice, help us to confront one another without hatred or bitterness, and to work together with mutual forbearance and respect; through Jesus Christ our Lord. *Amen.*

37. *For Our Daily Work* [Traditional]
Almighty God, you give us new life, new hope, and new opportunities with each returning day: Help us to use these blessings to the best of our capacity in doing

---

[vi] [Ed. Note: The collects referred to are these from Special Occasion 19. For Social Justice:

Almighty God, who created man in your own image: Grant us grace fearlessly to contend against evil, and to make no peace with oppression; and, that we may reverently use our freedom, help us to employ it in the maintenance of justice among men and nations, to the glory of your holy Name; through Jesus Christ our Lord, who lives and reigns with you and the Holy Spirit, one God, now and for ever. *Amen.*

Almighty God, who hast created man in thine own image: Grant us grace fearlessly to contend against evil, and to make no peace with oppression; and, that we may reverently use our freedom, help us to employ it in the maintenance of justice among men and nations, to the glory of thy holy Name; through Jesus Christ our Lord, who liveth and reigneth with thee and the Holy Spirit, one God, now and for ever. *Amen.*]

the work which we have to do; devoting ourselves wholly to your service, and putting our selfish interests aside to seek the welfare of our fellow men; for the sake of him who came among us as one who serves, your Son Jesus Christ our Lord. *Amen.*

    See also Services for Trial Use, p. 639.[vii]

38. *For Agriculture* [Traditional]
Almighty God, we thank you for making the earth fruitful to produce what is needed for the life and well-being of men: Bless those who work the fields; give us seasonable weather; and grant that we may all share the fruits of the earth rejoicing in your goodness; through Jesus Christ our Lord. *Amen.*

39. *For Industry*
Almighty God, whose Son Jesus Christ in his earthly life shared man's toil and hallowed his labor: Be present with your people where they work. Make those who direct the industries of this land responsive to your will, and keep them faithful in their trust. Give all men pride in what they do, a just return for their labor, and joy in serving you through serving others; through Jesus Christ, our Lord. *Amen.*

40. *For Those Whose Work Is Difficult*
Lord, you have taught us that we are members of one another: Hear our prayer for all who do the tedious, dirty, and dangerous work which is necessary to sustain our life; and grant that all who depend upon their service may remember them with thanks; through Jesus Christ our Lord. *Amen.*

41. *For the Unemployed*
Heavenly Father, we remember before you those who suffer want and anxiety from lack of work: Guide us so to use our public and private wealth, that the unemployed may be delivered from their trouble, and that, we may all find security in the well-being of this land; through Jesus Christ our Lord. *Amen.*

    [vii] [Ed. Note: The collects referred to are these from Special Occasion 22. For Vocation in Daily Work:

    Almighty God, heavenly Father, whose glory and handiwork are shown forth in the heavens and in the earth: Deliver us, we pray, in our several occupations from selfish love of riches, that we may do the work which you give us, with singleness of heart as your servants, and to the benefit of our fellow men; for the sake of him who came among us as one that serves, your Son Jesus Christ our Lord. *Amen.*

    Almighty God, heavely Father, who showest forth thy glory and handiwork in the heavens and in the earth: Deliver us, we beseech thee, in our several occupations from selfish love of riches, that we may do the work which thou givest us, with singleness of heart as thy servants, and to the benefit of our fellow men; for the sake of him who came among us as one that serveth, thy Son Jesus Christ our Lord. *Amen.*]

42. *For Schools and Colleges* (1) [Traditional]
Almighty God, behold with your gracious favor our universities, seminaries, colleges, and schools, that knowledge and wisdom may be increased among us. Bless all who teach and all who learn; and grant that in humility of heart they may ever look to you, the source of all truth; through Jesus Christ our Lord. *Amen.*

For Schools and Colleges (2)
O God, Source of all truth, Judge of all men: Bless the labors of those who study, those who teach, and those who add to the store of our knowledge. Show us how to transform learning into wisdom and technology into service, so that all our study may be dedicated to your glory; through Jesus Christ our Lord. *Amen.*

43. *For the Good Use of Leisure Time*
O God, in the course of this busy life, give us times of refreshment and peace; and grant that we may use that leisure to rebuild our bodies and renew our minds, so that our spirits may be opened to the goodness of your creation; through Jesus Christ our Lord. *Amen.*

44. *For Cities*
Father of mankind,
in your Word you have given us a vision of that holy city
in which there is neither pain nor death,
and to which the nations of the world bring their glory:
Behold and visit, we pray, the teeming cities of earth.
Renew the ties of mutual regard which form our civic life.
Send us honest and able leaders.
Enable us to eliminate poverty, prejudice, and oppression,
so that peace may prevail with righteousness, and justice with order.
And help us to make our cities the meeting-ground of cultures and races,
where men of different talents may find the fulfillment of their common humanity;
through Jesus Christ our Lord. *Amen.*

45. *For the Poor and Neglected*
Almighty and most merciful God, we remember before you all poor and neglected persons, whom it would be easy to forget; the homeless and the destitute; the old and the sick who have none to care for them. Let your fatherly goodness rest upon them. Heal those who are broken in body or spirit, and turn their sorrow to joy. Lift up the downhearted and cheer them with hope. When they are troubled, keep them from discouragement. When they are perplexed, save them from despair. Grant this, our Father, for the love of your Son, who for our sake became poor, even Jesus Christ our Lord. *Amen.*

fatherly goodness rest upon them. Heal those who are broken in body or spirit, and turn their sorrow to joy. Lift up the downhearted and cheer them with hope.

When they are troubled, keep them from discouragement. When they are perplexed, save them from despair. Grant this, our Father, for the love of your Son, who for our sake became poor, even Jesus Christ our Lord. *Amen.*

46. *For the Oppressed in the Land*

Look with pity, O heavenly Father, upon your people who live in our land with injustice, terror, disease, and death as their constant companions. Have mercy upon us. Help us to eliminate the cruelty of men to their neighbors. Strengthen those who spend their lives establishing equal protection of the law and equal opportunities for all; and grant that every one of us may enjoy a fair portion of this rich land which you have given us; through Jesus Christ our Lord. Amen.

47. *For Prisons and Prisoners*

Lord Jesus, for our sake you were condemned as a criminal: Visit our jails and prisons with your pity and judgment. Remember all prisoners [and especially those who are condemned to die]. Bring them to repentance, help them to amend their lives according to your will, and give them hope for their future. If any are held unjustly, forgive us, and teach us to improve our ways of justice. Remember also those who work in these institutions: keep them humane and compassionate; save them from becoming brutal or indifferent. And since what we do for those in prison, O Lord, we do for you, make us always conscious of the prisoners in our midst, and urgent to improve their lot. All this we ask for your mercy's sake. *Amen.*

48. *For Christian Service* [Traditional]

Another form of this prayer appears in Services for Trial Use, p. 637.[viii]

Lord, our heavenly Father, whose Son came not to be served but to serve: Bless all who, following in his steps, give themselves to the service of their fellows. Give them wisdom, patience, and courage to strengthen the weak and raise up those who fall; that, being inspired by your love, they may minister in your Name to the suffering, the friendless, and the needy; for the sake of your Son, who laid down his life for us, Jesus Christ our Savior. *Amen.*

[viii] [Ed. Note: The collects referred to are these from Special Occasion 20. For Social Service:

Heavenly Father, whose blessed Son came not to be served but to serve: Bless all, we pray, who, following in his steps, give themselves to the service of their fellow men; that with wisdom, patience, and courage, they may minister in his name to the suffering, the friendless, and the needy; for the love of him who laid down his life for us, your Son our Saviour Jesus Christ. *Amen.*

Heavenly Father, whose blessed Son came not to be ministered unto but to minister: Bless all, we pray thee, who, following in his steps, give themselves to the service of their fellow men; that with wisdom, patience, and courcage, they may minister in his Name to the suffering, the friendless, and the needy; for the love of him who laid down his life for us, thy Son our Savior Jesus Christ. *Amen.*]

49. *For a Right Attitude Toward Our Work*
O God,
as your Son, Jesus Christ, was obedient to his knowledge of your purposes for him,
help us to understand and obey your purposes for us,
and to discover the work we are best fitted to do.
And as he steadfastly rejected the temptation to use unworthy means,
teach us also to accept the discipline necessary to master our work,
and to work for the ends you desire,
to the honor of your holy Name. *Amen.*

50. *For the Right Use of God's Gifts* [Traditional]
Almighty God, your loving hand has given us all that we possess: Grant us grace that we may love you with all that we have, and be found faithful and acceptable stewards of your bounty; through Jesus Christ our Lord. *Amen.*

51. *For the Responsible Use of Money*
O Lord, your Son has taught us that from those to whom much is given, much will be required: Guide us to obtain our money honestly, neither injuring our neighbors nor ravaging your creation. And help us to use wisely what we have, for the well-being of our families and all people, and for the strengthening of your kingdom in justice, beauty, and peace; through Jesus Christ our Lord. *Amen.*

52. *For Those Who Influence Public Opinion*
Almighty God, you proclaim your truth in every age by many voices: Direct, in our time, we pray, those who speak where many listen and write what many read; that they may do their part in making the heart of this people wise, its mind sound, and its will righteous; to the honor of Jesus Christ our Lord. *Amen.*

Prayers for the Natural Order

53. *For Knowledge of God's Creation*
Almighty and everlasting God, you created the universe with its marvelous order; you made atoms, worlds, galaxies, and the infinite wonder of life: Grant that as we probe the mysteries of your creation, we may come to know you more truly, and more surely fulfill our role in your eternal purpose. In the Name of Jesus Christ our Lord. *Amen.*

54. *For the Harvest of Lands and Waters* [Traditional]
O Gracious Father, open your hand, we pray, and fill the hungry with good things. Let your breath go forth, that it may renew the face of the earth. Show us your loving-kindness, that our land may yield its fruit in abundance; and save us from selfish use of what you have given us, that all men everywhere may give thanks to you; through Jesus Christ our Lord. *Amen.*

55. *For the Conservation of Natural Resources* (1)
Almighty God, who gave man dominion over all your works: Teach us reverence for all created things. Give us grace so to employ the resources of nature that none may suffer from our abuse of them, and grant us such wisdom that generations yet to come may praise you for your bounty; in the Name of him through whom all things were made, Jesus Christ our Lord. *Amen.*

For the Conservation of Natural Resources (2)
Heavenly Father, generous Provider of all good gifts, teach men to live wisely on this fair earth. Bless our efforts to restore a healthful environment, to make the air clean, the water pure, and the soil rich. Let food abound on land and sea, and grant that it may be so distributed that hunger may threaten the world no more; through Jesus Christ our Lord. *Amen.*

56. *For the Exploration of Space*
Almighty God, Creator of all things, your dominion extends throughout the immensities of space: Guide and guard, we pray, those who seek to probe the mysteries of the universe. Save us all from that arrogance which attributes the achievements of this age to the ability of man alone, and grant that our courses through the sky may lead us to appreciate the majesty of your creation; through Jesus Christ our Lord. *Amen.*

57. *For the Responsible Use of Inventions and Discoveries*
Almighty and merciful God,
without you all things hasten to destruction and fall into nothingness:
Look upon us now with compassion,
for we have learned to unlock power from atoms
and lift ourselves into the boundless space of your creation.
Save us, lest we abuse these discoveries which you have put into our hands,
turning them to the world's misery and ruin.
Teach us to think your thoughts after you in fear and wonder,
and to use our knowledge for man's welfare and to your glory;
through Jesus Christ our Lord. *Amen.*

58. *For the Future of Mankind*
O God our heavenly Father,
you have blessed us and given us dominion over all the earth:
Increase our reverence before the mystery of life.
Give us new insight into your purposes for the human race,
and new wisdom and determination to provide for its future in obedience to your will;
through Jesus Christ our Lord. *Amen.*

59. *For Animals*
O God, you created all living things on the face of the earth and gave us dominion over them:
Grant that we may be faithful to this trust
in the way we treat all animals, both wild and tame.
Teach us to admire their beauty and to delight in their cunning;
to respect their strength and to wonder at their intelligence.
Grant that our use of them may be both merciful and wise.
So may we lend our voice to their praise of your goodness, which endures for ever. *Amen.*

Prayers for Family and Personal Life

60. *For Families* [Traditional]
O God our Father, bind together in your all-embracing love every family on earth. Banish anger and bitterness within them; nourish forgiveness and peace. Bestow upon parents such wisdom and patience that they may gently exercise the disciplines of love, and call forth from their children their greatest virtue and their highest skill. Instill in children such independence and self-respect that they may freely obey their parents, and grow in the joys of companionship. Open ears to hear the truth within the words another speaks; open eyes to see the reality beneath another's appearance; and make the mutual affection of families a sign of your kingdom; through Jesus Christ our Lord. *Amen.*

61. *For Living in Families When There is Conflict*
O God, the true Father of us all, look with compassion on all families living in tension, fear, or strife. Relieve their suspicions, calm their anger, and allay their anxiety. Help them to find the source of their conflicts, and to seek help from you and from those through whom you work; that the bonds of love and patience may be strengthened and rebuilt, and that they may live together in such a way that your Name may be honored and glorified among those around them; through Jesus Christ our Lord. *Amen.*

62. *For Children*
Almighty God, whose compassion embraces all men, we beseech you for the world's children.

May those whose small bodies are undernourished
    or diseased be fed and made whole;
May those whose minds are dull and unchallenged
    come alive;
May those whose homes are broken by strife find
    peace and security.

Protect in all children, O Lord, their special grace of spontaneity; and keep from despair those who know failure or frustration. In due time bring them, your children and our brothers, to their full human stature; through Jesus Christ our Lord. *Amen.*

63. *For the Care of Children* [Traditional]
Almighty God, heavenly Father, you have blessed us with the joy and care of children: Give us calm strength and patient wisdom as we bring them up, so that we may teach them to love whatever is just and true and good, following the example of our Savior Jesus Christ. *Amen.*

64. *For Young Persons* (1)
Lord Jesus Christ, you increased in wisdom and stature as you grew to manhood: Be a strong companion and guide to all young persons seeking their true freedom as children of God. Establish them in honor and courage. Direct them in the paths of love. And grant that as they grow in age, they may grow in faith and in knowledge of that abundant life which you have promised to all your servants. *Amen.*

For Young Persons (2)
God our Father,
you see your children growing up in an unsteady and confusing world: Show them that your ways give more life than the ways of the world, and that following you is better than chasing selfish goals. Help them to take failure not as a measure of their worth, but as the chance for a new start. Give them strength to hold their faith in you, and to keep alive their joy in your creation; through Jesus Christ our Lord. *Amen.*

65. *For Married Couples*
Almighty God, Giver of life and love: Bless those (or, *N.* and *N.*) whom you have joined in holy Matrimony. Grant them wisdom and devotion in the ordering of their life together, that each may be to the other a strength in need, a counsellor in perplexity, a comfort in sorrow, and a companion in joy. And so knit their wills together in your will, and their spirits in your Spirit, that they may show forth your love and abide in your peace all the days of their life; through Jesus Christ our Lord. *Amen.*

66. *For the Aged* (1)
Remember, O Lord, we pray,
the men and women who reach the summit of their years.
Teach them to lay aside former responsibilities without regret
and to enjoy new leisure with delight.
Keep their minds open and make their hearts young.
Sustain them in health, surround them with love,

and crown their days with such a living sense of your presence
that they may be prepared to see you face to face
in your heavenly kingdom;
through Jesus Christ our Lord. *Amen.*

For the Aged (2)
Look with mercy, O God our Father, on all those whose increasing years bring them weakness, distress, or isolation. Provide for them homes of dignity and peace; give them understanding helpers; and, as their strength diminishes, increase their faith and their assurance of your love. This we ask in the Name of Jesus Christ our Lord. *Amen.*

67. *For a Birthday* (1)
O God our Father, bless your child *N.* as *his* years increase: In *his* seeking, guide *him*; in *his* striving, sustain *him*; in danger and temptation, guard *him*. Give *him* a thankful heart, and grant that *he* may find *his* freedom in doing your will; through Jesus Christ our Lord. *Amen.*

For a Birthday (2)
O God, our times are in your hand: Look with favor, we pray, on your servant *N.* as *he* begins another year. Grant that *he* may grow in wisdom and grace, and daily strengthen *his* trust in your goodness all the days of *his* life; through Jesus Christ our Lord. *Amen.*

68. *For the Absent* [Traditional]
O God, whose fatherly care reaches to the ends of the earth: We humbly pray for those whom we love, now absent from us. Defend them from all dangers of body and spirit; and grant that both they and we, by drawing nearer to you, may be bound together by your love in the fellowship of the people of God; through Jesus Christ our Lord. *Amen.*

69. *For Those We Love* [Traditional]
Almighty God, we entrust all who are dear to us to your never-failing care and love, for this life and the life to come; knowing that you are doing for them better things than we can desire or pray for; through Jesus Christ our Lord. *Amen.*

70. *For Travelers*
O God, our heavenly Father, whose glory fills the whole creation, and whose presence we find wherever we go: Preserve those who travel, [in particular . . .]; surround them with your loving care; protect them from every danger; and bring them in safety to their journey's end; through Jesus Christ our Lord. *Amen.*

71. *For Sick Persons* (1) [Traditional]
Merciful God, giver of life and health: Bless *N.*, your *servant*, and those who minister to *him* your healing gifts, that *he* may be restored to full health and a whole spirit; through Jesus Christ our Lord. *Amen.*

For Sick Persons (2)
Father of mercies and God of all comfort, our only help in time of need, we humbly pray you to relieve your sick *servant N.*, for whom our prayers are desired. Look upon *him* with your mercy; comfort *him* with a sense of your goodness; preserve *him* from temptation; and give *him* patience in *his* affliction. In your good time restore *him* to health; enable *him* to live the rest of *his* life in your love and to your glory; and grant that finally *he* may abide with you in everlasting life; through Jesus Christ our Lords. *Amen.*

    See also *Services for Trial Use, p. 635.*

72. *For One Critically Ill* [Traditional]
Hear us, O Lord, as we pray to you on behalf of your servant *N.* As *his* bodily strength decreases, let *his* faith grow strong; and comfort *him* with the assurance of your forgiveness and the hope of your eternal kingdom; through Jesus Christ our Lord. *Amen.*

73. *For a Sick Child* [Traditional]
O heavenly Father, watch with us over your child *N.* (*or*, your servant *N.*) for whom we offer our prayers in *his* sickness. Grant that *he* may be restored to that perfect health which you alone can give; through Jesus Christ our Lord. *Amen.*

74. *For One About to Undergo an Operation* [Traditional]
Almighty God our heavenly Father, graciously comfort your *servant N.* in *his* suffering and bless the means made use of for *his* cure. Fill *his* heart with confidence, so that even if *he* is afraid, *he* may put his trust in your goodness and power; through Jesus Christ our Lord. *Amen.*

75. *For the Mentally Ill* [Traditional]
O heavenly Father, have mercy on all who are disturbed in mind or spirit. Restore them to strength of mind and cheerfulness of heart, and sustain them in health and peace; through Jesus Christ our Lord. *Amen.*

76. *For Those Who Are Addicted*
O blessed Lord, you ministered to all who came to you: Look with compassion, we pray, upon those who have lost their health and freedom by addiction. Restore to them the assurance of your unfailing mercy; remove from them the fears that

beset them; strengthen their wills that they may overcome their weakness; and to those who care for them, give understanding patience and persevering love. *Amen.*

77. *For Hospitals and Healing Ministries*
Almighty God, whose blessed Son Jesus Christ went about healing all manner of sickness among the people: Continue, we pray, his gracious work among us; bless and provide for our hospitals; grant to physicians, surgeons, nurses and all who serve with them, wisdom and skill, sympathy and patience; and give your blessing to all who work to prevent suffering; through Jesus Christ our Lord. *Amen.*

78. *For a Person in Trouble or Bereavement* [Traditional]
Merciful Father, you have taught us in your holy Word that you do not willingly afflict or grieve the children of men: Look with pity upon the sorrows of your servants (*or*, your servant *N.*) for whom our prayers are desired. Remember *them*, Lord, in mercy; nourish *them* with patience; comfort *them* with a sense of your goodness; lift up your countenance upon *them*, and give *them* peace; through Jesus Christ our Lord. *Amen.*

> See also the Collect for the Monday in Holy Week, Services for Trial Use, p. 508.[ix]

79. *For Those Who Mourn* (1) [Traditional]
Almighty God, Father of mercies and giver of all comfort: Deal graciously with those who mourn, that, casting every care on you, they may know the strength and consolation of your love; through Jesus Christ our Lord. *Amen.*

For Those Who Mourn (2)
Give faith and courage, O Lord, to all who mourn, that they may have strength to meet the days to come with steadfastness and patience; not sorrowing as those without hope, but in thankful remembrance of your great goodness in past years, and in the sure expectation of a joyful reunion with those they love; this we ask in the Name of Jesus Christ our Savior. *Amen.*

For Those Who Mourn (3)
O Heavenly Father, you have given us a sure faith and a lively hope: Help us to live as those who trust in your fatherly care, in the communion of saints, the

---

[ix] [Ed. Note: This is the collect for Monday in Holy Week:

Almighty God, whose most dear Son went not up to joy but first he suffered pain, and entered not into glory before he was crucified: Mercifully grant that we, walking in the way of the cross, may find it none other than the way of life and peace; through Jesus Christ your Son our Lord. *Amen.*

(The collects for both rites are identical.)]

forgiveness of sins, and the resurrection to everlasting life. Confirm this faith and hope in us all the days of our life; through Jesus Christ our Lord. *Amen.*

80. *For Dying in Faith* [Traditional]
O God, whose days are without end, and whose mercies cannot be numbered: Make us, we pray, deeply sensible of the shortness and uncertainty of human life; and let your Holy Spirit lead us in holiness and righteousness all our days: that, when we shall have served you in our generation, we may be gathered to our fathers, having the assurance of a good conscience; in the communion of the holy Catholic Church; in the confidence of a sure faith; in the comfort of a certain hope; in favor with you, our God, and in perfect charity with the world. All this we ask through Jesus Christ our Lord. *Amen.*

81. *For the Dead* (1) [Traditional]
Almighty God, we remember before you today your faithful *servant N.*; and we pray that as you have brought *him* to your nearer presence, *he* may continue in your joyful service; so that *he* with your servants everywhere may share your eternal victory; through Jesus Christ our Lord. *Amen.*

For the Dead (2)
Almighty God, whose love extends to realms we cannot reach: We commend to your care those who have departed from us but not from you. Grant to them the unending joys of your glorious kingdom of light and peace, in the blessed company of all your faithful people in every time and place; and grant to us, who mourn the dead, the grace to abide in your will with our spirits strengthened and our faith renewed; through Jesus Christ our Lord. *Amen.*

For the Dead (3)
We commend to your merciful care, O heavenly Father, your faithful servants now departed (*or*, your faithful servant *N.*).
You redeemed *them* through Christ; grant *them* pardon and peace.
You created *them* to praise you for ever;
summon *them* to everlasting life.
You bring your kingdom to its glorious consummation; grant that *they* may continually work the good purposes of your loving will; through Jesus Christ our Lord. *Amen.*

82. *On Memorial Days* [Traditional]
Almighty God, you hold in your hands both the living and the dead: We remember before you all those who have laid down their lives in the service of our country. Grant them your mercy and the light of your presence; and, that their death may not have been in vain, increase in us the will to work unceasingly for justice and peace among men and nations; through Jesus Christ our Lord. *Amen.*

83. *For Guidance* (1) [Traditional]
Direct us, O Lord, in all our doings with your most gracious favor and further us with your continual help; that in all our work, begun, continued, and ended in you, we may glorify your Name, and finally obtain everlasting life; through Jesus Christ our Lord. *Amen.*

For Guidance (2)
O God, you guide the humble of heart to a right judgment in all things, and you dispel the ignorance of godly men by the light of your truth: Grant us, in all our doubts and uncertainties, the grace to seek your will, so that we may turn from the way of error, and in your light see light, and in your straight path never stumble; through Jesus Christ our Lord. *Amen.*

84. *For Quiet Confidence* [Traditional]
O God of peace, you have taught us that in returning and rest we shall be saved, in quietness and confidence shall be our strength: By the might of your Spirit lift us to your presence, where we may be still and know that you are God; through Jesus Christ our Lord. *Amen.*

85. *For Trustfulness* [Traditional]

Another form of this prayer appears in Services for Trial Use, p. 491.[x]

O most loving Father, you will us to give thanks for all things, to dread nothing but losing you, and to trust you since you care for us: Save us from faithless fears and worldly anxieties, and grant that no clouds of this mortal life may hide from us that immortal love which you have shown us in your Son, Jesus Christ our Lord. *Amen.*

86. *Prayers of Self-Dedication* (1) [Traditional]
Draw our hearts to you, O God, and guide our minds; fill our imaginations and control our wills; make us wholly yours, wholly dedicated to your service. Then use us as you will, for your glory, and for the welfare of your people; through Jesus Christ our Lord. *Amen.*

Prayers of Self-Dedication (2)
Make us channels of your grace, O Lord, that our wills may conform to your will and our choices reflect your love to your people; so that your law may be fulfilled on earth as it is in heaven; through Jesus Christ our Lord. *Amen.*

Prayers of Self-Dedication (3)
Lord, you have given all for us. Help us to give all for you. Amen.

---

[x] [Ed. Note: This is the collect for ??:]

87. *For Self-Mastery*
O Lord, help us to be masters of ourselves that we may be the servants of others; through Jesus Christ our Lord and Master. *Amen.*

88. *For Self-Acceptance*
God, give us the serenity to accept the things we cannot change, the courage to change the things we can, and the wisdom to distinguish the one from the other. *Amen.*

89. *A Prayer of Love (Attributed to St. Francis)*
Lord, make us instruments of your peace.
Where there is hatred, let us sow love;
Where there is injury, pardon;
Where there is discord, union;
Where there is doubt, faith;
Where there is despair, hope;
Where there is darkness, light;
Where there is sadness, joy.

Grant that we may not so much seek to be consoled
    as to console;
    To be understood as to understand;
    To be loved as to love.
For it is in giving that we receive,
    It is in pardoning that we are pardoned,
    And it is in dying that we are born to eternal life. *Amen.*

Other Prayers

90. *On Sunday* (1) [Traditional]
O God, you make us glad every week in our remembrance of the glorious resurrection of Christ Jesus, your Son: Renew us this day through our worship, that the days to come may be spent in your service; through the same Jesus Christ our Lord. *Amen.*

On Sunday (2)
O God our King,
by the resurrection of your Son Jesus Christ on the first day of the week,
you conquered sin,
put death to flight,
and gave us the hope of everlasting life:
Redeem all our days by this victory;
forgive our sins,

banish our fears,
make us bold to praise you and to do your will,
and steel us to wait for the consummation of your kingdom on the last great Day;
through the same Jesus Christ our Lord. *Amen.*

91. *In the Morning* (1) [Traditional]

O God, the King eternal, whose light divides the day from the darkness, and turns the shadow of death into the morning: Drive far from us all wrong desires, incline our hearts to keep your law, and guide our feet into the way of peace; that, having done your will with cheerfulness during the day, we may, when night comes, rejoice to give you thanks; through Jesus Christ our Lord. *Amen.*

In the Morning (2)

We thank you, Father, for our rest during the past night and for the gift of a new day. Grant that we may so pass its hours in the perfect freedom of your service that, when evening comes, we may again give you thanks; through Jesus Christ our Lord. *Amen.*

92. *In the Evening* (1) [Traditional]

O Lord, support us all the day long, until the shadows lengthen, and the evening comes, and the busy world is hushed, and the fever of life is over, and our work is done. Then in your mercy, grant us a safe lodging, and a holy rest, and peace at the last; through Jesus Christ our Lord. *Amen.*

In the Evening (2)

O God, the life of mortal men, the light of the faithful, the strength of those who labor, and the repose of the dead: We thank you for the blessings of the day that is past, and humbly ask for your protection through the coming night. Bring us in safety to the morning hours; through him who died and rose again for us, your Son, our Savior Jesus Christ. *Amen.*

93. *Before Worship* (1) [Traditional]

Almighty God, from whom every good prayer comes: Give us the spirit to praise you and thank you and call upon your Name, that our hearts may be warmed within us and our minds enlightened. Grant that we may worship you now in beauty, truth, and love; through Jesus Christ our Lord. *Amen.*

Before Worship (2)

Assist us mercifully, O Lord, in our prayers, and direct us toward everlasting salvation: that among all the changes and chances of this mortal life, your ready help may always defend us; through Jesus Christ our Lord. *Amen.*

Before Worship (3)
Quiet our minds, O God, and gladden our hearts; that, as we come together to worship you, we may be open to your presence and find that this place is the very gate of heaven; through Jesus Christ our Lord. *Amen.*

94. *Before Sermons* (1)
Let the words of my mouth and the meditation of our hearts be always acceptable in your sight, O Lord, our strength and our redeemer. *Amen.*

Before Sermons (2)
Come, O Holy Spirit, come.
Come as the wind and cleanse;
come as the fire and burn;
convert and consecrate our lives
to our great good and your great glory;
through Jesus Christ our Lord. *Amen.*

Before Sermons (3)
Take my lips, O Lord, and speak through them; take our minds and think with them. Take our hearts and set them on fire; through Jesus Christ our Lord. *Amen.*

95. *Before Receiving Communion*
Be present, be present, O Jesus, our good High Priest, as you were present with your disciples; and be known to us in the breaking of bread; who live and reign with the Father and the Holy Spirit, now and for ever. *Amen.*

See also the Prayer of Humble Access, Services for Trial Use, p. 51.[xi]

96. *After Receiving Communion* (1)

Another form of this prayer appears in Services for Trial Use, p. 616.[xii]

[xi] [Ed. Note: We do not presume to come to this thy Table, O merciful Lord, trusting in our own righteousness, but in thy manifold and great mercies. We are not worthy so much as to gather up the crumbs under thy Table. But thou art the same Lord whose property is always to have mercy. Grant us therefore, Gracious Lord, so to partake of the Body and Blood of thy dear Son Jesus Christ, that we may be cleansed from all our sins, and may evermore dwell in him, and he in us. *Amen.*]

[xii] [Ed. Note: The collects referred to are these from Special Occasion 3. Of the Holy Eucharist:

God our Father, whose Son our Lord Jesus Christ gave us in this wonderful sacrament the memorial of his passion: Grant us so to reverence the sacred mysteries of his Body and Blood, that we may also discern within ourselves the fruit of his redemption, who now lives and reigns with you in the unity of the Holy Spirit, one God, for ever and ever. *Amen.*

God our Father, whose Son our Lord Jesus Christ hath given us in this wonderful sacrament the memorial of his passion: Grant us so to reverence the sacred mysteries of his Body and Blood, that we may ever perceive within ourselves the fruit of his redemption, who now liveth and reigneth with thee in the unity of the Holy Spirit, one God, for ever and ever. *Amen.*]

O Lord Jesus Christ, in this wonderful sacrament you have given us a memorial of your passion: Grant that we may so reverence the sacred mysteries of your Body and Blood that we may ever discern within ourselves the fruit of your redeeming work; who live and reign on high with the Father and the Holy Spirit, one God, now and for ever. *Amen.*

After Receiving Communion (2)
Almighty God, we offer you our souls and bodies to be a living sacrifice through Jesus Christ our Lord. Send us into the world in the power of your Spirit, to live and work for your praise and glory. *Amen.*

> *See also the Collect for the Nineteenth Sunday after Pentecost, Services for Trial Use, p. 561.*

97. *For the Answering of Prayer* [Traditional]
Almighty God, you have promised to heed the petitions of those who ask in the Name of Jesus your Son: Hear the prayers which we have now made to you; and grant that what we have asked according to your will, we may obtain according to your mercy; through Jesus Christ our Lord. *Amen.*

98. *After Worship* (1) [Traditional]
Grant, O Lord, that your Word, which we have heard this day with our ears, we may believe in our hearts and show forth in our lives to the honor and praise of your Name; through Jesus Christ our Lord. *Amen.*

After Worship (2)
We thank you, Lord, for opening our ears to your Word
and our eyes to your glory.
We thank you for the good news
of a redeemed creation
and the vision of a new mankind.
Send us forth in the power of your Spirit
to live our lives in your world
according to this revelation of your will;
through Jesus Christ our Lord. *Amen.*

99. *Grace at Meals* (1) [Traditional]
For these and all his mercies, God's holy Name be praised and blessed through Jesus Christ our Lord. *Amen.*

Grace at Meals (2)
Blessed are you, O Lord God, King of the Universe, for you give us food to sustain our lives and make our hearts glad; through Jesus Christ our Lord. *Amen.*

Prayers, Thanksgivings, and Litanies 45

Grace at Meals (3)
Blessed are you, O Lord our God, King of the Universe, for you bring forth bread from the earth. *Amen.*
Blessed are you, O Lord our God, King of the Universe, for you create the fruit of the vine. *Amen.*

Grace at Meals (4)
Give us grateful hearts, our Father, for all your mercies, and make us mindful of the needs of others; through Jesus Christ our Lord. *Amen.*

Grace at Meals (5)
Grant, O Lord, that our fellowship may be the revelation of your presence, and turn our daily bread into bread of life; through Jesus Christ our Lord. *Amen.*

Grace at Meals (6)
Give thanks to the Lord, for he is good;
for his love endures for ever;
through Jesus Christ our Lord. *Amen.*

Grace at Meals (7)
Taste and see that the Lord is good;
happy is the man who trusts in him;
through Jesus Christ our Lord. *Amen.*

Grace at Meals (8)
The eyes of all wait upon you, O Lord:
and you give them their food in due season.
You open wide your hand,
and satisfy the needs of every living creature.
Glory to the Father, and to the Son, and to the Holy Spirit:
as in the beginning, so now, and for ever. Amen.

Grace at Meals (9)
Be present at our table, Lord;
Be here and everywhere adored.
Thy creatures bless, and grant that we
May feast in Paradise with thee. *Amen.*

100. *A Blessing* (1)
The Lord bless us and keep us.
The Lord make his face to shine upon us and be gracious to us.
The Lord lift up his countenance upon us and give us peace,
Now and for ever. *Amen.*

A Blessing (2)
The God of peace, who brought again from the dead our Lord Jesus Christ, the great Shepherd of the sheep, through the blood of the everlasting covenant: Make you perfect in every good work to do his will, working in you that which is well pleasing in his sight; through Jesus Christ, to whom be glory for ever and ever. Amen.

Thanksgivings

General Thanksgivings

1. *The General Thanksgiving* [Traditional]
Almighty God, Father of all mercies,
we your unworthy servants give you humble thanks
for all your goodness and loving-kindness to us
and to all men.
We bless you for our creation, preservation,
and all the blessings of this life;
but above all for your incomparable love
in the redemption of the world
by our Lord Jesus Christ;
for the means of grace, and for the hope of glory.

And, we pray,
give us such an awareness of your mercies,
that with truly thankful hearts
we may make known your praise,
not only with our lips, but in our lives,
by giving up our selves to your service,
and by walking before you in holiness and
righteousness all our days;
through Jesus Christ our Lord,
to whom, with you and the Holy Spirit,
be all honor and glory throughout all ages.
Amen.

2. *A General Thanksgiving*
Accept, O Lord, our thanks and praise for all that you have done for us. We thank you for the splendor of the whole creation, for the beauty of this world, for the wonder of life, and for the mystery of love.

We thank you for the blessing of family and friends, and for the loving care which surrounds us on every side.

We thank you for setting us at tasks which demand our best effort, and for leading us to accomplishments which satisfy and delight us.

We thank you even for the disappointments and failures which lead us to acknowledge our dependence on you alone.

Above all, we thank you for your Son, Jesus Christ; for the truth of his word and the example of his, life, for his steadfast obedience, by which he overcame temptation; for his dying, through which he overcame death; and for his rising to life again, in which we are raised to the life of your kingdom.

Grant us the gift of your Spirit, so that we can know him and make him known; and through him, at all times and in all places, may give thanks to you in all things. *Amen.*

3. *For the Mission of the Church*
Almighty God, you sent your Son, Jesus Christ, to reconcile the world to yourself. We praise and bless you for those whom you have sent in the power of the eternal Spirit to preach the Gospel to all nations. We thank you for gathering together by their prayers and labors a community of love in all parts of the earth, and that in every place your servants call upon your Name; for the kingdom and the power and the glory are yours for ever. *Amen.*

4. *For the Saints and Faithful Departed* (1)
O God of both the living and the dead, we praise your holy Name for all your servants who have finished their course in faith [especially . . .]; and we pray that, encouraged by their examples and strengthened by their fellowship, we may be partakers with them of the inheritance of the saints in light; through the merits of your Son, Jesus Christ our Lord. *Amen.*

For the Saints and Faithful Departed (2)
We give thanks to you, O Lord our God, for all your servants and witnesses of time past:
Abraham, the father of believers,
Moses, Samuel, Isaiah, and all the prophets,
John the Baptist, the forerunner,
Mary, the Mother of our Lord,
Peter and Paul and all the apostles,
Stephen the first martyr, and all the martyrs and saints, in every age and in every land.
In your mercy, O Lord our God, give us, with them, hope in your salvation and in the promise of eternal life in your kingdom. Through Jesus Christ, our Lord, the first-born of many brethren. *Amen.*

Thanksgivings for National Life

5. For the Nation

The responses in italics may be omitted.

Almighty God, giver of all good things,
We thank you for the natural majesty and beauty of this land. They restore us, though we often destroy them.
   Heal us.
We thank you for the great resources of this nation. They make us rich, though we often exploit them.
   Forgive us.
We thank you for the men and women who have made this country strong. They are models for us, though we often fall short of them.
   Inspire us.
We thank you for the torch of liberty which has been lit in this land. It has drawn people here from every nation, though we have often hidden from its light.
   Enlighten us.
We thank you for the faith we have inherited in all its rich variety. It sustains our life, though we have been faithless again and again.
   Renew us.
Help us, O Lord, to finish the good work here begun. Strengthen our efforts to blot out ignorance and prejudice, and to abolish poverty and crime. And hasten the day when all our people, with many voices, in one united chorus, will glorify your holy Name. *Amen.*

6. For Heroic Service

O Judge of the nations, we remember before you with grateful hearts the men and women of our country who in the day of decision ventured much for the liberties we now enjoy. Grant that we may not rest until all the people of this land share the benefits of true freedom and gladly accept its disciplines. This we ask in the Name of Jesus Christ our Lord. *Amen.*

7. For Negotiating Peace

Eternal God, Ruler of nations and Father of all men: By your laws we learn to live in honor and justice with our neighbors. We thank you for the patience and goodwill, the tact and perception, the skill, the understanding, and the endless labor of those on opposite sides of this conflict who now meet face to face to negotiate an end to strife. Grant them perseverance in their task until our present hostilities are ended, to the lasting glory of your Name. *Amen.*

8. *For the Restoration of Peace*
Almighty God, whose Name is Love: With full hearts we thank you for peace restored, and for the light which shines through the darkness of the world's sin. We thank you for preserving our lives in the perils and dangers through which we have passed, and for opening before us a new opportunity to establish justice among our brothers. Give us grace to love all men as your Son loved us, and so make us worthy to live in peace, both now and for ever. *Amen.*

9. *For the Restoration of Domestic Peace*
O God of justice and peace, we thank you for the settlement of strife recently accomplished among us. Grant that the terms of agreement may be implemented in good faith, to our mutual benefit and to the honor of your holy Name; through Jesus Christ our Lord. *Amen.*

Thanksgivings for the Social Order

10. *For the Diversity of Races and Cultures*
O God, our Father and Creator, we thank you for the wonderful diversity of races and cultures in the world. Enrich our lives by ever-widening circles of fellowship, and show us your presence in those most alien to us, until our knowledge of your love is made perfect in our love for all our brothers; through Jesus Christ our Lord. *Amen.*

11. *For the Widening Vision of Social Justice*
O God of righteousness, we thank you for the faith we inherit. It gives us the vision of a world where children of God are not ground down in oppression but lifted up in freedom.

We thank you for the gift of your love. It demands
    that the human person must not be bound in
    misery but liberated in joy.
We thank you for the abundance of the earth. It makes
    possible a society of persons not equal in
    poverty but diverse in wealth.
We thank you for the pricking of conscience. It makes
    us lay the foundations for such a world,
    not tomorrow but today.
We thank you in the Name of Jesus Christ our Lord. *Amen.*

12. *For Peacemakers*
Lord Jesus Christ, O Prince of Peace, you have revealed to us the vision of one world where all live together as children of one Father: We thank you for those who, following in your footsteps, have drawn our hearts to an understanding of

common needs, and have challenged us to live generously. Confirm in us our purpose to obey your will, that our world may become the kingdom of your righteousness, now and for ever. *Amen.*

Thanksgivings for the Natural Order

13. *For the Creation*

We give you thanks, most gracious God, for the beauty of earth and sky and sea; for the richness of mountains, plains, and rivers; for the songs of birds and the radiance of flowers. We praise your Name for planting in us a sense of responsibility for this bounty, so that we may safeguard parklands and wilderness for posterity. Grant that we may continue to grow in our grateful enjoyment of your abundant creation, to the honor and glory of your Majesty, now and for ever. *Amen.*

14. *For the Harvest* [Traditional]

O God, in your never-failing providence there is a time to plant and a time to reap: We praise you and thank you for the coming of the harvest in yet another year; for the increase of the earth and the gathering in of its fruits, and for all the blessings you have bestowed upon this nation. Give us such a lively sense of your great mercy toward us, that we may serve you all our days with humble, thankful, and obedient hearts; through Jesus Christ our Lord. *Amen.*

Thanksgivings in Family and Personal Life

15. *For the Birth of a Child*

O God, our heavenly Father, we thank you that you have brought your servant *N.* safely through childbirth and have blessed this family with the gift of a son (*or*, a daughter, *or*, children). Grant that by your grace, *his* parents, honoring each other and obeying your will, may make their home an image of your kingdom and cherish *him* in the likeness of your love; through Jesus Christ our Lord. *Amen.*

16. *For the Gift of a Child*

Heavenly Father, you sent your own Son into this world as a little child: We give you our humble thanks. for this new life entrusted to our care. Help us to remember that we are all your children, and so to love and nurture *N.*, your child, that *he* may attain to that full stature intended for *him* in your eternal kingdom; for the sake of your dear Son Jesus Christ our Lord. *Amen.*

> *See also the prayers in the service of Thanksgiving for the Birth of a Child, Services for Trial Use, p. 325.*

17. *For the Restoration of Health*

Almighty God and heavenly Father, we thank you for healing your servant *N.*, on whose behalf we praise and bless your Name. Grant, O Lord, through your help that *he* may live in this world according to your will, and also inherit everlasting life in the world to come; through Jesus Christ our Lord. *Amen.*

18. *For Safe Travel*

Heavenly Father, we thank you for this journey (*or,* these journeys) safely ended, and for the many persons who have served us in our travel. We thank you for your guiding hand, preserving us from dangers, seen and unseen, along the way, and for your presence at every destination. Grant that our wisdom in ordering our lives may increase as fast as our skill in conquering distance, so that all our journeys may be undertaken with care and ended with praise; through Jesus Christ our Lord. *Amen.*

Litanies

1. *A Bidding Litany*

For use as a general intercession, or on special occasions.

Any of the clauses in this litany may be omitted, and others added, as the occasion requires.

Good Christian people:
Let us pray for Christ's holy Catholic Church, the blessed company of all faithful people.

Let us pray that God will strengthen it in purity of faith, in holiness of life, and in perfectness of love.

And let us pray that God will restore to it the witness of visible unity.

V. Sanctify your Church, O Lord,
R. *That we all may be one.*

Let us pray for all the ministers of God's holy Word and Sacraments, that they may faithfully exercise their pastoral office.

In particular, let us pray for Bishops [especially *N.*, our Presiding Bishop, and *N.* (*N.*), our Bishop(s)], Priests [especially . . .], and Deacons [especially . . .], that they may shine as lights in the world and worthily represent our Savior Christ before men.

V. Clothe your ministers with righteousness,
R. *And let your people sing for joy.*

Let us pray that able persons will offer themselves to serve God in Church and State.

Let us pray for all schools, colleges, and seminaries, and for all who maintain and support them, that true religion and useful learning may increase and flourish among us.

V. Make us to understand your ways, O Lord,
R. *And teach us to walk in your paths.*

Let us pray for the President of the United States and for the Governor of this State (or Commonwealth), and for all in positions of authority, that they may serve you by governing this people well.

V. Lord, keep this nation under your care,
R. *And guide us in the way of justice and truth.*

Let us pray for all the people of this land, that they live in the true faith and fear of God, and in justice and brotherly love toward one another.

V. Lord, save your people,
R. *Bless us, for we are yours.*

Let us pray for all who travel by land, sea, or air; for prisoners and captives; for all who are in sickness or sorrow; for all who have fallen into sin; for all who, through temptation, ignorance, helplessness, grief, trouble, fear, or the near approach of death, especially need our prayers.

V. Let not the needy, O Lord, be forgotten,
R. *Nor the hope of the poor be taken away.*

Let us pray also for rain and sunshine; for the fruits of the earth; for the products of all honest industry; for the helpful inventions of science and the developments of technology which ease labor or increase delight; and for all good gifts, temporal and spiritual, to us and to all men.

V. Show us your mercy, O Lord,
R. *And grant us your salvation.*

Finally, let us praise and thank our God: Father, Son, and Holy Spirit, for the wonderful grace and virtue declared in all his saints, who have been the instruments of his grace and the lights of the world in their times;

And let us pray that we may have, grace to follow their examples in this life, and to share with them the life of God's eternal kingdom.

V. You are worthy, O Lord our God, to receive glory and honor and power;
R. *You are worthy to receive blessing and praise, now and for ever. Amen.*

If the Lord's Prayer is not used elsewhere in the service, it follows here.

2. *A Litany of Thanksgiving*

This Litany is provided for optional use on Thanksgiving Day and at other times in place of the Prayer of Intercession at the Holy Eucharist (Services for Trial Use, p. 602).
For use at any time after the Collects at Morning or Evening Prayer, or separately.

Let us give thanks to God our Father for all his gifts so freely bestowed upon us:
For the beauty and wonder of his creation, in earth and sky and sea,

We thank you, Lord.

For all that is gracious in the lives of men and women, revealing the image of Christ, We thank you, Lord.
For our daily food and drink, our homes and families, and our friends,

We thank you, Lord.

For minds to think, and hearts to love, and hands to serve,

We thank you, Lord.

For health and strength to work, and leisure to rest and play,

We thank you, Lord.

For the brave and courageous who are patient in suffering, and faithful in adversity,

We thank you, Lord.

For all valiant seekers after truth, liberty, and justice,

We thank you, Lord.

For the communion of saints, in all times and places,

We thank you, Lord.

Above all, let us give thanks for the great promises and mercies given to us in Christ Jesus our Lord:

To him be praise and glory, with the Father and the Holy Spirit, now and for ever. Amen.

3. A Litany for the Mission of the Church
For use after the Collects of Morning or Evening Prayer, or separately.

O Father, Creator, from whom the whole family in heaven and earth is named,
> *Have mercy on us.*

O Son, Redeemer, through whom the world is reconciled to the Father,
> *Have mercy on us.*

O Holy Spirit, Sanctifier, whose glory fills the world and searches the deep things of God,
> *Have mercy on us.*

O Holy, blessed, and glorious Trinity, one God,
> *Have mercy on us.*

From blind hearts and petty spirits, that refuse to see the need of all mankind for your love,
> *Good Lord, deliver us.*

From pride, self-sufficiency, and the unwillingness to admit our need of your compassion,
> *Good Lord, deliver us.*

From discouragement in the face of pain and disappointment, and from lack of persistence and thoroughness,
> *Good Lord, deliver us.*

By your baptism into the sins of the world,
> *Good Lord, forgive us.*

By your abundant feeding of the multitudes,
> *Good Lord, nourish us.*

By your suffering and death, which broke down the dividing walls of hostility among men,
> *Good Lord, reconcile us.*

By your glorious resurrection and ascension,
> *Good Lord, renew us.*

By your commission to the Apostles,
> *Good Lord, send us forth.*

By the coming of the Holy Spirit, who unites all things in heaven and earth,
> *Good Lord, make us one.*

Strengthen and encourage all who do your work in lonely and dangerous places.
> *Hear us, good Lord.*

Open the hearts and hands of many for the support of your Church in every place.
> *Hear us, good Lord.*

Touch our eyes, that we may see the glory of God in all creation.
Hear us, good Lord.

Touch our ears, that we may hear from every mouth the wonderful works of God.
Hear us, good Lord.

Touch our lips, that we may tell in every tongue the wonderful works of God.
Hear us, good Lord.

Touch our hands, that we may do the truth which you have taught us.
Hear us, good Lord.

Touch our feet, that we may go for you into all parts of the world.
Hear us, good Lord.

If the Lord's Prayer is not used elsewhere in the service, it follows here. This collect may be added:

The Collect
O God, without whom our labor is in vain, and with whom the least of your children go forth as the mighty: Prosper all work undertaken according to your will; and grant to all whom you send a pure intention, patient faith, sufficient success upon earth, and the blessedness of serving you in heaven; through Jesus Christ our Lord. *Amen.*

4. *A Litany for the Ministry*

For use at Ordinations (see Services for Trial Use, pp. 459-462); or after the collects at Morning or Evening Prayer; or separately.

God the Father,
Have mercy on us.
God the Son,
Have mercy on us.
God the Holy Spirit,
Have mercy on us.
Holy Trinity, one God,
Have mercy on us.
We humbly pray that you will hear us, O Lord; and that you will send peace to the whole world, which you have reconciled to yourself by the ministry of your Son, Jesus,
Lord, hear our prayer.
That you will guide all in civil authority to establish justice and maintain it for all men,
Lord, hear our prayer.

That you will heal the divisions of your visible Church, that all may be one,
Lord, hear our prayer.
That you will grant to your People the forgiveness of sins, and give us grace to amend our lives,
Lord, hear our prayer.
That you will lead every member of your Church in his particular vocation and ministry to serve you in a true and godly life,
Lord, hear our prayer.
That you will raise up able ministers for your Church, that the Gospel may be made known to all people,
Lord, hear our prayer.
That you will inspire all Bishops, Priests, and Deacons with your love, that they may hunger for truth, and thirst after righteousness,
Lord, hear our prayer.
That you will fill them with compassion, and move them to care for all your people,
Lord, hear our prayer.

At the ordination of a bishop the following is said:

That you will bless our brother *N.*, elected bishop in your Church, and pour your grace upon *him*, that *he* may faithfully fulfill the duties of this Ministry, build up your Church, and glorify your Name,
Lord, hear our prayer.

At the ordination of deacons or of priests is said:

That you will bless your servant(s), *N. (N.)*, now to be admitted to the Order of Deacons (*or*, Priests), and pour your grace upon *him*, that *he* may faithfully fulfill the duties of this Ministry, build up your Church, and glorify your Name,
Lord, hear our prayer.

As appropriate, the following suffrage is added, adapted when necessary.

That you will bless *his family* (the members of his household *or* community), and adorn them with all Christian virtues,
Lord, hear our prayer.
That by the indwelling of your Holy Spirit you will sustain those who have been called to the ministry of your Church, and encourage them to persevere to the end,
Lord, hear our prayer.
That we, with [your blessed servant, St. _____ and] all your saints who have served you in the past, may be gathered into your unending kingdom,
Lord, hear our prayer.

Except at an Ordination, the Litany is concluded with the Lord's Prayer (if not used elsewhere in the service), and the following collect, or some other suitable one.

The Collect
O God, as you have always nourished and protected your Church, raise up for us good and faithful ministers of your Word and Sacraments, stewards of the mysteries of Christ; and grant that your people, instructed by their teaching and inspired by their example, may be guided to serve you truly and to know you more and more as you revealed yourself in Christ Jesus, your Son, our Lord. *Amen.*

5. *A Litany for Personal Life* (The Southwell Litany)

Originally composed and particularly suitable for retreats and quiet days.

> Lord, open our minds to see ourselves as you see us,
> or even as others see us and we see others;
> And from all unwillingness to know our infirmities,
> > *Save us and help us, O Lord.*

> From moral weakness, from hesitation,
> from fear of men and dread of responsibility:
> > Strengthen us with courage to speak the truth
> > in love and self-control;
> And alike from the weakness of hasty violence
> and from the weakness of moral cowardice,
> > *Save us and help us, O Lord.*

> From weakness of judgment,
> from the indecision that can make no choice,
> and from the irresolution that carries no choice
> > into act:
> > Strengthen our eye to see and
> > our will to choose the right;
> And from losing opportunities to serve you,
> and from perplexing ourselves and others
> > with uncertainties,
> > *Save us and help us, O Lord.*

> From infirmity of purpose,
> from want of earnest care and interest,
> from sluggish indolence and slack indifference,
> and from all spiritual deadness of heart,
> > *Save us and help us, O Lord.*

From dullness of conscience, from feeble sense of duty,
from thoughtless disregard of consequences to others,
from a low idea of the obligations of our calling,
and from all half-heartedness in our service,
    Save us and help us, O Lord.

From weariness in continuing struggles,
from despondency in failure and disappointment,
from overburdened sense of unworthiness,
from morbid fancies of imaginary back-slidings:
    Raise us to a lively hope in your mercy
        and in the power of faith;
And from all exaggerated fears and vexations,
    Save us and help us, O Lord.

From self-conceit, vanity, and boasting,
from delight in supposed success and superiority:
    Raise us to the modesty and humility
        of true sense and taste and reality;
And from all the harms and hindrances
        of offensive manners and self-assertion,
    Save us and help us, O Lord.

From affectation and untruth,
    conscious or unconscious,
from pretence and hypocrisy,
from impulsive self-adaptation to the moment
    to please persons or make
    circumstances easy:
    Strengthen us to true simplicity;,
And from all false appearances,
    Save us and help us, O Lord.

From love of flattery, from over-ready belief in praise,
from dislike of criticism,
and from the comfort of self-deception
    in persuading ourselves
        that others think better of us than we are,
    Save us and help us, O Lord.

From all love of display and sacrifice to popularity,
from thinking of ourselves and forgetting you
    in our worship
    Hold our minds in spiritual reverence;

And from self-glorification in all our words and works,
Save us and help us, O Lord.

From pride and self-will,
from the desire to have our own way in all things,
from overweening love of our own ideas
    and blindness to the value of others,
from resentment against opposition
    and contempt for the claims of others:
  Enlarge the generosity of our hearts
    and enlighten the fairness of
    our judgments;
And from all selfish arbitrariness of temper,
Save us and help us, O Lord.

From jealousy, whether of equals or superiors,
from grudging others success,
from impatience of submission and eagerness
    for authority:
  Give us the spirit of brotherhood
    to share loyally with fellow-workers
    in all true proportion;
And from all insubordination to just law and proper
    authority,
Save us and help us, O Lord.

From all hasty utterances of impatience,
from the retort of irritation and the taunt of sarcasm,
from all infirmity of temper in provoking
    or being provoked,
and from all idle words that may do hurt,
Save us and help us, O Lord.

In all times of temptation to follow pleasure,
    to leave duty for amusement,
    to indulge in distraction, dissipation,
    dishonesty, or debt,
    or to degrade our high calling and forget
    our solemn vows;
And in all times of frailty in our flesh,
Save us and help us, O Lord.

In all times of ignorance and perplexity
    as to what is right and best to do:

Direct us with wisdom to judge aright,
>   and order our ways
>   and overrule our circumstances
>   by your good Providence;
> And in our mistakes and misunderstandings,
>   *Save us and help us, O Lord.*

In times of doubts and questionings,
>   when our belief is perplexed by new
>   learning,
>   and our faith is strained
>   by doctrines and mysteries beyond our
>   understanding:
> Give us the faithfulness of learners,
>   and the courage of believers in your truth;
> And alike from stubborn rejection of new revelations
> and from hasty assurance that we are wiser
>   than our fathers,
>   *Save us and help us, O Lord.*

From strife, partisanship, and division,
from magnifying our certainties to condemn
>   all differences,
from building our systems to exclude all challenges,
and from all arrogance in our dealings with
>   other persons,
>   *Save us and help us, O Lord.*

Give us knowledge of ourselves:
>   our power and weaknesses, our spirit,
>   our sympathy,
>   our imagination, our knowledge, our truth;
> Teach us by the standard of your Word,
>   by the judgments of others,
>   by examinations of ourselves;
> Give us an earnest desire to strengthen ourselves
>   continually
>   by study, by diligence, by prayer and
>   meditation;
> And from all fancies, delusions, and prejudices
>   of habit, or temper, or society,
>   *Save us and help us, O Lord.*

Give us true knowledge of others,
> in their difference from us and in their
> likeness to us,
that we may deal with their real selves —
> measuring their feelings by our own,
> but patiently considering their
> varied lives
> and thoughts and circumstances;
And in all our dealings with them,
from false judgments of our own,
from misplaced trust and distrust,
from misplaced giving and refusing,
from misplaced praise and rebuke,
> *Save us and help us, O Lord.*

Chiefly we pray that we may know you
> and see you in all your works,
> always feel your presence near,
> hear you and know your call:
> Let your Spirit be our will, your Word our word;
And in all our shortcomings and infirmities,
may we have sure faith in your mercy.
> *Save us and help us, O Lord.*

Finally, we pray, blot out our past transgressions,
heal the evils of our past negligences and ignorances,
and help us to amend our past mistakes and
> misunderstandings:
> Uplift our hearts to new love,
> > new energy, new devotion,
> > that we may be unburdened
> > from the grief and shame of past
> > unfaithfulness,
> > and go forth in your strength
> > to persevere through success and failure,
> > through good report and evil report,
> > even to the end;
And in all time of our tribulation,
and in all time of our prosperity,
> *Save us and help us, O Lord.*

Here may follow the Lord's Prayer, if it is not used elsewhere in the service, and the Grace.

6. *A Litany for Healing*

For use at any time of intercession for the sick.

God the Father, whose will for all men is health and salvation;
Have mercy on us.

God the Son, who came that we might have life and have it more abundantly;
Have mercy on us.

God the Spirit, whose temple our bodies are;
Have mercy on us.

Holy Trinity, in whom we live, and move, and have our being;
Have mercy on us.

Son of David, you healed all who came to you in faith;
Heal your people, Lord.

Son of Man, you sent forth your disciples to preach the Gospel and heal the sick;
Heal your people, Lord.

Son of God, you pardon our sins and heal our infirmities;
Heal your people, Lord.

Eternal Christ, your abiding Spirit renews our minds;
Heal your people, Lord.

Lord Jesus, your holy Name is a medicine of healing and a pledge of eternal life;
Heal your people, Lord.

We pray that you will hear us, O Lord; and that you will grant your grace to make the sick well;
Hear us, and make us whole.

That you will give patience, courage, and faith to all who are disabled by injury or sickness;
Hear us, and make us whole.

That you will give speedy healing, relief from pain, and fearless confidence to all sick children;
Hear us, and make us whole.

That you will grant your strengthening presence to all who are about to undergo an operation;
Hear us, and make us whole.

That you will sustain those who face long illness, bearing them up as on eagles' wings;
Hear us, and make us whole.

That you will comfort those who endure continual pain, pouring upon them the sweet balm of your Spirit;
Hear us, and make us whole.

That you will grant to all sufferers the refreshment of quiet sleep;
Hear us, and make us whole.

That you will abide with all who are lonely or despondent, having no one to comfort them;
Hear us, and make us whole.

That you will restore all who are in mental darkness to soundness of mind and cheerfulness of heart;
Hear us, and make us whole.

That by sickness endured and sickness observed you will teach us our mortality, that we may prepare for death with fortitude and meet it with hope;
Hear us, and make us whole.

That you will give your wisdom in ample measure to doctors and nurses, that with knowledge, skill, and patience, they may minister to the sick;
Hear us, and make us whole.

That you will guide by your good Spirit all who search for the causes of sickness and disease;
Hear us, and make us whole.

Jesus, Lamb of God:
Have mercy on us.
Jesus, bearer of our sins:
Have mercy on us.
Jesus, redeemer of the world:
Give us your peace.

If the Lord's Prayer is not used elsewhere in the service, it follows here. This collect may be added:

The Collect

Almighty God, giver of life and health: Your Son came into this ailing world to make your children whole. Send your blessing on all who are sick and on all who minister to them; that when they are restored to health of body and mind, they may give thanks to you in your Church; through the same Jesus Christ our Lord. *Amen.*

7. A Litany for the Dying or the Dead

For use at any time of intercession for the dying or the departed.

> God the Father,
>   *Have mercy on your servant(s).*
>
> God the Son,
>   *Have mercy on your servant(s).*
>
> God the Holy Spirit,
>   *Have mercy on your servant(s).*
>
> Holy Trinity, one God,
>   *Have mercy on your servant(s).*
>
> From all evil, from all sin, from all tribulation,
>   *Good Lord, deliver him.*
>
> By your Incarnation, by your Cross and Passion, by your Death and Burial,
>   *Good Lord, deliver him.*
>
> By your Resurrection and Ascension, and by the coming of the Holy Spirit,
>   *Good Lord, deliver him.*
>
> We sinners pray that you will hear us, O Lord God; that you will deliver the soul(s) of your servant(s) from every fear, from the power of evil, and from eternal death,
>   *Hear us, good Lord.*
>
> That you will mercifully pardon all his sins,
>   *Hear us, good Lord.*
>
> That you will grant him a place of refreshment and everlasting blessedness,
>   *Hear us, good Lord.*
>
> That you will give him joy and gladness in your kingdom, with the saints in light,
>   *Hear us, good Lord.*

Jesus, Lamb of God:
> *Have mercy on him.*

Jesus, bearer of our sins:
> *Have mercy on him.*

Jesus, redeemer of the world:
> *Give him your peace.*

Lord, have mercy.
> *Christ, have mercy.*

Lord, have mercy.

If the Lord's Prayer is not used elsewhere in the service, it follows here. This collect may be added:

The Collect
Deliver your servant(s), O Sovereign Lord, from all evil, and set him free from every bond; that he may rest with all your saints in the eternal habitations; where with the Father and the Holy Spirit you live and reign, one God, for ever and ever. *Amen.*

The following Commendation may be added if appropriate:

Into your hands, O merciful Savior, we commend your servant *N*. Acknowledge, we humbly beseech you, a sheep of your own fold, a lamb of your own flock, a sinner of your own redeeming. Receive *him* into the arms of your mercy, into the blessed rest of everlasting peace, and into the glorious company of the saints in light. *Amen.*

In Traditional Language

Prayers

Prayers for the World

1. *For Joy in God's Creation* [Contemporary]
O heavenly Father, who hast filled the world with beauty: Open our eyes to behold thy gracious hand in all thy works; that rejoicing in thy whole creation, we may learn to serve thee with gladness; for the sake of him by whom all things were made, thy Son, Jesus Christ our Lord. *Amen.*

2. *For All Sorts and Conditions of Men* [Contemporary]
O God, the Creator and Preserver of all mankind, we humbly beseech thee for all sorts and conditions of men; that thou wouldest be pleased to make thy ways known unto them, thy saving health unto all nations. More especially we pray for thy holy Church universal; that it may be so guided and governed by thy good Spirit, that all who profess and call themselves Christians may be led into the way of truth, and hold the faith in unit of spirit, in the bond of peace, and in righteousness of life. Finally, we commend to thy fatherly goodness all those who are in any way afflicted, or distressed, in mind, body, or estate; [especially those for whom our prayers are desired] that it may please thee to comfort and relieve them according to their several necessities; giving them patience under their sufferings, and a happy issue out of all their afflictions. And this we beg for Jesus Christ's sake. *Amen.*

5. *For Peace Among the Nations* [Contemporary]
Almighty God, our heavenly Father, guide, we beseech thee, the nations of the world into the way of justice and truth, and establish among them that peace which is the fruit of righteousness, that they may become the kingdom of our Lord and Savior Jesus Christ. *Amen.*

Prayers for the Church

8. *For the Church* [Contemporary]
Gracious Father, we pray for thy holy Catholic Church. Fill it with all truth, in all truth with all peace. Where it is corrupt, purify it. Where it is in error, direct it. Where in any thing it is amiss, reform it. Where it is right, strengthen it. Where it is in want, provide for it. Where it is divided, reunite it; for the sake of Jesus Christ, thy Son, our Savior. *Amen.*[1]

9. *For the Mission of the Church* [Contemporary]

Another form of this prayer appears in Services for Trial Use, p. 628.[xiii]

[xiii] [Ed. Note: The collects referred to are these from Special Occasion 14. For the Mission of the Church I:

O God, who made of one blood all nations of men to dwell on the face of the whole earth, and sent your blessed Son to preach peace to those who are far and to those who are near: Grant that all men everywhere may seek after you and find you; bring the nations into your fold, pour out your Spirit upon all mankind, and hasten your kingdom; through Jesus Christ your Son our Lord, who lives and reigns with you and the Holy Spirit, one God, now and for ever. *Amen.*

O God, who hast made of one blood all nations of men to dwell on the face of the whole earth, and didst send thy blessed Son to preach peace to those who are far off and to those who are nigh: Grant that all men everywhere may seek after thee and find thee; bring the nations into thy fold, pour out thy Spirit upon all mankind, and hasten thy kingdom; through Jesus Christ thy Son our Lord, who liveth and reigneth with thee and the Holy Spirit, one God, now and for ever. *Amen.*]

Prayers, Thanksgivings, and Litanies 67

O God, who hast made of one blood all nations of men to dwell on the face of the whole earth, and didst send thy blessed Son to preach peace to those who are far off and those who are near: Grant that all men everywhere may seek after thee and find thee. Bring the nations into thy fold, pour out thy Spirit upon all flesh, and hasten thy kingdom; through the same thy Son, Jesus Christ our Lord. *Amen.*

10. *For Clergy and People* [Contemporary]
Almighty and everlasting God, from whom cometh every good and perfect gift: Send down upon our Bishops, and other Clergy, and upon the Congregations committed to their charge, the healthful Spirit of thy grace; and, that they may truly please thee, pour upon them thy continual blessing. Grant this, O Lord, for the honor of our Advocate and Mediator, Jesus Christ. *Amen.*

16. *For the Unity of the Church* (1) [Contemporary]
O God, the Father of our Lord Jesus Christ, our only Savior, the Prince of Peace: Give us grace seriously to lay to heart the great dangers we are in by our unhappy divisions. Take away all hatred and prejudice, and whatever else may hinder us from godly union and concord; that as there is but one Body and one Spirit, and one hope of our calling, one Lord, one Faith, one Baptism, one God and Father of us all, so we may be all of one heart and of one soul, united in one holy bond of truth and peace, of faith and charity, and may with one mind and one mouth glorify thee; through Jesus Christ our Lord. *Amen.*

For the Unity of the Church (2)
O Lord Jesus Christ, who saidst unto thine Apostles, "Peace I leave with you, my peace I give unto you": Regard not our sins, but the faith of thy Church; and grant to it that peace and unity which is according to thy will, who livest and reignest with the Father and the Holy Spirit, one God, world without end. *Amen.*

18. *For the Ordained Ministry* [Contemporary]
Almighty God, the giver of all good gifts, who of thy divine providence hast appointed various Orders in thy Church: Give thy grace, we humbly beseech thee, to all who are [now] called to any office and ministration for thy people; and so replenish them with the truth of thy doctrine, and endue them with holiness of life, that they may faithfully serve before thee to the glory of thy great Name, and to the benefit of thy holy Church; through Jesus Christ our Lord, who liveth and reigneth with thee in the unity of the Holy Spirit, one God, now and ever. *Amen.*

See also Services for Trial Use, pp. 624-627.

20. *For Christian Education* [Contemporary]

Another form of this prayer appears in Services for Trial Use, p. 623.[xiv]

Almighty God, our heavenly Father, who hast committed to thy holy Church the care and nurture of thy children: Enlighten with thy wisdom those who teach and those who learn, that, rejoicing in the knowledge of thy truth, we may worship thee and serve thee from generation to generation; through Jesus Christ our Lord. *Amen.*

24. For Those About to Receive the Laying on of Hands [Contemporary]
O God, who through the teaching of thy Son Jesus Christ didst prepare the disciples for the coming of the Holy Spirit: Make ready the hearts and minds of thy servants who at this time are seeking to be strengthened by the gifts of the Holy Spirit through the laying on of hands, that drawing near with penitent and faithful hearts, they may evermore be filled with the power of his divine indwelling; through the same Jesus Christ our Lord. *Amen.*

Prayers for the State

25. *For Our Country* [Contemporary]
Almighty God, who hast given us this good land for our heritage: We humbly beseech thee that we may always prove ourselves a people mindful of thy favor and glad to do thy will. Bless this land with honorable industry, sound learning, and pure manners. Save us from violence, discord, and confusion; from pride and arrogance, and from every evil way. Defend our liberties, and fashion into one united people the multitudes brought hither out of many kindreds and tongues. Fill with the spirit of wisdom those to whom in thy Name we entrust the authority of government, that there may be justice and peace at home, and that, through obedience to thy laws, we may show forth thy praise among the nations of the earth. In the time of prosperity, fill our hearts with thankfulness, and in the day of trouble, suffer not our trust in thee to fail; all which we ask through Jesus Christ our Lord. *Amen.*

[xiv] [Ed. Note: The collects referred to are these from Special Occasion 12. For Education:

Almighty God, the fountain of all wisdom: Enlighten by your Holy Spirit those who teach and those who learn, that, rejoicing in the knowledge of your truth, they may worship and serve you from generation to generation; through Jesus Christ our Lord, who lives and reigns with you in the unity of the holy Spirit, one God, now and for ever. *Amen.*

Almighty God, the fountain of all wisdom: Enlightenby thy Holy Spirit those who teach and those who learn, that, rejoicing in the knowledge of thy truth, they may worship and serve thee from generation to generation; through Jesus Christ our Lord who liveth and reigneth with thee in the unity of the same Spirit, one God, now and for ever. *Amen.*]

26. *For the President of the United States and All in Civil Authority* [Contemporary]
O Lord our Governor, whose glory is in all the world: We commend this nation to thy merciful care, that being guided by thy Providence, we may dwell secure in thy peace. Grant to the President of the United States, the Governor of this State (or Commonwealth), and to all in authority, wisdom and strength to know and to do thy will Fill them with the love of truth and righteousness; and make them ever mindful of their calling to serve this people in thy fear; through Jesus Christ our Lord, who liveth and reigneth with thee and the Holy Spirit, one God, world without end. *Amen.*

27. *For Congress or a State Legislature* [Contemporary]
O God, the fountain of wisdom, whose statutes are good and gracious, and whose law is truth: We beseech thee so to guide and bless our Senators and Representatives in Congress assembled (*or*, in the Legislature of this State or Commonwealth), that it may enact such laws as shall please thee, to the glory of thy Name and the welfare of this people; through Jesus Christ our Lord. *Amen.*

28. *For Courts of Justice* [Contemporary]
Almighty God, who sittest in the throne judging right: We humbly beseech thee to bless the courts of justice and the magistrates in all this land; and give unto them the spirit of wisdom and understanding, that they may discern the truth, and impartially administer the law in the fear of thee alone; through him who shall come to be our Judge, thy Son our Savior, Jesus Christ. *Amen.*

Prayers for the Social Order

35. *For Social Justice* [Contemporary]

> *This prayer also appears in Services for Trial Use, p. 636.*[xv]

Almighty God, who hast created man in thine own image: Grant us grace fearlessly to contend against evil, and to make no peace with oppression; and, that we may reverently use our freedom, help us to employ it in the maintenance of justice

---

[xv] [Ed. Note: The collects referred to are these from Special Occasion 19. For Social Justice:

Almighty God, who created man in your own image: Grant us grace fearlessly to contend against evil, and to make no peace with oppression; and, that we may reverently use our freedom, help us to employ it in the maintenance of justice among men and nations, to the glory of your holy Name; through Jesus Christ our Lord, who lives and reigns with you and the Holy Spirit, one God, now and for ever. *Amen.*

Almighty God, who hast created man in thine own image: Grant us grace fearlessly to contend against evil, and to make no peace with oppression; and, that we may reverently use our freedom, help us to employ it in the maintenance of justice among men and nations, to the glory of thy holy Name; through Jesus Christ our Lord, who liveth and reigneth with thee and the Holy Spirit, one God, now and for ever. *Amen.*]

among men and nations, to the glory of thy holy Name; through Jesus Christ our Lord. *Amen.*

37. *For Our Daily Work* [Contemporary]

Another form of this prayer appears in services for Trial Use, p. 639.[xvi]

Almighty God, our heavenly Father, who declarest thy glory and showest forth thy handiwork in the heavens and in the earth: Deliver us, in our several occupations, from the selfish love of riches, that we may do the work which thou givest us to do, in truth, in beauty, and in righteousness, with singleness of heart as thy servants, and to the benefit of our fellow-men; for the sake of him who came among us as one that serveth, thy Son Jesus Christ our Lord. *Amen.*

38. *For Agriculture* [Contemporary]
Almighty God, who hast blessed the earth that it should be fruitful and bring forth whatever is needed for the life of man: Bless those who work in the fields, and grant such seasonable weather that we may all share the fruits of the earth, and ever rejoice in thy goodness; through Jesus Christ our Lord. *Amen.*

42. *For Schools and Colleges* [Contemporary]
Almighty God, behold with thy gracious favor our universities, seminaries, colleges, and schools, that knowledge and wisdom may be increased among us. Bless all who teach and all who learn; and grant that in humility of heart they may ever look unto thee, who art the source of all truth; through Jesus Christ our Lord. *Amen.*

45. *For the Poor and Neglected* [Contemporary]
O God, almighty and merciful, who healest those that are broken in heart, and turnest the sadness of the sorrowful to joy: Let thy fatherly goodness be upon all that thou hast made. Remember in thy pity such as are this day destitute, homeless, or forgotten of their fellow men. Bless those whose increasing years are a

---

[xvi] [Ed. Note: The collects referred to are these from Special Occasion 22. For Vocation in Daily Work:

Almighty God, heavenly Father, whose glory and handiwork are shown forth in the heavens and in the earth: Deliver us, we pray, in our several occupations from selfish love of riches, that we may do the work which you give us, with singleness of heart as your servants, and to the benefit of our fellow men; for the sake of him who came among us as one that serves, your Son Jesus Christ our Lord. *Amen.*

Almighty God, heavely Father, who showest forth thy glory and handiwork in the heavens and in the earth: Deliver us, we beseech thee, in our several occupations from selfish love of riches, that we may do the work which thou givest us, with singleness of heart as thy servants, and to the benefit of our fellow men; for the sake of him who came among us as one that serveth, thy Son Jesus Christ our Lord. *Amen.*]

burden, or who have no one to care for them. Lift up those who are cast down. Cheer with hope all neglected and unhappy people. Though they be troubled on every side, keep them from discouragement; though they be perplexed, save them from despair. Grant this, O Lord, for the love of him who for our sakes became poor, thy Son, our Savior Jesus Christ. *Amen.*

48. *For Christian Service* [Contemporary]

Another form of this prayer appears in Services for Trial Use, p. 637.[xvii]

O Lord, our heavenly Father, whose blessed Son came not to be ministered unto, but to minister: Bless all who, following in his steps, give themselves to the service of their fellow men. Give them wisdom, patience, and courage to strengthen the weak and raise up those who fall; that, being inspired by thy love, they may worthily minister in thy Name to the suffering, the friendless, and the needy; for the sake of him who laid down his life for us, the same thy Son, our Savior Jesus Christ. *Amen.*

50. *For the Right Use of God's Gifts* [Contemporary]
Almighty God, whose loving hand hast given us all that we possess: Grant us grace that we may honor thee with our substance; and, remembering the account which we must one day give, may be faithful stewards of thy bounty; through Jesus Christ our Lord. *Amen.*

Prayers for the Natural Order

54. *For the Harvest of Lands and Waters* [Contemporary]
O gracious Father, who openest thine hand and fillest all things living with plenteousness: Bless the lands and the waters, and so multiply the harvest of the world. Let thy breath go forth that it may renew the face of the earth. Show thy loving-kindness, that our land may give her increase; and save us from selfish use of what thou givest, that all men everywhere may give thanks unto thee; through Christ our Lord. *Amen.*

[xvii] [Ed. Note: The collects referred to are these from Special Occasion 20. For Social Service:

Heavenly Father, whose blessed Son came not to be served but to serve: Bless all, we pray, who, following in his steps, give themselves to the service of their fellow men; that with wisdom, patience, and courage, they may minister in his name to the suffering, the friendless, and the needy; for the love of him who laid down his life for us, your Son our Saviour Jesus Christ. *Amen.*

Heavenly Father, whose blessed Son came not to be ministered unto but to minister: Bless all, we pray thee, who, following in his steps, give themselves to the service of their fellow men; that with wisdom, patience, and courcage, they may minister in his Name to the suffering, the friendless, and the needy; for the love of him who laid down his life for us, thy Son our Savior Jesus Christ. *Amen.*]

Prayers for Family and Personal Life

60. *For Families* [Contemporary]
Almighty God, our heavenly Father, who settest the solitary in families: We commend to thy continual care the homes in which thy people dwell. Put far from them, we beseech thee, every root of bitterness, the desire of vainglory, and the pride of life. Fill them with faith, virtue, knowledge, temperance, patience, godliness. Knit together in constant affection those who, in holy wedlock, have been made one flesh; turn the hearts of the parents to the children and the hearts of the children to the parents; and so enkindle fervent charity among us all, that we may be evermore kindly affectioned one to another; through Jesus Christ our Lord. *Amen.*

63. *For the Care of Children* [Contemporary]
Almighty God, heavenly Father, who hast blessed us with the joy and care of children: Give us light and strength so to train them, that they may love whatever is true and pure and lovely and of good report, following the example of our Savior Jesus Christ. *Amen.*

68. *For the Absent* [Contemporary]
O God, whose fatherly care reacheth to the uttermost parts of the earth: We humbly beseech thee graciously to behold and bless those whom we love, now absent from us. Defend them from all dangers of soul and body; and grant that both they and we, drawing nearer to thee, may be bound together by thy love in the communion of thy Holy Spirit, and in the fellowship of thy saints; through Jesus Christ our Lord. *Amen.*

69. *For Those We Love* [Contemporary]
Almighty God, we entrust all who are dear to us to thy never-failing care and love, for this life and the life to come; knowing that thou art doing for them better things than we can desire or pray for; through Jesus Christ our Lord. *Amen.*

71. *For Sick Persons* (1) [Contemporary]
O merciful God, giver of life and health: Bless, we pray thee, thy servant *N.* and those who minister to *him* of thy healing gifts; that *he* may be restored to fullness of health and wholeness of spirit; through Jesus Christ our Lord. *Amen.*

For Sick Persons (2)
O Father of mercies and God of all comfort, our only help in time of need: We humbly beseech thee to behold, visit, and relieve thy sick servant *N.*, for whom our prayers are desired. Look upon *him* with the eyes of thy mercy; comfort *him* with a sense of thy goodness; preserve *him* from temptation; and give *him* patience under *his* affliction. In thy good time restore *him* to health, and enable *him* to lead the rest of *his* life in thy love and to thy glory; and grant that finally *he* may dwell with thee in life everlasting; through Jesus Christ our Lord. *Amen.*

See also Services for Trial Use, p. 635.

72. *For One Critically Ill* [Contemporary]
Hear, O Lord, we beseech thee, these our prayers, as we call upon thee on behalf of this thy servant *N.*; and bestow upon *him* the help of thy merciful consolation; through Jesus Christ our Lord. *Amen.*

73. *For a Sick Child* [Contemporary]
O heavenly Father, watch with us, we pray thee, over thy sick child *N.* (*or*, thy servant *N.*) for whom our prayers are offered, and grant that *he* may be restored to that perfect health which is thine alone to give; through Jesus Christ our Lord. *Amen.*

74. *For One About To Undergo an Operation* [Contemporary]
Almighty God our heavenly Father, we beseech thee graciously to comfort thy servant *N.* in *his* suffering and to bless the means made use of for *his* cure. So fill *his* heart with confidence that even when *he* is afraid, *he* yet may put his trust in thee; through Jesus Christ our Lord. *Amen.*

75. *For the Mentally Ill* [Contemporary]
O heavenly Father, we beseech thee to have mercy upon all thy children who are living in mental darkness. Restore them to strength of mind and cheerfulness of spirit, and give them health and peace; through Jesus Christ our Lord. *Amen.*

78. *For a Person in Trouble or Bereavement* [Contemporary]
O merciful Father, who hast taught us in thy holy Word that thou lost not willingly afflict or grieve the children of men: Look with pity upon the sorrows of thy servant for whom our prayers are offered. Remember *him*, O Lord, in mercy; nourish *his* soul with patience; comfort *him* with a sense of thy goodness; lift up thy countenance upon *him*, and give *him* peace; through Jesus Christ our Lord. *Amen.*

See also the Collect for the Monday in Holy Week, Services for Trial Use p. 508.[xviii]

79. *For Those Who Mourn* [Contemporary]
Almighty God, Father of mercies and giver of all comfort: Deal graciously, we pray thee, with those who mourn, that, casting every care on thee, they may know the consolation of thy love; through Jesus Christ our Lord. *Amen.*

[xviii] [Ed. Note: This is the collect for Monday in Holy Week:

Almighty God, whose most dear Son went not up to joy but first he suffered pain, and entered not into glory before he was crucified: Mercifully grant that we, walking in the way of the cross, may find it none other than the way of life and peace; through Jesus Christ your Son our Lord. *Amen.*

(The collects for both rites are identical.)]

80. *For Dying in Faith* [Contemporary]
O God, whose days are without end, and whose mercies cannot be numbered: Make us, we beseech thee, deeply sensible of the shortness and uncertainty of human life; and let thy Holy Spirit lead us in holiness and righteousness all our days; that, when we shall have served thee in our generation, we may be gathered unto our fathers, having the testimony of a good conscience; in the communion of the Catholic Church; in the confidence of a certain faith; in the comfort of a reasonable, religious, and holy hope; in favor with thee our God, and in perfect charity with the world. All which we ask through Jesus Christ our Lord. *Amen.*

81. *For the Dead* [Contemporary]
Almighty God, we remember this day before thee thy faithful *servant N.*; and we pray thee that, having opened to *him* the gates of larger life, thou wilt receive *him* more and more into thy joyful service; that *he* may win with thee and thy servants everywhere, the eternal victory; through Jesus Christ our Lord. *Amen.*

82. *On Memorial Days* [Contemporary]
Almighty God, our heavenly Father, in whose hands are the living and the dead: We give thee thanks for all thy servants who have laid down their lives in the service of our country. Grant to them thy mercy and the light of thy presence; and give us such a lively sense of thy righteous will that the work which thou hast begun in them may be perfected through us; through Jesus Christ our Lord. *Amen.*

83. *For Guidance* (1) [Contemporary]
Direct us, O Lord, in all our doings with thy most gracious favor and further us with thy continual help; that in all our works begun, continued, and ended in thee, we may glorify thy holy Name, and finally, by thy mercy, obtain everlasting life; through Jesus Christ our Lord. *Amen.*

For Guidance (2)
O God, by whom the meek are guided in judgment, and light riseth up in darkness for the godly: Grant us, in all our doubts and uncertainties, the grace to ask what thou wouldest have us to do, that the Spirit of wisdom may save us from all false choices, and that in thy light we may see light, and in thy straight path may not stumble; through Jesus Christ our Lord. *Amen.*

84. *For Quiet Confidence* [Contemporary]
O God of peace, who hast taught us that in returning and rest we shall be saved, in quietness and in confidence shall be our strength: By the might of thy Spirit lift us, we pray thee, to thy presence, where we may be still and know that thou art God; through Jesus Christ our Lord. *Amen.*

85. *For Trustfulness* [Contemporary]

Another form of this prayer appears in Services for Trial Use, p. 491.[xix]

O most loving Father, who willest us to give thanks for all things, to dread nothing but the loss of thee, and to cast all our care on thee who carest for us: Preserve us from faithless fears and worldly anxieties, and grant that no clouds of this mortal life may hide from us the light of that love which is immortal, and which thou hast manifested unto us in thy Son, Jesus Christ our Lord. *Amen.*

86. *A Prayer of Self-Dedication* [Contemporary]
Almighty and eternal God, so draw our hearts to Thee, so guide our minds, so fill our imaginations, so control our wills, that we may be wholly thine, utterly dedicated unto thee; and then use us, we pray thee, as thou wilt, but always to thy glory and the welfare of thy people; through our Lord and Savior Jesus Christ. Amen.

Other Prayers

90. *On Sunday* [Contemporary]
O God, who makest us glad with the weekly remembrance of the glorious resurrection of thy Son our Lord: Renew us this day through our worship of thee, that the days to come may be spent in thy service; through the same Jesus Christ our Lord. *Amen.*

91. *In the Morning* [Contemporary]
O God, the King eternal, who dividest the day from the darkness, and turnest the shadow of death into the morning: Drive far off from us all wrong desires, incline our hearts to keep thy law, and guide our feet into the way of peace; that, having done thy will with cheerfulness while it was day, we may, when the night cometh, rejoice to give thee thanks; through Jesus Christ our Lord. *Amen.*

92. *In the Evening* (1) [Contemporary]
O Lord, support us all the day long, until the shadows lengthen, and the evening comes, and the busy world is hushed, and the fever of life is over, and our work is done. Then in thy mercy, grant us a safe lodging, and a holy rest, and peace at the last. *Amen.*

In the Evening (2)
O God, who art the life of mortal men, the light of the faithful, the strength of those who labor, and the repose of the dead: We thank thee for the timely

---

[xix] [Ed. Note: This is the collect for ??:]

blessings of the day, and humbly beseech thy merciful protection all the night. Bring us, we pray thee, in safety to the morning hours; through him who died for us and rose again, thy Son, our Savior Jesus Christ. *Amen.*

93. *Before Worship* (1) [Contemporary]

O Almighty God, who pourest out on all who desire it, the spirit of grace and of supplication: Deliver us, when we draw near to thee, from coldness of heart and wanderings of mind, that with steadfast thoughts and kindled affections, we may worship thee in spirit and in truth; through Jesus Christ our Lord. *Amen.*

Before Worship (2)

Assist us mercifully, O Lord, in these our supplications and prayers, and dispose the way of thy servants toward the attainment of everlasting salvation; that, among all the changes and chances of this mortal life, they may ever be defended by thy gracious and ready help; through Jesus Christ our Lord. *Amen.*

97. *For the Answering of Prayer* [Contemporary]

Almighty God, who hast promised to hear the petitions of those who ask in thy Son's Name: We beseech thee mercifully to incline thine ears to us who have now made our prayers and supplications unto thee; and grant that those things which we have faithfully asked according to thy will, may effectually be obtained, to the relief of our necessity, and to the setting forth of thy glory; through Jesus Christ our Lord. *Amen.*

98. *After Worship* [Contemporary]

Grant, we beseech thee, Almighty God, that the words which we have heard this day with our outward ears, may, through thy grace, be so grafted inwardly in our hearts, that they may bring forth in us the fruit of good living, to the honor and praise of thy Name; through Jesus Christ our Lord. *Amen.*

99. *Grace at Meals* [Contemporary]

Give us grateful hearts, our Father, for all thy mercies, and make us mindful of the needs of others; through Jesus Christ our Lord. *Amen.*

100. *A Blessing* (1) [Contemporary]

The Lord bless us, and keep us. The Lord make his face to shine upon us, and be gracious unto us. The Lord lift up his countenance upon us, and give us peace, both now and evermore. *Amen.*

A Blessing (2)

The God of peace, who brought again from the dead our Lord Jesus Christ, the great Shepherd of the sheep, through the blood of the everlasting covenant: Make you perfect in every good work to do his will, working in you that which is well pleasing in his sight; through Jesus Christ, to whom be glory for ever and ever. *Amen.*

Thanksgivings

The numbering of the Thanksgivings which follow corresponds to the numbering in the Contemporary Language section. As pointed out in the Introduction (p. 14), not all the material in that section has a corresponding version in traditional language.

1. *The General Thanksgiving* [Contemporary]
Almighty God, Father of all mercies,
we thine unworthy servants,
do give thee most humble and hearty thanks
for all thy goodness and loving-kindness to us,
and to all men.

We bless thee for our creation, preservation,
and all the blessings of this life;
but above all for thine inestimable love
in the redemption of the world by our Lord Jesus Christ
for the means of grace, and for the hope of glory.

And, we beseech thee, give us that due sense
of all thy mercies,
that our hearts may be unfeignedly thankful;
And that we show forth thy praise,
not only with our lips, but in our lives,
by giving up our selves to thy service,
and by walking before thee
in holiness and righteousness
all our days;
through Jesus Christ our Lord,
to whom, with thee and the Holy Spirit,
be all honor and glory, world without end.
Amen.

14. *For the Harvest* [Contemporary]
Most gracious God, by whose knowledge the depths are broken up and the clouds drop down the dew: We yield thee hearty thanks and praise for the return of seedtime and harvest, for the increase of the ground and the gathering in of its fruits, and for all the other blessings of thy merciful providence bestowed upon this nation and people. Give us a just sense of these great mercies, such as may appear in our lives by an humble, holy, and obedient walking before thee all our days; through Jesus Christ our Lord, to whom, with thee and the Holy Spirit, be all glory and honor, world without end. *Amen.*

17. *For the Restoration of Health* [Contemporary]
Almighty God and heavenly Father, we give thee humble thanks for that thou hast been graciously pleased to deliver from his sickness thy servant *N.*, in whose behalf we bless and praise thy Name. Grant, O gracious Father, that *he*, through thy help, may live in this world according to thy will, and also be partaker of everlasting glory in the life to come; through Jesus Christ our Lord. *Amen.*

The Litany and other Prayers from the Prayer Book of 1928

1. *The Litany*

> *To be said or sung, kneeling, standing, or in procession; before the Eucharist or after the Collects of Morning or Evening Prayer; or separately; especially in Lent and on Rogation Days.*

> O God the Father, Creator of heaven and earth,
> > *Have mercy upon us.*
> O God the Son, Redeemer of the world,
> > *Have mercy upon us.*
> O God the Holy Ghost, Sanctifier of the faithful,
> > *Have mercy upon us.*
> O holy, blessed, and glorious Trinity, one God,
> > *Have mercy upon us.*
> Remember not, Lord, our offences, nor the offences of our forefathers; neither reward us according to our sins: Spare us, good Lord, spare thy people, whom thou hast redeemed with thy most precious blood, and by thy mercy preserve us forever,
> > *Spare us, good Lord.*

> From all evil; from sin; from inordinate and sinful affections; and from all the deceits of the world, the flesh, and the devil,
> > *Good Lord, deliver us.*

> From all blindness of heart; from pride, vainglory, and hypocrisy; and from envy, malice, and hatred,
> > *Good Lord, deliver us.*

> From all oppression, sedition, and rebellion; from all false doctrine, heresy, and schism; from hardness of heart, and contempt of thy Word and Commandment,
> > *Good Lord, deliver us.*

From lightning, and tempest; from earthquake, fire, and flood; from plague, pestilence, and famine; from battle and murder, and from dying unprepared,
Good Lord, deliver us.

By the mystery of thy holy Incarnation; by thy Baptism, Fasting, and Temptation,
Good Lord, deliver us.

By thine Agony and Bloody Sweat; by thy Cross and Passion; by thy precious Death and Burial; by thy glorious Resurrection and Ascension; and by the Coming of the Holy Ghost,
Good Lord, deliver us.

In all time of our tribulation; in all time of our prosperity; in the hour of death, and in the day of judgment,
Good Lord, deliver us.

We sinners do beseech thee to hear us, O Lord God, and that it may please thee to rule and govern thy holy Church Universal in the right way,
We beseech thee to hear us, good Lord.

That it may please thee so to rule the hearts of thy servants, the President of the United States, and all others in authority, that they may do justice, and love mercy, and walk in the paths of truth,
We beseech thee to hear us, good Lord.

That it may please thee to enlighten all Bishops, Priests, and Deacons, with true knowledge and understanding of thy Word, and that both by their preaching and living they may set it forth, and show it accordingly,
We beseech thee to hear us, good Lord.

That it may please thee to send forth laborers into thy harvest, and to extend thy Church over all the earth,
We beseech thee to hear us, good Lord.

That it may please thee to bless and keep all thy people,
We beseech thee to hear us, good Lord.

That it may please thee to give us an heart to love and fear thee, and diligently to live after thy commandments,
We beseech thee to hear us, good Lord.

That it may please thee to give us true repentance; to forgive us all our sins, negligences, and ignorances; and to endue us with the grace of thy Holy Spirit to amend our lives according to thy holy Word,
We beseech thee to hear us, good Lord.

That it may please thee to strengthen such as do stand; and to comfort and help the weak-hearted; and to raise up those who fall; and finally to beat down Satan under our feet,
We beseech thee to hear us, good Lord.

That it may please thee to help, support, and strengthen all who are in danger, need, and tribulation,
We beseech thee to hear us, good Lord.

That it may please thee to preserve all who travel by land, by water, or by air; all women in child-birth, all sick persons and young children; and to show thy pity upon all prisoners and captives,
We beseech thee to hear us, good Lord.

That it may please thee to defend, and provide for, the fatherless children, and widows, and all who are desolate and oppressed,
We beseech thee to hear us, good Lord.

That it may please thee to have mercy upon all mankind,
We beseech thee to hear us, good Lord.

That it may please thee to make wars to cease in all the world; to give to all nations unity, peace, and concord; and to bestow upon all peoples the liberty to serve thee without fear,
We beseech thee to hear us, good Lord.

That it may please thee to forgive our enemies, persecutors, and slanderers, and to turn their hearts,
We beseech thee to hear us, good Lord.

That it may please thee to bring into the way of truth all such as have erred, and are deceived,
We beseech thee to hear us, good Lord.

That it may please thee to give and preserve to our use the fruits of the earth, so that in due time we may enjoy them,
We beseech thee to hear us, good Lord.

That it may please thee to grant to all the faithful departed eternal life and peace,
We beseech thee to hear us, good Lord.

That it may please thee to grant that with all thy Saints we may attain to thy heavenly kingdom,
We beseech thee to hear us, good Lord.

Son of God, we beseech thee to hear us.
Son of God, we beseech thee to hear us.

O Lamb of God, who takest away the sins of the world,
Have mercy upon us.

O Lamb of God, who takest away the sins of the world,
Have mercy upon us.

O Lamb of God, who takest away the sins of the world,
Grant us thy peace.

Lord, have mercy upon us.		Kyrie eleison.
Christ, have mercy upon us.	or	*Christe eleison.*
Lord, have mercy upon us.		Kyrie eleison.

When the Holy Communion or Ante-communion is to follow immediately, the Litany is concluded at this point and the Communion Service begins with the Salutation and Collect of the Day. The Prayer of Intercession within the Eucharist is then omitted.

On all other occasions the Litany continues as follows:

Our Father, who art in heaven, Hallowed be thy. Name. Thy kingdom come. Thy will be done, On earth as it is in heaven. Give us this day our daily bread. And forgive us our trespasses, As we forgive those who trespass against us. And lead us not into temptation, But deliver us from evil. *Amen.*

O Lord, let thy mercy be showed upon us,
   As we do put our trust in thee.
The Lord be with you.
   And with thy spirit.
Let us pray.

The Litany concludes with this or some other Collect.

Almighty God, who hast promised to hear the petitions of those who ask in thy Son's Name: We beseech thee to incline thine ear to us who have now made our supplications unto thee; and grant that those things which we have asked faithfully according to thy will, may be obtained effectually, to the relief of our necessity, and to the setting forth of thy glory; through Jesus Christ our Lord, to whom, with thee and the Holy Ghost, be all honor and glory, world without end. Amen.

2. A Bidding Prayer

> *For use before or after Sermons, or on special occasions.*
> *Any of the clauses of this Prayer may be omitted, or others added, as occasion may require.*

Good Christian People, I bid your prayers for Christ's holy Catholic Church, the blessed company of all faithful people; that it may please God to confirm and strengthen it in purity of faith, in holiness of life, and in perfectness of love, and to restore to it the witness of visible unity; and more especially for that branch of the same planted by God in this land, whereof we are members; that in all things it may work according to God's will, serve him faithfully, and worship him acceptably.

Ye shall pray for the President of these United States, and for the Governor of this State, and for all that are in authority; that all, and every one of them, may serve truly in their several callings to the glory of God, and the edifying and well-governing of the people, remembering the account they shall be called upon to give at the last great day.

Ye shall also pray for the ministers of God's Holy Word and Sacraments; for Bishops [and herein more especially for the Bishop of this Diocese], that they may minister faithfully and wisely the discipline of Christ; likewise for all Priests and Deacons [and herein more especially for the Clergy here residing], that they may shine as lights in the world, and in all things adorn the doctrine of God our Savior.

And ye shall pray for a due supply of persons fitted to serve God in the Ministry and in the State; and to that end, as well as for the good education of all the youth of this land, ye shall pray for all schools, colleges, and seminaries of sound and godly learning, and for all whose hands are open for their maintenance; that whatsoever tends to the advancement of true religion and useful learning may for ever flourish and abound.

Ye shall pray for all the people of these United States, that they may live in the true faith and fear of God, and in brotherly charity one towards another.

Ye shall pray also for all who travel by land, sea, or air; for all prisoners and captives; for all who are in sickness or in sorrow; for all who have fallen into grievous sin; for all who, through temptation, ignorance, helplessness, grief, trouble, dread, or the near approach of death, especially need our prayers.

Ye shall also praise God for rain and sunshine; for the fruits of the earth; for the products of all honest industry; and for all his good gifts, temporal and spiritual, to us and to all men.

Finally, ye shall yield unto God most high praise and hearty thanks for the wonderful grace and virtue declared in all his saints, who have been the choice vessels of his grace and the lights of the world in their several generations; and pray unto God, that we may have grace to direct our lives after their good examples; that, this life ended, we may be made partakers with them of the glorious resurrection, and the life everlasting.

And now, brethren, summing up all our petitions, and all our thanksgivings, in the words which Christ hath taught us, we make bold to say,

Our Father, who art in heaven, Hallowed be thy Name. Thy kingdom come. Thy will be done, On earth as it is in heaven. Give us this day our daily bread. And forgive us our trespasses, As we forgive those who trespass against us. And lead us not into temptation, But deliver us from evil. For thine is the kingdom, and the power, and the glory, for ever and ever. *Amen.*

3. *A Collect for Peace*
O God, who art the author of peace and lover of concord, in knowledge of whom standeth our eternal life, whose service is perfect freedom: Defend us thy humble servants in all assaults of our enemies; that we, surely trusting in thy defence, may not fear the power of any adversaries, through the might of Jesus Christ our Lord. *Amen.*

4. *For a General or Diocesan Convention*
Almighty and everlasting God, who by the Holy Spirit didst preside in the council of the blessed Apostles, and hast promised, through thy Son Jesus Christ, to be with thy Church to the end of the world: We beseech thee to be with the Council of thy Church [here] assembled in thy Name and Presence. Save us from all error, ignorance, pride, and prejudice; and of thy great mercy, so direct, sanctify, and govern us in our work by the mighty power of thy Holy Spirit, that the Gospel of Christ may be truly preached, truly received, and truly followed, in all places, to the breaking down the kingdom of sin, Satan, and death; till at length the whole of thy dispersed sheep, being gathered into one fold, shall become partakers of everlasting life; through the merits and death of Jesus Christ our Savior. *Amen.*

5. *For the President of the United States and All in Civil Authority* (1)
O Lord, our heavenly Father, the high and mighty Ruler of the universe, who dost from thy throne behold all the dwellers upon earth: Most heartily we beseech thee, with thy favor to behold and bless thy servant, The President of the United States, and all others in authority; and so replenish them with the grace of thy Holy Spirit, that they may always incline to thy will and walk in thy way. Endue them plenteously with heavenly gifts; grant them in health and prosperity long to live; and finally, after this life, to attain everlasting joy and felicity; through Jesus Christ our Lord. *Amen.*

For the President of the United States and all in Civil Authority (2)
Almighty God, whose kingdom is everlasting and power infinite: Have mercy upon this whole land; and so rule the hearts of thy servants, The President of the United States, The Governor of this State (*or*, Commonwealth), and all others

in authority, that they, knowing whose ministers they are, may above all things seek thy honor and glory; and that we and all the People, duly considering whose authority they bear, may faithfully and obediently honor them, according to thy blessed Word and ordinance; through Jesus Christ our Lord, who with thee and the Holy Ghost liveth and reigneth ever, one God, world without end. *Amen.*

6. *For the Army*
O Lord God of Hosts, stretch forth, we pray thee, thine almighty arm to strengthen and protect the soldiers of our country. Support them in the day of battle, and in the time of peace keep them safe from all evil; endue them with courage and loyalty; andg rant that in all things they may serve without reproach; through Jesus Christ our Lord. *Amen.*

7. *For the Navy*
O Eternal Lord God, who alone spreadest out the heavens, and rulest the raging of the sea: Vouchsafe to take into thy almighty and most gracious protection our country's Navy, and all who serve therein. Preserve them from the dangers of the sea, and from the violence of the enemy; that they may be a safeguard unto the United States of America, and a security for such as pass on the seas upon their lawful occasions; that the inhabitants of our land may in peace and quietness serve thee our God, to the glory of thy Name; through Jesus Christ our Lord. *Amen.*

8. *In Time of Dearth, Drought, or Storm*
O God, heavenly Father, whose gift it is that the rain doth fall and the earth bring forth her increase: Behold the afflictions of thy people [in. . .]; deliver us from the immoderate weather from which we suffer; increase the fruits of the earth by thy heavenly benediction; and grant that the scarcity which now threatens us may, through thy goodness, be mercifully turned into plenty; for the love of Jesus Christ our Lord. *Amen.*

9. *A In Time of Crisis*
O God, merciful and compassionate, who art ever ready to hear the prayers of those who put their trust in thee: Graciously hearken to us who call upon thee, and grant us thy help in this our need; through Jesus Christ our Lord. *Amen.*

General Intercessions from the Holy Eucharist 1970

The following forms of intercession, appointed for use at the Eucharist (Services for Trial Use, pp. 93-112), may also be used after the Collects at Morning or Evening Prayer, or separately.

The intercessions may be introduced with a sentence of invitation related to the Season or to themes emphasized in the rest of the service.

When a briefer form of Prayer is desired, some or all of the petitions marked with an asterisk may be omitted.

Collects suitable to conclude these intercessions will be found on pp. 169-170.

General Intercession I

With all our heart and with all our mind, let us pray to the Lord, saying, "Lord, have mercy".

*For the peace from above, for the loving kindness of God, and for the salvation of our souls, let us pray to the Lord.
Lord, have mercy.

For the peace of the world, for the welfare of the holy Church of God, and for the unity of all mankind, let us pray to the Lord.
Lord, have mercy.

For our Bishop, and for all the clergy and people,
let us pray to the Lord.
Lord, have mercy.

For our President, for the leaders of the nations, and for all in authority,
let us pray to the Lord.
Lord, have mercy.

For this city (town, village, _____), for every city and community, and for those who live in them,
let us pray to the Lord.
Lord, have mercy.

*For seasonable weather, and for an abundance of the fruits of the earth,
let us pray to the Lord.
Lord, have mercy.

* For the good earth which God has given us, and for the wisdom and will to conserve it,
let us pray to the Lord.
Lord, have mercy.

* For those who travel on land, on water, in the air, or through outer space,
let us pray to the Lord.
Lord, have mercy.

For the aged and infirm, for widows and orphans, and for the sick and the suffering,

let us pray to the Lord.
Lord, have mercy.

For the poor and the oppressed, for prisoners and captives, and for all who remember and care for them,
let us pray to the Lord.
Lord, have mercy.

For all who have died in the hope of the resurrection, and for all the departed,
let us pray to the Lord.
Lord, have mercy.

* For deliverance from all danger, violence, oppression, and degradation,
let us pray to the Lord.
Lord, have mercy.

* For the absolution and remission of our sins and offenses,
let us pray to the Lord.
Lord, have mercy.

* That we may end our lives in faith and hope, without suffering and without reproach,
let us pray to the Lord.
Lord, have mercy.

* Defend us, deliver us, and in your compassion protect us, O Lord, by your grace.
Lord, have mercy.

In the Communion of Saints, let us commend ourselves, and one another, and all our life to Christ our God.
To you, O Lord our God.

A brief silence is then observed.
The Litany is concluded with the following or some other prayer:

Concluding Prayer in Contemporary Language
Lord Jesus Christ, you have given us grace at this time with one accord to make our common supplication, and have promised that when two or three are agreed together in your Name you will grant their requests: Fulfill now, O Lord, our desires and petitions, as may be best for us; granting us in this world knowledge of your truth, and in the world to come life everlasting; through your mercy, O Christ, to whom with the Father and the Holy Spirit be honor and glory for ever and ever. Amen.

A Concluding Prayer in Traditional Language
Lord Jesus Christ, who hast given us grace at this time with one accord to make our common supplication, and hast promised that when two or three are agreed together in thy Name thou wilt grant their requests: Fulfill now, O Lord, our desires and petitions, as may be best for us; granting us in this world knowledge of thy truth, and in the world to come life everlasting; through thy mercy, O Christ, to whom with the Father and the Holy Spirit be honor and glory for ever and ever. *Amen.*

General Intercession II

In the course of the silence after each bidding, the People offer their own prayers, either silently or aloud.

I ask your prayers for God's people throughout the world: for our Bishop(s) _____; for this gathering; and for all ministers and people.
  Pray, brothers and sisters, for the Church.

  Silence

I ask your prayers for peace among men; for goodwill among nations; and for the well-being of all people.
  Pray, brothers and sisters, for justice and peace.

  Silence

I ask your prayers for the poor, the sick, the hungry, the oppressed, and those in prison.
  Pray, brothers and sisters, for those in any need or trouble.

  Silence

I ask your prayers for all who seek God, or a deeper knowledge of him.
  Pray, brothers and sisters, that they may find and be found of him.

  Silence

I ask your prayers for the departed [especially _____].
  Pray, brothers and, sisters, for those who have died.

  Silence
  Members of the congregation may ask the prayers or the thanksgivings of those present.

* I ask your prayers for . . .

* I ask your thanksgiving for . . .
   Give thanks, brothers and sisters, for God's great goodness.

   Silence

Praise God for those in every generation in whom Christ has been honored [especially _____ whom we remember today]. And pray that we may have grace to glorify Christ in our own day.

   Silence
   A concluding prayer is then added. For suggestions see pp. 96-97.

General Intercession III [Contemporary]

   After the invitation to prayer, the Leader and People pray responsively.

Father, we pray for thy holy Catholic Church:
   That we all may be one.
Grant that every member of the Church may truly and humbly serve thee:
   That thy Name may be glorified by all people.
We pray for all Bishops, Priests and Deacons:
   That they may be faithful stewards of thy holy mysteries.
We pray for all who govern and hold authority in the nations of the world:
   That there may be peace and justice among men.
May we seek to do thy will in all that we undertake:
   That we may be blest in all our works.
Have compassion on those who suffer from any grief or trouble:
   That they may be delivered from their distress.
Grant rest eternal to the departed:
   Let light perpetual shine upon them.
We praise thee for all thy saints who have entered into joy:
   May we also come to share in thy heavenly kingdom.
Let us pray in silence for our own needs and those of others.

   Silence
   The following or some other prayer is then added:

Almighty God, the fountain of all wisdom, who knowest our necessities before we ask, and our ignorance in asking: We beseech thee to have compassion upon our infirmities; and those things which for our unworthiness we dare not, and for our blindness cannot ask, mercifully give us for the sake of thy Son Jesus Christ our Lord. *Amen.*

General Intercession III [Traditional]

After the invitation to prayer, the Leader and People pray responsively.

Father, we pray for your holy Catholic Church:
That we all may be one.

Grant that every member of the Church may truly and humbly serve you:
That your Name may be glorified by all people.

We pray for all Bishops, Priests and Deacons:
That they may be faithful ministers of your Word and Sacraments.

We pray for all who govern and hold authority in the nations of the world:
That there may be peace and justice among men.

Give us courage to do your will in all that we undertake:
That we may be blest in all our works.

Have compassion on those who suffer from any grief or trouble:
That they may be delivered from their distress.

Give to the departed eternal rest:
Let your light shine upon them for ever.

We praise you for all your saints who have entered into joy:
May we also come to share in your heavenly kingdom.

Let us pray in silence for our own needs and those of others.

Silence
The following or some other prayer is then added:

Almighty God, to whom our needs are known before we ask, help us to ask only what accords with your will; and those good things which we dare not, or in our blindness cannot ask, grant us for, the sake of your Son, Jesus Christ our Lord. *Amen.*

General Intercession IV

The Leader may expand any paragraph with specific petitions. A short period of silence follows each paragraph. The periods of silence may be concluded as follows:

Lord, in your mercy
Hear our prayer.

Let us pray for the whole Church of God in Christ Jesus, and for all men according to their needs.

Silence

Grant, Almighty God, that we who confess your Name may be united in your truth, live together in your love, and show forth your glory in the world.

Silence

Direct this and every nation into the ways of justice and peace, that we may honor all men, and seek the common good.

Silence

Save and comfort those who suffer, that they may hold to you through good and ill, and trust in your unfailing love.

Silence

Remember, Lord, those who have died in the peace of Christ, and those whose faith is known to you alone, and deal with us and them according to your great mercy.

Silence

Grant these our prayers, O merciful Father, for the sake of your Son, our Savior Jesus Christ. *Amen.*

General Intercession V

In peace, let us pray to the Lord,
saying "Lord, have mercy" (or, "Kyrie eleison").

For the peace of the world, that a spirit of respect and forbearance may grow among nations and peoples, we pray to you, O Lord.

Here and after every petition the People respond:

Kyrie eleison. or *Lord, have mercy.*

For the holy Church of God, that it may be filled with truth and love, and be found without fault at the Day of your Coming, we pray to you, O Lord.

For *N.* our Presiding Bishop, for *N.* (*N.*) our own Bishop(s), for all Bishops and other Ministers, and for all the holy People of God,
we pray to you, O Lord.

*For all who fear God and believe in his Christ, that our divisions may cease and all may be one as you, Lord, and the Father are one,
we pray to you, O Lord.

*For the mission of the Church, that in faithful witness it may preach the Gospel to the ends of the earth,
we pray to you, O Lord.

*For those who do not yet believe, and for those who have lost their faith, that they may receive the light of the Gospel,
we pray to you, O Lord.

For those in positions of public trust, [especially   that they may serve justice, and promote the dignity and freedom of all men,
we pray to you, O Lord.

*For a blessing upon the labors of men, and for the right use of the riches of creation, that mankind may be freed from famine and disaster,
we pray to you, O Lord.

For the poor, the persecuted, the sick, and all who suffer; for refugees, prisoners, and all who are in danger: that they may be relieved and protected,
we pray to you, O Lord.

For this Congregation; [for those who are present, and for those who are absent,] that we may be delivered from hardness of heart, and show forth your glory in all that we do,
we pray to you, O Lord.

*For our enemies and those who wish us harm; and for all whom we have injured or offended,
we pray to you, O Lord.

*For ourselves; for the forgiveness of our sins, and for the grace of the Holy Spirit to amend our lives,
we pray to you, O Lord.

For all who have commended themselves to our prayers: for our families, friends, and neighbors; that being freed from anxiety, they may live in joy, peace, and health,
we pray to you, O Lord.

*For _____
we pray to you, O Lord.

For all who have died in the faith of Christ, that, with all the saints, they may have rest in that place where there is no pain or grief, but life eternal,
we pray to you, O Lord.

Rejoicing in the fellowship of [the ever-blessed Virgin Mary, (blessed N.) and] all the saints, let us commend ourselves, and one another, and all our life to Christ our God

> To you, O Lord our God.

> *Silence*
> *The Litany is concluded with this doxology:*

For yours is the majesty, O Father, Son, and Holy Spirit; yours is the kingdom and the power and the glory, now and for ever. *Amen.*

> *or else with this or some other prayer:*

O Lord our God, accept the fervent prayers of your people; in the multitude of your mercies, look with compassion upon us and all who, turn to you for help: For you are gracious, O lover of men; and to you we give glory, Father, Son, and Holy Spirit, now and for ever. *Amen.*

General Intercession VI

> *For use on Good Friday or on other occasions of particular solemnity. The specific petitions that are indented may be adapted by addition or omission, as appropriate, at the discretion of the Minister. The collects which follow each period of silent prayer are customarily said by the Priest. Each collect is printed twice: first in contemporary and then in traditional language.*

Let us pray for all men everywhere according to their need, and for the people of God in every place.

Let us pray for the holy Catholic Church of Christ throughout the world;

> For its unity in witness and service
> For all Bishops and other Ministers and the people whom they serve
> For N., our Bishop, and all the people of this Diocese
> For all Christians in this community
> For those preparing to be baptized
> [particularly,]

that God will confirm his Church in faith, increase it in love, and preserve it in peace.

Silence

[Contemporary] Almighty and everlasting God, by whose Spirit the whole company of your faithful people is governed and sanctified: Receive our prayers which we now offer before you for all members of your holy Church, that in their vocation and ministry they may truly and devoutly serve you, to the glory of your Name; through our Lord and Savior Jesus Christ. *Amen.*

[Traditional] Almighty and everlasting God, by whose Spirit the whole body of the Church is governed and sanctified: Receive our supplications and prayers, which we offer before thee for all members of thy holy Church, that every member of the same, in his vocation and ministry, may truly and godly serve thee; through our Lord and Savior Jesus Christ. *Amen.*

Let us pray for all nations and peoples of the earth, and for those in authority among them;

> For N., the President of the United States
> For the Congress and the Supreme Court For the Members and representatives of the United Nations
> For all who serve the common good of men

that by God's help they may seek justice and truth, and live in peace and concord.

Silence

[Contemporary] Almighty God, from whom all thoughts of truth and peace proceed: We pray you to kindle in the hearts of all men the true love of peace; and guide with your pure and peaceable wisdom those who take counsel for the nations of the earth, that in tranquillity your kingdom may go forward, until the earth is filled with the knowledge of your love; through Jesus Christ our Lord. *Amen.*

[Traditional] Almighty God, from whom all thoughts of truth and peace proceed: Kindle, we pray thee, in the hearts of all men the true love of peace; and guide with thy pure and peaceable wisdom those who take counsel for the nations of the earth; that in tranquillity thy kingdom may go forward, till the earth is filled with the knowledge of thy love; through Jesus Christ our Lord. *Amen.*

Let us pray for all who suffer, and are afflicted in body or in mind;

> For the hungry and the homeless, the destitute and the oppressed
> For the sick, the wounded, and the crippled

> For those in loneliness, fear, and anguish
> For those who face temptation, doubt, and despair
> For prisoners and captives, and those in mortal danger
> For the sorrowful and bereaved

that God in his mercy will comfort and relieve them, and grant them the knowledge of his love, and stir up in us the will and patience to minister to their needs.

Silence

[Contemporary] Gracious God, you see all the suffering, injustice, and misery which abound in this world. We implore you to look mercifully upon the poor, the oppressed, and all who are burdened with pain and sorrow. Fill our hearts with your compassion, and give us strength to serve them in their need, for the sake of him who suffered for us, our Savior Jesus Christ. *Amen.*

[Traditional] Gracious God, who seest all the suffering, injustice, and misery which abound in this world: We beseech thee to look mercifully upon the poor, the oppressed, and all who are burdened with pain and sorrow. Fill our hearts with thy compassion, and give us strength to serve them in their need, for the sake of him who suffered for us, our Savior Jesus Christ. *Amen.*

Let us pray for all who, whether in ignorance or in disbelief, have not received the gospel of Christ;

> For those who have never heard the word of Christ
> For those who have lost their faith
> For those hardened by sin or indifference
> For the contemptuous and the scornful
> For those who are enemies of the Cross of Christ,
> and persecutors of his disciples

that God will open their hearts to the truth, and lead them to faith and obedience.

Silence

[Contemporary] Merciful God, who made all men and hate nothing that you have made; nor do you desire the death of a sinner, but rather that he should be converted and live: Have mercy upon all who know you not as you are revealed in the Gospel of your Son. Take from them all ignorance, hardness of heart, and contempt of your Word. Bring all men home, good Lord, to your fold, so that they may be one flock under the one shepherd, your Son Jesus Christ our Lord. *Amen.*

[Traditional] Merciful God, who hast made all men, and hatest nothing that thou hast made, nor desirest the death of a sinner, but rather that he should be converted and live: Have mercy upon all who know thee not as thou art revealed in the Gospel of thy Son. Take from them all ignorance, hardness of heart, and contempt of thy Word; and so bring them home, blessed Lord, to thy fold, that they may be made one flock under one shepherd, Jesus Christ our Lord. *Amen.*

Let us commit ourselves to our God, and pray for the grace of a holy life, that, with all who have departed this world and have died in the faith, we may be accounted worthy to enter into the fullness of the joy of our Lord, and receive the crown of life in the day of resurrection.

Silence

[Contemporary] O God of unchangeable power and eternal light: Look favorably on your whole Church, that wonderful and sacred mystery. By the tranquil operation of your providence, carry out the work of man's salvation. Let the whole world see and know that things which were cast down are being raised up, and things which had grown old are being made new, and that all things are being renewed to the perfection of him through whom all things were made, your Son our Lord Jesus Christ, who lives and reigns with you, in the unity of the Holy Spirit, one God, for ever and ever. Amen.

[Traditional] O God of unchangeable power and eternal light: Look favorably upon thy whole Church, that wonderful and sacred mystery; and by the tranquil operation of thy providence, carry out the work of man's salvation. Let the whole world see and know that things which were cast down are being raised up, and things which had grown old are being made new, and that all things are being renewed unto the perfection of him through whom all things were made, thy Son our Lord Jesus Christ, who liveth and reigneth with thee in the unity of the Holy Spirit, one God, for ever and ever. Amen.

General Intercession VII

The Leader and People pray responsively

In peace, we pray to you, Lord God:

For all people in their daily life and work;
For our families, friends, and neighbors, and for those who are alone.

For this community, the nation, and the world;
For all who work for justice, freedom, and peace.

For the just and proper use of your creation;
For the victims of hunger, fear, injustice and oppression.

For all who are in danger, sorrow, or any kind of trouble;
For those who minister to the sick, the friendless, and the needy.

For the peace and unity of the Church of God;
For all who proclaim the Gospel, and all who seek the Truth.

For Bishops and other Ministers, [especially for *N.* our Presiding Bishop, and *N.*(*N.*) our Bishop(s)];
For all who serve God in his Church.

For the special needs and concerns of this congregation.
>*Those present may add their own petitions*

Hear us, Lord;
For your mercy is great.

We thank you, Lord, for all the blessings of this life.
>*The People may add their own thanksgivings*

We will exalt you, O God our King;
And praise your Name for ever and ever.

We pray for all who have died, [especially _____], that they may have a place in your eternal kingdom.

Lord, let your loving-kindness be upon them;
Who put their trust in you.

*We pray to you also for the forgiveness of our sins.
>*Leader and People*

Have mercy upon us, most merciful Father:
In your compassion forgive us our sins,
known and unknown,
things done and left undone:
And so uphold us by your Spirit
that we may live and serve you
in newness of life,
to the honor and glory of your Name.
>*A concluding prayer is then added. For suggestions see below.*

Concerning the Collect at the Prayers

When a Collect concludes the Intercession, a suitable one is selected, such as:

a. *a collect appropriate to the Season or occasion being celebrated;*
b. *a collect expressive of some special need in the life of the local congregation;*

c. *a collect for the mission of the Church;*
d. *a general collect such as one of the following:*

Lord, hear the prayers of your people; and what we have asked faithfully, grant that we may obtain effectually, to the glory of your Name; through Jesus Christ our Lord. *Amen.*

Heavenly Father, you have promised to hear what we ask in the Name of your Son: We pray you, accept and fulfill our petitions, not as we ask in our ignorance, nor as we deserve in our sinfulness, but as you know and love us in your Son, Jesus Christ our Lord. *Amen.*

Almighty and eternal God, ruler of all things in heaven and earth: Mercifully accept the prayers of your people, and strengthen us to do your will; through Jesus Christ our Lord. *Amen.*

Hasten, O Father, the coming of your Kingdom; and grant that we your servants, who now live by faith, may with joy behold your Son at his coming in glorious majesty; even Jesus Christ, our only Mediator and Advocate. *Amen.*

Lord Jesus Christ, you said to your Apostles, "Peace I give to you; my own peace I leave with you": Regard not our sins, but the faith of your Church, and give to us the peace and unity of that heavenly City where, with the Father and the Holy Spirit, you live and reign now and for ever. *Amen.*

O God, you have brought us near to an innumerable company of angels, and to the spirits of just men made perfect: Grant us during our earthly pilgrimage to abide in their fellowship, and in our heavenly country to become partakers of their joy; through Jesus Christ our Lord. *Amen.*

God grant to the living—grace;
to the departed—rest;
to the church, the nation, and all mankind—peace and concord;
and to us and all his servants—life everlasting. *Amen.*

A History of Intercessory Prayer in Christian Worship[12]

The basic Biblical authorization for intercessions on behalf of those not directly a part of the life and structure of the Church is found in the injunction of I Timothy 2:1. It reads (RSV): "First of all, then, I urge that supplications, prayers, intercessions, and thanksgivings be made for all men, for kings and all who are in high position, that we may lead a quiet and peaceable life, godly and respectful in every way." This has formed the basis for the introductory relative clause of the Prayer for the Whole

State of Christ's Church ever since it appeared in this form at the opening of the 1549 canon. The prayer itself was a gathering together of the propitiatory petitions and memorials of the Sarum Mass scattered through the canon and elsewhere (the post-offertory prayer, the stranded Oremus which marks the lost "prayer of the veil" or even a litany, *Te Igitur, Memento, Communicantes, Hanc Igitur, Memento etiam*). Such intercessions were primarily for the Church and its people (*"in primus . . . pro ecclesia tua sancta catholica"*) and only indirectly for the world. The Prayer for the Whole State reflects this in its Christian rulers." The breadth which this originally implied is lost as the reality of an established Church, set in a situation which could be described as "Christendom", steadily recedes.

By and large the same inwardness is found in the New Testament, where intercession relates almost exclusively to the needs of the Christian fellowship, at that time clearly demarked from "the world." Notable expression is given to this limitation in John 17:9, where the words are attributed to Christ, "I am praying for them; I am not praying for the world but for those whom thou hast given me." The extension in verse 20 is only to those who will later be a part of the Church, "Those who are to believe in me through their word." Prayer for the world outside the Church tended to be for the benefit of the Church — as is reflected in the Collect for the Fifth Sunday after Trinity (STU, 9 Pentecost), a Leonine-based prayer itself echoing the passage from Timothy.[xx]

Intercessions for the living and commemorations and prayers for the departed have been associated primarily with the Eucharist. They became associated with the consecration or with the offering of the consecrated elements as a sacrifice, as the efficacy of such an offering came to be developed from the fourth century on (cf. St. Cyril of Jerusalem). Behind the Reformation move to place the intercessions in an earlier part of the service lie historical precedents, though it may be questioned whether antiquity determined the move. Even in the "Gallican position" adopted by Cranmer in 1552 there lies a development of anticipated-propitiation found still in the offertory prayers of the Roman Mass. The new position served its purpose only because in 1552 there was no offertory in the sense of an offering of gifts.

The rubric on page 71 of the American Prayer Book of 1928 which provides for the use of the Bidding Prayer or "other authorized intercessions" before the offertory (as a part of "ante-Communion") moves toward the restoration of

---

[xx] [Ed. Note: Grant, O Lord, we pray, that the course of this world may be so peaceably ordered by your governance, that your Church may serve you in all joy and peace; through Jesus Christ our Lord, who lives and reigns with you and the Holy Spirit, one God, now and for ever. *Amen.*

Grant, O Lord, we beseech thee, that the course of this world may be so peaceably ordered by thy governance, that thy Church may joyfully serve thee in all godly quietness; through Jesus Christ our Lord, who liveth and reigneth with thee and the Holy Spirit, one God, now and for ever. *Amen.*]

an earlier arrangement. The place of "pre-Eucharistic" prayers has been noted by the Vatican Council's Constitution on the Sacred Liturgy. Provision is made in Chapter II, 53, for the restoration to the mass of "the common prayer" or "the prayer of the faithful", in which "the people are to take part", after the Gospel and the homily. The *Instruction on the Liturgy* of the Sacred Congregation of Rites devotes a whole section (IV.56) to its implementation. The Prayer of the Faithful is, "for the interim", to be placed after the isolated "Oremus" before the Offertory.[13] It is there laid down that, provided the celebrant takes the "words of introduction and the concluding prayer", the intentions or invocations may be chanted by a deacon or a cantor or other qualified server." It is also to be noted that the Constitution explicitly extends the range of intercessions beyond the Church, "for the civil authorities, for those oppressed by various needs, for all mankind, and for the salvation of the entire world." It finds no other Biblical basis for this than the one we have already noted (*Constitution*, note 39).

These observations about the scope of the intercessions, their place in the service, and the manner of leading them, though they pertained strictly speaking to the Eucharist when it was the only truly corporate and public rite of the Church, nevertheless indicate principles which may be applied also to intercessory prayer in other public services as well Whether we can trace Dom Gregory Dix' "synaxis" as a separate service, it is of interest to note where the intercessions have been placed and the scope of them.

It is impossible to be dogmatic about the pre-Nicene prayers of the Church since they actually were or were permitted to be free compositions. The *Didache* in the "broken-bread" prayer and in what appears to be a post-communion or post-agape prayer limits the scope to the Church (IX.4; X.5). Justin Martyr's description of second century worship, where the newly baptized share for the first time the prayers of the Church, includes common prayers "for all men everywhere." On Sundays the prayers follow the reading of Scripture and the sermon, but no example is given nor list of contents (*Apology* I. lxv, lxvii). No mention is made of intercession as such in Hippolytus. For the contents and intentions we have to turn to the classical liturgies of the fourth century. Here, for example, in the so-called "Clementine Liturgy", the prayers follow the series of dismissals and are the first items designed for "the faithful", though they precede the Kiss of Peace. The prayers of the faithful at this point were an activity of the whole gathering (after the others had withdrawn) and normally consisted of a series of biddings by the Deacon, followed perhaps by silent prayer, by a response of the people, and by a "collect" or a "benediction" by the celebrant (usually the Bishop). The Clementine series begins, "Let us pray for the peace and welfare of the world", and is extended

---

13. This "interim" arrangement continued in use until the promulgation of the revised *Ordo Missae* in 1969. In the revised *Ordo*, the Prayer of the Faithful follows the Nicene Creed and is considered an integral part of the Liturgy of the Word.

to enemies and persecutors, but as enemies and persecutors of Christians. When prayer was bid for "those without" it was that they might be converted.

An examination of the great liturgies does not give us any confidence that the Church as a general rule practised intercession for the world apart from the Church or for the benefit of the faithful. Where prayer is offered for the world it is for the world, under a Christian (or "orthodox") emperor, or king, true to the faith of an established Christendom. For example, the prayer in Sarapion for fruitfulness prays that God will bless all the earth, but it is also a prayer for "thy holy and only Catholic Church."

The arrangement of intercessions at the Eucharist is only indirectly our concern in this study. It has been dealt with in other studies. The development of "occasional prayers" as such is a feature of the progress of the peculiarly Anglican form of worship. Especially on Sundays, it belongs with the amalgamation of Morning Prayer, Litany, and Holy Communion, or with the making of Morning Prayer into a form of Sunday (Divine) Worship by adding to its basic structure as a daily office, elements taken from the Holy Communion. The basic structure is seen in the 1549 Matins, beginning with the Lord's Prayer and the versicle, "Open thou our lips," and ending with the "third collect." To this there came to be added in 1552 a penitential introduction, and from 1662 on after the last collect, the opportunity for "occasional" intercessions and thanksgivings. By common practice, though not by Prayer Book provision, the service came to be completed by adding from the Communion a sermon, an offering, and a blessing. The office proper ends with the Grace. The development and topical coverage of the occasional prayers to be said between the Collects and the Grace may be seen in the various Prayer Books.

At first, in 1549, there were two prayers placed with the six collects, one or more of which were to be said after the offertory when there was no Communion. The additional prayers were For Rain and For Fair Weather, and thiis remind us of Sarapion and the Egyptian liturgies. In the 1549 book there was a prayer For the King in the ante-Communion and there was the Prayer for the Whole State at the start of the canon. There was also the Litany of 1544 with its broad coverage, based on an originally Syrian custom, which became a part of many Eucharistic rites but also had a separate development in the form of processions. In 1552 the Prayer for the Whole State acquired its "Gallican" position after the Offertory (though there was no offering as such) and the prayers For Rain and For Fair Weather were omitted from the ante-Communion prayers and added after the Litany. They were to be said "if the time require," along with prayers In Time of Dearth or Famine (two), In Time of War, and In Time of Any Common Plague or Sickness.

For a wider range of explicit prayers we have to go beyond the Books of Common Prayer to books of private prayer and devotion published apart from the first Prayer Book. A good example is the *Primer or Book of Private Prayer needful to be used of all Christians*, authorized and set forth in 1553. It contained the Catechism, graces for table, a form of preparation for prayer, and orders for family prayer. The latter were structured on the pattern of Matins and Evensong and the Litany, to which were added the prayers already mentioned, a prayer For One that is Sore Sick and the collects from the ante-Communion. There was also a section headed, "Sundry Godly Prayers for Diverse Purposes", which began with three alternate prayers for the King, one for the King's Council, one for judges, one for Bishops, Spiritual Pastors and Ministers of God's Word, and proceeded to prayers for various "estates" of men which will be found in the list starting with "For Gentlemen". A further section, headed "General Prayers," included more personal devotions for Christian graces, gifts, dispositions and the like. These features of the *Primer* suggest the Family Prayer section in the American Book, introduced in 1789 before the Psalter, and the "Additional Prayers" added in 1928. The contents of the primers perhaps imply that it was conceived to he the duty of Christian families and individuals rather than for the gathered Church, to pray for the world at large.

In some editions of the 1552 Book a section of "Godly Prayers" is found after the Psalter, and as appendices to the Elizabethan Books. These are prayers of a personal nature often in the form of longer meditations rather than collects. From 1560 on there were frequently issued "occasional forms of prayer" to be used publicly during the Queen's reign which mark critical periods at home and abroad.

In the 1662 Prayer Book provision was made for saying the Prayer for the King (a feature of the Communion service) after the third collect at Morning and Evening Prayer, followed by prayers For the Royal Family, and For the Clergy and People, ending with the "Prayer of St. Chrysostom" and the Grace. Following the Litany there also appeared a section of "Prayers and Thanksgivings upon Several Occasions," from which the term "Occasional Prayers" arises since they are to be said, as 1549 put it, "if the time require." This corresponds to the "Prayers and Thanksgivings" of the 1928 Book in position though not, of course, in scope.

The tendency to add prayers to this section of the Book has been constant and natural and it may be traced in other Books. As with the 1553 *Primer* and earlier or later collections of Private Prayers, official or semi-official, there is a proper policy of adding prayers to fit the conditions of the time. The 1928 American Book added a whole section of such prayers to Family Prayers. With changed social conditions and the combined effect of a decline in formal family worship and an increase in somewhat informal "family services" in the church, the Prayer Book services of Family Prayer have largely fallen out of use. Their function was taken over by publications such as those by the Forward Movement sponsored by General Convention, which publishes manuals of which *Prayers New and Old* is a fine example. *Services for Trial Use*, of course, has proposed a new style of family prayer. Meanwhile, some of the Additional Prayers from the 1928 Prayer Book and some from these subsequent collections have made their way into the public worship of the Church where they have survived a kind of "trial use," and the Commission has included a number of them in this present collection.

Appendices

A Selected Bibliography

Only books from which prayers have been drawn for this collection or which have been otherwise used for this study are included in this list.

Anthologies

Ahrens, Hermann C., Jr.	*Tune In*, Pilgrim Press, 1968
	The Armed Forces Prayer Book,
Episcopal Church	The Church Pension Fund, 1951
	Prayers New and Old,
Forward Movement	Forward Movement Publications, 1937
	After the Third Collect,
Milner-White, E.	Mowbray, 1952
	Occasional Prayers Reconsidered,
Milner-White, E.	SPCK, 1930
McNutt, Frederic B.	*The Prayer Manual*, Mowbray, 1951
Oosterhuis, Huub	*Your Word is Near*, Newman, 1968
	Book of Prayers for Church and Home,
Paine, Howard, and Thompson, Bard	Christian Education Press, 1963
Rodenmayer, Robert N.	*The Pastor's Prayer Book*, Oxford, 1960
Suter, J. W.	*Prayers for a New World,*
	Scribner's, 1964
Suter, J.W.	*Uncommon Prayers*, Seabury, 1955
Tileston, Mary Wilder	*Prayers Ancient and Modern,*
	Little, Brown & Co., Boston, 1921

Prayer Books of the Anglican Communion

Canada
The Book of Common Prayer and Administration of the Sacraments and other Rites and Ceremonies of the Church according to the use of the Anglican Church of Canada. (version of 1959) The University Press, Cambridge, 1959

England
The Book of Common Prayer and Administration of the Sacraments ... according to the use of the Church of England. Together with The Psalter. (version of 1662) SPCK, London, 1935

Ireland
The Book of Common Prayer and Administration of the Sacraments and other rites and ceremonies, together with The Psalter. (version of 1926) SPCK, Dublin, 1949

South Africa
A Book of Common Prayer and Administration of the Sacraments, set forth by authority for use in the Church of the Province of South Africa. (version of 1954) Oxford University Press, London, 1959

United States
The Book of Common Prayer and Administration of the Sacraments and other Rites and Ceremonies of the Church, according to the use of the Protestant Episcopal Church in the United States of America. Together with The Psalter or Psalms of David. (version of 1928) The Church Pension Fund, New York, 1945

Related Sources

The Grey Book
A new prayer book. Proposals for the revision of the Book of Common Prayer and additional services and prayers. Oxford University Press, London, 1923/37

"The Deposited Book"
The Book of Common Prayer with the Additions and Deviations Proposed in 1928. (Church of England) Oxford University Press, London, 1928

Services for Trial Use
Alternatives to Prayer Book Services authorized for trial use by the General Convention of the Episcopal Church, 1970. The Church Hymnal Corporation, New York, 1971

Church of South India
The Book of Common Worship, Church of South India. Oxford University Press, London, 1963

Consultation on Church Union (COCU)
An Order of Worship for the Proclamation of the Word of God and the Celebration of the Lord's Supper with Commentary. Recommended to the churches for experimental use by the Commission on Worship and the Executive Committee the Consultation on Church Union. Forward Movement Publications, 1968

For information regarding the authorship or source of prayers in the American Book of Common Prayer, reference should be made to Shepherd, Massey Hamilton, Jr., The Oxford American Prayer Book Commentary, Oxford University Press. New York, 1950.

Key to Abbreviations

A full description of the books referred to below will be found in the Bibliography on p. 102 ff.

AFPB	Armed Forces Prayer Book
ATC	After the Third Collect
BCP	American Book of Common Prayer, 1928
BCPCan	Canadian Book of Common Prayer, 1959
BCPEng	Proposed English Book of Common Prayer, 1928
BCPIre	Irish Book of Common Prayer, 1926
BCPAfr	South African Book of Common Prayer, 1954
BPCH	Book of Prayers for Church and Home
CSI	Church of South India Book of Common Worship
DC-IV	Drafting Committee for Prayers and Thanksgivings of the Standing Liturgical Commission; the appended initials indicate the member of the committee who wrote the original version of the prayer: JB — James Birney CP — Charles Price CR — Caroline Rose JRZ — J. Robert Zimmerman
MHS	Massey H. Shepherd, Jr.
OPR	Occasional Prayers Reconsidered
PAM	Prayers Ancient and Modern
PM	The Prayer Manual
PNO	Prayers New and Old
PNW	Prayers for a New World
PPB	The Pastor's Prayer Book
SLC	Standing Liturgical Commission This notation denotes that the prayer was generated by a discussion of the whole commission; the appended name indicates the chief author of the original version of the prayer.
STU	Services for Trial Use
UP	Uncommon Prayers

Index of Sources

Prayers taken from the 1928 American Book of Common Prayer are marked simply BCP. No attempt has been made to identify them further, since information

Prayers, Thanksgivings, and Litanies 105

regarding authorship is readily available in works like the *Oxford American Prayer Book Commentary*. New prayers are traced to the anthology from which the Drafting Committee drew the text and to the original authors when possible.

Nearly all the prayers in the collection underwent revision at the hands of the Drafting Committee and again by the Liturgical Commission itself. Each source, consequently, should be marked revised. This annotation is omitted, however, to avoid tiresome repetition.

A key to the abbreviations used in these pages will be found on page 104.

Prayers

1. For Joy in God's Creation	BCP
2. For All Sorts and Conditions of Men	BCP
3. For the Human Family	DC-IV; CP
4. For Peace (1)	ATC (8b); E. Milner-White
For Peace (2)	ATC (8a); OPR
5. For Peace Among the Nations	BCP
6. For Those Who Work for Peace	BCPEng 1928, p. 128; Francis Paget, Bishop of Oxford
7. For Our Enemies	*The Living Church*, Sept. 8, 1968. 157/10, p. 11
8. For the Church	BCP; William Laud; rev. MHS
9. For the Mission of the Church (1)	BCP
For the Mission of the Church (2)	DC-IV; CR
10. For Clergy and People	BCP
11. For the Diocese	SLC; based on a prayer of A. J. Mason, PM(565)
12. For the Parish	PNO, p. 62
13. For a Church Convention or Meeting	SLC
14. For the Election of a Bishop or Rector	BCPEng 1928, p. 125
15. For the Presiding Bishop	PNO, p. 60
16. For the Unity of the Church (1)	BCP
For the Unity of the Church (2)	BCP
17. For the Church in a Changing World	PM(541); unknown
18. For the Ordained Ministry	STU, p. 624
19. For the Supply of Candidates for the Ordained Ministry	SLC; Boone Porter
20. For Christian Education	BCP

21.	For Monastic Orders and Vocations	Bonnell Spencer, OHC
22.	For a Retreat	Richard M. Benson, SSJE
23.	For Those About to be Baptized	DC-IV; CP
24.	For Those About to Receive the Laying on of Hands	BCP
25.	For Our Country	BCP
26.	For the President	BCP
27.	For Congress or a State Legislature	BCP
28.	For Courts of Justice	BCP
29.	For Sound Government	DC-IV; CR
30.	For Local Government	BCPCan, p. 50
31.	For an Election	PNO, p. 70
32.	For Those in the Armed Forces	AFPB, p. 55
33.	For Those Who Suffer for Conscience' Sake	DC-IV; CP
34.	For Fellow-Citizens Abroad	DC-IV; CR
35.	For Social Justice (1)	BCP
	For Social Justice (2)	Unknown
36.	In Struggles for Social Justice	The Grey Book, p. 84
37.	For Our Daily Work	BCP
38.	For Agriculture	BCP
39.	For Industry	BCPCan, p. 53
40.	For Those Whose Work is Difficult	BCPCan, p. 54
41.	For the Unemployed	PM(717); Industrial Christian Fellowship
42.	For Schools and Colleges (1)	BCP
	For Schools and Colleges (2)	DC-IV; CR
43.	For the Good Use of Leisure Time	DC-IV; JB
44.	For Cities	DC-IV; JRZ
45.	For the Poor and Neglected	BCP
46.	For the Oppressed in the Land	DC-IV, CR
47.	For Prisons and Prisoners	DC-IV; CP
48.	For Christian Service	BCP
49.	For a Right Attitude Toward Our Work	DC-IV; CR
50.	For the Right Use of God's Gifts	BCP

Prayers, Thanksgivings, and Litanies 107

51. For the Responsible Use of Money	SLC; CP
52. For Those Who Influence Public Opinion	PPB(424); *The Boys' Prayer Book*; E. Milner-White
53. For Knowledge of God's Creation	DC-IV; JRZ
54. For the Harvest of Lands and Waters	BCP
55. For the Conservation of Natural Resources(1)	Charles W. F. Smith
For the Conservation of Natural Resources (2)	DC-IV; CR
56. For the Exploration of Space	DC-IV; JRZ
57. For the Responsible Use of Inventions	PM(690); F. B. McNutt; based on phrases of Abp. Garbett
58. For the Future of Mankind	SLC
59. For Animals	DC-IV; CP
60. For Families (Contemporary)	DC-IV; CP
For Families (Traditional)	BCP
61. For Living in Families When There is Conflict	Brooke Bushong, CA
62. For Children	SLC; Virginia Harbour
63. For the Care of Children	BCP
64. For Young Persons (1)	DC-IV; CP
For Young Persons (2)	Brooke Bushong, CA
65. For Married Couples	PBCH(203); Angus Dun
66. For the Aged (1)	SLC; CP
For the Aged (2)	Charles and Ivy Smith
67. For a Birthday (1)	PPB(98); R. Rodenmayer
For a Birthday (2)	SLC; CP
68. For the Absent	BCP
69. For Those We Love	BCP
70. For Travelers	BCPCan, p. 54
71. For Sick Persons (1)	BCP
For Sick Persons (2)	BCP
72. For One Critically Ill	BCP
73. For a Sick Child	BCP
74. For One About to Undergo an Operation	BCP

75. For the Mentally Ill	BCP
76. For Those Who are Addicted	Charles W. F. Smith
77. For Hospitals and Healing Ministries	BCPCan, p. 55
78. For a Person in Trouble or Bereavement	BCP
79. For Those Who Mourn (1)	BCP
For Those Who Mourn (2)	BCPIre, p. 49
For Those Who Mourn (3)	BCPAfr, p. 479
80. For Dying in Faith	BCP
81. For the Dead (1)	BCP
For the Dead (2)	PM(821); based on an anonymous prayer
For the Dead (3)	PM(819); based on a prayer of R. W. D. Lee
82. On Memorial Days	BCP
83. For Guidance (1)	BCP
For Guidance (2)	BCP
84. For Quiet Confidence	BCP
85. For Trustfulness	BCP
86. Prayers of Self-Dedication (1)	PM(255); William Temple in *Basic Convictions*
Prayers of Self-Dedication (2)	DC-IV; CR
Prayers of Self-Dedication (3)	PM(246); *The Daily Service, Revised Edition*; G. W. Briggs
87. For Self-Mastery	PM(68); Alex. Patterson
88. For Self-Acceptance	UP, p. 33; Reinhold Niebuhr
89. A Prayer of Love (Attributed to St. Francis)	PPB(588)
90. On Sunday (1)	BCP
On Sunday (2)	SLC; CP
91. In the Morning (1)	BCP
In the Morning (2)	BCPCan, p. 728; Daybreak Office of the Eastern Church
92. In the Evening (1)	BCP
In the Evening (2)	BCP
93. Before Worship (1)	BCP

Prayers, Thanksgivings, and Litanies   109

Before Worship (2)	BCP
Before Worship (3)	PPB(330); unknown
94. Before Sermons (1)	Psalm 19
Before Sermons (2)	PPB(348); unknown
Before Sermons (3)	PAM; W. H. H. Aitken
95. Before Receiving Communion	CSI, p. 14; Mozarabic Liturgy
96. After Receiving Communion (1)	PPB(365); St. Thomas Aquinas; Tr. MHS
After Receiving Communion (2)	DC-IV; JRZ
97. For the Answering of Prayer	BCP
98. After Worship (1)	BCP
After Worship (2)	SLC; CP
99. Grace at Meals (1)	Unknown
Grace at Meals (2)	*Authorized Daily Prayer Book* (Jewish), adapted
Grace at Meals (3)	*Authorized Daily Prayer Book* (Jewish)
Grace at Meals (4)	BCP
Grace at Meals (5)	Henry Sylvester Nash
Grace at Meals (6)	Psalm 118:1
Grace at Meals (7)	Psalm 34:8
Grace at Meals (8)	Psalm 145
Grace at Meals (9)	BPCH(347); John Wesley
100. A Blessing (1)	BCP
A Blessing (2)	BCP

Thanksgivings

1. The General Thanksgiving	BCP
2. A General Thanksgiving	DC-IV; CP
3. For the Mission of the Church	DC-IV; CR
4. For the Saints and Faithful Departed (1)	DC-IV; CR
For the Saints and Faithful Departed (2)	COCU Liturgy, 1968, p. 26; Taizé Liturgy
5. For the Nation	DC-IV; CR
6. For Heroic Service	DC-IV; CR

7. For Negotiating Peace	DC-IV; CR
8. For the Restoration of Peace	DC-IV; CR
9. For the Restoration of Domestic Peace	DC-IV; CR
10. For the Diversity of Races and Cultures	DC-IV; CR
11. For the Widening Vision of Social Justice	DC-IV; CR
12. For Peacemakers	DC-IV; CR
13. For the Creation	DC-IV; CR
14. For the Harvest	BCP
15. For the Birth of a Child	DC-IV; CR
16. For the Gift of a Child	DC-IV; CR
17. For the Restoration of Health	BCP
18. For Safe Travel	DC-IV; CR

Litanies

1. A Bidding Litany	BCP adapted; based on an idea of H. Francis Hines
2. A Litany of Thanksgiving	STU, p. 602
3. A Litany for the Mission of the Church	*Calendar of Prayer for Missions*, 1961-1962; *Overseas Mission Review*, vol. iv, no. 3, Whitsunday, 1959
4. A Litany for the Ministry	STU, p. 459
5. A Litany for Personal Life	(The Southwell Litany) George Ridding, first Bishop of Southwell; *A Litany of Remembrance*, from George Ridding, Schoolmaster and Bishop, by his wife Lady Laura Ridding, Edward Arnold, London, 1908, Appendix II, pp. 352-355; adapted by Rt. Rev. Charles Williams as *The Southwell Litany*, published in an undated pamphlet by Forward Movement; rev. DC-IV, CP and MHS
6. A Litany for Healing	*Prayer Book Studies III*; Morton Stone

7. A Litany for the Dying or the Dead   BCP

The Litany and Other Prayers from the 1928 Prayer Book
The Litany in this section is the version, slightly altered, from *Prayer Book Studies V.* The source of all the other prayers is BCP.

General Intercessions from the Holy Eucharist 1970
The sources of these intercessions are described in *Prayer Book Studies 21: The Holy Eucharist*, The Church Hymnal Corporation, New York, 1970, Vol. 6, p. 14.

Disposition of the Prayers, Thanksgivings, and Litanies of the 1928 Prayer Book

Morning Prayer	appears in this collection as:
For the President	
O Lord, our heavenly Father	1928 Prayers 5
O Lord our Governor	Prayer 26
For Clergy and People	Prayer 10
For all Conditions of Men	Prayer 2
A General Thanksgiving	Thanksgiving 1
A Prayer of St. Chrysostom	Collect, General Intercession I

Evening Prayer	
For the President	1928 Prayers 5
(Others as in Morning Prayer)	

Prayers and Thanksgivings	
A Prayer for Congress	Not included
For a State Legislature	Prayer 2
For Courts of Justice	Prayer 28
For Our Country	Prayer 25
At Meetings of Convention	1928 Prayers 4
For the Church	Prayer 8
For the Unity of God's People	Prayer 16
For Missions	
O God, who hast made of one blood	Prayer 9
Almighty God, whose compassions	Not included

For Those Who are to be Admitted into Holy Orders	
Almighty God, our heavenly Father	Not included
Almighty God, giver of all good	Prayer 18
For the Increase of the Ministry	Not included (cf. Prayer 19)
For Fruitful Seasons	
Almighty God, who hast blessed	Prayer 38
O Gracious Father, who openest	Prayer 54
For Rain	Not included
For Fair Weather	Not included
In Time of Dearth and Famine	1928 Prayers 8
In Time of War and Tumults	Not included
In Time of Calamity	1928 Prayers 9
For the Army	1928 Prayers 6
For the Navy	1928 Prayers 7
Memorial Days	Prayer 82
For Schools, Colleges, and Universities	Prayer 42
For Religious Education	Prayer 20
For Children	Not included (cf. Prayer 62)
For Those About to be Confirmed	Prayer 24
For Christian Service	Prayer 48
For Social Justice	Prayer 35
For Every Man in his Work	Prayer 37
For the Family of Nations	Prayer 5
In Time of Great Sickness and Mortality	Not included
For a Sick Person	Prayer 71
For a Sick Child	Prayer 73
For a Person Under Affliction	Prayer 78
For a Person or Persons Going to Sea	Not included
For Prisoners	Not included (cf. Prayer 47)
A Bidding Prayer	1928 Prayers 2 (cf. Litany 1)
Collects	
O Lord Jesus Christ	Prayer 16 (cf. page 97)
Assist us mercifully	Prayer 93
Grant, we beseech thee,	Prayer 98

Prayers, Thanksgivings, and Litanies   113

Direct us, O Lord,	Prayer 83
Almighty God, the fountain of all wisdom	Collect, General Intercession III
Almighty God, who hast promised	Prayer 97 (cf. page 81)

Thanksgivings

A Thanksgiving to Almighty God for the Fruits of the Earth	Thanksgiving 14
The Thanksgiving of Women after Childbirth	Not included (cf. Thanksgiving 15)
For Rain	Not included
For Fair Weather	Not included
For Plenty	Not included
For Peace and Deliverance	Not included (cf. Thanksgiving 8)
For Restoring Peace at Home	Not included (cf. Thanksgiving 9)
For a Recovery from Sickness	Not included
For a Child's Recovery from Sickness	Thanksgiving 17
For a Safe Return from a journey	Not included (cf. Thanksgiving 18)

The Litany   1928 Prayers 1

The Order for the Visitation of the Sick

A Prayer for Recovery	Not included (cf. Prayer 71)
A Prayer for Healing	Not included
A Thanksgiving for the Beginning of a Recovery	Not included
For a Sick Person when there appeareth but small hope of Recovery	Not included
For the Despondent	Not included
A Prayer which may be said by the Minister in behalf of all present	Prayer 80
A Commendatory Prayer for a Sick Person at the Point of Departure	Not included
Litany for the Dying	Litany 7
An Absolution	Not included
A Commendation	Not included (See STU, p. 363)
A Commendatory Prayer	Litany 7 (Prayer 72 in the present collection is the third collect in the Office of Visitation in the 1928 Prayer Book.)

The Ordinal
Litany for Ordinations   Not included (cf. Litany 4)

Forms of Prayer to be Used in Families
Morning Prayer   Not included (See STU, p. 302)
Evening Prayer   Not included (See STU, p. 304)

Additional Prayers
For the Spirit of Prayer   Prayer 93
In the Morning
  O God, the King Eternal   Prayer 91
  Almighty God, who alone gavest Not included
At Night
  O Lord, support us   Prayer 92
  O God, who art the life   Prayer 92
Sunday Morning   Prayer 90
For Quiet Confidence   Prayer 84
For Guidance   Prayer 83
For Trustfulness
  O Most loving Father   Prayer 85
  O Heavenly Father   Not included
For Joy in God's Creation   Prayer 1
For the Children   Prayer 63
For the Absent   Prayer 68
For Those We Love   Prayer 69
For the Recovery of a Sick Person   Prayer 71
For One About to Undergo an Operation   Prayer 74
For a Birthday   Not included (cf. Prayer 67)
For an Anniversary of One Departed   Prayer 81
For Those in Mental Darkness   Prayer 75
For a Blessing on the Families of the Land   Prayer 60
For all Poor, Homeless and Neglected Folk   Prayer 45
For Faithfulness in the Use of This World's Goods   Prayer 50

Prayers, Thanksgivings, and Litanies 115

A General Intercession   Not included
Grace Before Meat
  Bless, O Father   Not included
  Give us grateful hearts   Prayer 99

(For the disposition of the Collects of the Prayer Book, see Prayer Book Studies 19, Vol. 2., pp. 82-89.)

Acknowledgments

Grateful acknowledgment for permission to use copyrighted material is extended to the following authors, publishers, and copyright holders:

> E. Milner-White, *After the Third Collect*, A. R. Mowbray & Co. Ltd., The Alden Press, Oxford
>
> E. Milner-White, *The Occasional Prayers in the 1928 Book Reconsidered*, SPCK
>
> *The Book of Common Prayer, Proposed 1928*, Oxford University Press, Central Board of Finance, Church of England, London
>
> *The Living Church*, Vol. 157, no. 10, The Living Church, Milwaukee, Wisconsin
>
> *Prayers New and Old*, Forward Movement Publications, Cincinnati, Ohio
>
> Frederic B. McNutt, *The Prayer Manual*, A. R. Mowbray & Co. Ltd., The Alden Press, Oxford
>
> *The Book of Common Prayer*, 1959, Anglican Church of Canada, Toronto
>
> *The Grey Book*, Oxford University Press, London
>
> Robert N. Rodenmayer, *The Pastor's Prayer Book*, Oxford University Press, New York
>
> *The Book of Common Prayer*, 1926, SPCK, General Synod of the Church of Ireland, Dublin
>
> *A Book of Common Prayer—South Africa*, Oxford University Press, London, copyright by the Bishop of St. John's, Port Elizabeth, South Africa
>
> William Temple, *Basic Convictions*, Macmillan, London and Basingstoke
>
> G. W. Briggs, *The Daily Service Revised Edition*, Oxford University Press, London
>
> J. W. Suter, *Uncommon Prayers*, Seabury Press, New York
>
> Mary Wilder Tileston, *Prayers Ancient and Modern*, Little, Brown and Company, Boston
>
> Consultation on Church Union, *An Order of Worship*, Forward Movement Publications, Cincinnati, Ohio
>
> *The Southwell Litany*, Forward Movement Publications, Cincinnati, Ohio

Every effort has been made to trace the copyright owners of prayers included in this collection. If, in spite of these efforts, any copyrighted material has been included without due permission or acknowledgment, a sincere apology is herewith extended to the copyright owner. Future editions of this Study will rectify any such omission brought to the attention of the Standing Liturgical Commission of the Episcopal Church.

General Index

This Index was prepared to assist Ministers and other leaders of worship in finding quickly a topical prayer or one remembered only by some striking or familiar phrase. The selection of entries is somewhat arbitrary. No attempt has been made to index the contents of the litanies and general intercessions because of the great variety of topics covered in each, but themes from the prayers at the end of the litanies and intercessions have been included in the Index.

The numbers refer to pages. The following symbols identify the nature and style of the various items:

- P Prayer
- T Thanksgiving
- (c) Contemporary language
- (t) Traditional language

Abraham, the father of believers ... T, (c) 47
Abroad, fellow-citizens ... P, (c) 28
Absent, for the ... P, (c) 36, (t) 72
Addicted, for those who are ... P, (c) 37
Afflicted, those who are in any way ... P, (c) 19, (t) 66
Aged, for the ... P, (c) 35
Agriculture, for ... P, (c) 29, (t) 70
Air clean again, make the ... P, (c) 33
All sorts and conditions of men ... P, (c) 19, (t) 66
Animals, for ... P, (c) 34
Armed Forces, for those in ... P, (c) 27
Army, for the ... P, (t) 84
Author of Peace and lover of concord ... P, (t) 83

Baptized, for those about to be ... P, (c) 24
Be present, be present, O Jesus ... P, (c) 43
Bereavement, for a person in trouble or ... P, (c) 38, (t) 73
Better things than we can desire or pray for ... P, (c) 36, (t) 72
Bidding Litany, a ... (c) 51
Bidding Prayer, a ... (t) 82

Birthday, for a ... P, (c) 36
Bishop, to choose a ... P, (c) 22
Bishops and other clergy, for ... P, (c) 27, (t) 67
Blessed are you, O Lord our God (Grace at meals) ... P, (c) 44
Blessing, a ... (c) 45, (t) 76
Blessings of this life, all the .. T, (c) 46, (t) 77
Blood of the everlasting covenant ... P, (c) 46, (t) 76
Body and Blood, reverence the sacred mysteries of your ... P, (c) 44
Born again by water and the Spirit ... P, (c) 24
Breaking of the bread, be known to us in the ... P, (c) 43

Care of children, for the ... P, (c) 35, (t) 72
Catholic Church, communion of (for dying in faith) ... P, (c) 39, (t) 74
Changes and chances of this mortal life ... P, (c) 42, (t) 76
Channels of your grace, make us ... P, (c) 40
Child, for a sick ... P, (c) 37, (t) 73
[Child], the gift of a ... T, (c) 50
Childbirth, safely through ... T, (c) 50
Children, care and nurture of ... P, (c) 23-24, (t) 68
[Children], for the world's ... P, (c) 62
[Children], growing up in an unsteady and confusing world ... P, (c) 35
Christian education ... P, (c) 23-24, (t) 68
Christian service, for ... P, (c) 31 (t) 71
Christians, all who profess and call themselves ... P, (c) 19, (t) 66
Church, a litany for the mission of the ... (c) 54
[Church], for the mission of the ... P, (c) 21, (t) 66-67 T, (c) 47
[Church], for your holy Catholic ... P, (c) 20, (t) 66
[Church], sustain your, in a changing world ... P, (c) 23
[Church], that wonderful and sacred mystery ... P, (c) 95, (t) 95
[Church], unity of ... P, (c) 22, (t) 67
Church convention or meeting ... P, (c) 22
Cities, for ... P, (c) 30
Civil Authority, all in ... P, (c) 26, (t) 69 P, (t) 83
Colleges, for schools and ... P, (c) 30, (t) 70
Come, Holy Spirit, come ... P, (c) 43
Comfort, giver of all (for those who mourn) ... P, (c) 38, (t) 73
Commendation of the Dying ... P, (c) 65
Communion, after receiving   P, (c) 44
[Communion], before receiving .. P, (c) 43
Compassion, fill our hearts with . P, (c) 94, (t) 94
Condemned to die, those who are (for prisoners) .. P, (c) 31
Confidence, for quiet . P, (c) 40, (t) 74

Congregations committed to their charge, .. P, (c) 21, (t) 67
Congress, for .. P, (c) 42, (t) 69
Conscience' sake, those who suffer for ... P, (c) 27
Conservation of natural resources, for the ... P, (c) 33
Council of thy Church (conventions) ... P, (t)
Country, for our ... P, (c) 25, (t) 68
Courage to change the things we can ... P, (c) 41
Courts of justice, bless the ... P, (c) 41, (t) 69
Creation, enjoyment of your abundant ... T, (c) 50
[Creation], for knowledge of God's ... P, (c) 32
[Creation], joy in God's ... P, (c) 18, (t) 65
[Creation], thank you for the splendor of the whole ... T, (c) 46
Crisis, in time of ... P, (t) 84
Critically ill, for one ... P, (c) 37, (t) 73
Cultures, for the diversity of races and ... T, (c) 49
Cure, bless the means made use of ... P, (c) 37, (t) 73

Daily work, for our ... P, (c) 28, (t) 70
Dangerous work, for all who do ... P, (c) 29
Day, gift of a new ... P, (c) 42
Day that is past, blessings of the ... P, (c) 42
Dead, a litany for the ... (c) 64
[Dead], for the ... P, (c) 39, (t) 74
Deal graciously with those who mourn ... P, (c) 38, (t) 73
Death of a sinner, nor (do you) desire the ... P, (c) 95, (t) 95
Diocese, you have called us in this ... P, (c) 21
Direct us, O Lord, in all our doings ... P, (c) 40, (t) 74
Discoveries, responsible use of ... P, (c) 33
Dispose the way of thy servants .. P, (t) 76
Distressed, those who are in any way ... P, (c) 19, (t) 66
Disturbed in mind or spirit, all who are ... P, (c) 37
Dying, a litany for the ... (c) 64
Dying in faith, for our ... P, (c) 39, (t) 80
Doubts and uncertainties, in all our ... P, (c) 40, (t) 74

Earth, renew the face of ... P, (c) 32, (t) 71
Education, Christian ... P, (c) 24, (t) 68
Election, for an (civic) .. P, (c) 27
Enemies, for our ... P, (c) 20
Entrust all who are dear to us ... P, (c) 36, (t) 72
Environment, restore a healthful ... P, (c) 33
Evening, in the ... P, (c) 42, (t) 75

Prayers, Thanksgivings, and Litanies   119

Evil, fearlessly to contend against ... P, (c) 28, (t) 69
Executive Council and Staff ... P, (c) 22

Faith, confidence of (for dying in faith) ... P, (c) 39, (t) 74
Faithful departed, for the Saints and ... T, (c) 47
Faithful stewards of your bounty ... P, (c)32, (t) 71
Families, for ... P, (c) 34, (t) 72
[Families] when there is conflict ... P, (c) 34
Father of all mercies ... T, (c) 46, (t) 77
Fear, all families living in ... P, (c) 37
Fears, from faithless ... P, (c) 40, (t) 75
Food in due season, you give them their ... P, (c) 45
Forgiveness, the power of (mission of Church) ... P, (c) 21
Freedom, that we may rightly use ... P, (c) 28
[Freedom], that we may reverently use ... P, (t) 69
[Freedom], all young persons seeking their true ... P, (c) 34
[Freedom], whose service is perfect ... P, (t) 83
Friendless, minister in your Name to the ... P, (c) 31, (t) 71
Friends, family and ... T, (c) 46
Fruits of the earth ... P, (c) 70, (t) 84
Fulfill now, O Lord, our desires and petitions ... P, (c) 86, (t) 87

Gates of larger life, having opened to him the ... P, (t) 74
Gathering in of its fruits (for the harvest) ... T, (c) 32, (t) 77
General Intercessions ... (c) (t) 84 ff.
Gospel of Christ may be truly preached (Church conventions) .. P, (t) 83
Government, for local ... P, (c) 27
[Government], those to whom we entrust authority of .. P, (c) 25, (t) 68
Governor of this State ... P, (c) 69, (t) 83
Governors of States ... P, (c) 26
Grace at meals ... P, (c) 44, (t) 76
Grace at this time to make our common supplication ... P, (c) 86, (t) 86
Grateful hearts, give us .. P, (c) 45, (t) 76
Great Litany, the ... (t) 78
Guidance, for ... P, (c) 40, (t) 74

Harvest, for the ... T, (c) 86, (t) 77
Harvest of lands and waters, for the ... P, (c) 32, (t) 71
Hasten, O Father, the coming of your Kingdom ... P, (c) 97
Healing, a litany for ... (c) 62
[Healing], thank you for ... T, (c) 51
Healing gifts, those who minister ... P, (c) 37, (t) 72

Healing ministries, for hospitals and ... P, (c) 38
Health, for the restoration of ... T, (c) 51, (t) 78
[Health], giver of life and ... P, (c) 37
[Health], restore him to ... P, (c) 37, (t) 72
Heroic service, for ... T, (c) 48
Holy Spirit, ready to receive the blessing of (laying on of hands) ... P, (c) 25 (t) 68
Home, an image of your kingdom ... T, (c) 50
Homeless, for the ... P, (c) 30, (t) 70
Homes in which thy people dwell ... P, (t) 72
Hope of glory ... T, (c) 46, (t) 77
Hospitals and healing ministries, for ... P, (c) 38
Human family, look with compassion on the ... P, (c) 19
Human rights may be safeguarded ... P, (c) 26-27

Ignorance, not as we ask in our ... P, (c) 97
Ill, for one critically ... P, (c) 37, (t) 73
Image, you made us in your own ... P, (c) 19
Industry, for ... P, (c) 29
Injustice, for those who live in our land with ... P, (c) 31
[Injustice], you see all the ... P, (c) 94, (t) 94
Instruments of your peace, make us ... P, (c) 41
Into your hands, O merciful Savior ... P, (c) 65
Inventions and discoveries, responsible use of ... P, c 33
Intercessions, General ... (c) (t) 84 ff.

Jails, visit our ... P, (c) 31
Journeys, undertaken with care and ended with praise ... T, (c) 51
Journey's end, bring them (travelers) in safety to ... P, (c) 36
Joy, companion in (married couples) ... P, (c) 35
Joy in God's creation ... P, (c) 18, (t) 65
Judges of our courts ... P, (c) 26
Just men made perfect, spirits of ... P, (c) 97
Justice, for courts of ... P, (c) 26, (t) 69
[Justice], teach us to improve our ways of ... P, (c) 31
[Justice], that there may be (for our country) ... P, (t) 68

Kingdom of glory prepared for them (Baptism) ... P, (c) 25
Knowledge, those who add to ... P, (c) 30

Labor, a just return for .. P, (c) 29
Lamb of your own flock .. P, (c) 65
Laying on of hands, for those about to receive ... P, (c) 25, (t) 68

Learn, bless all who .. p, .(c) 30, (t) 70
Leisure time, good use of ... P, (c) 30
Liberties, preserve and increase our .. P, (c) 25
[Liberties], defend our ... P, (t) 68
Life and health, giver of ... P, (c) 72
Light, in your light see ... P, (c) 40, (t) 74
Light of the faithful ... P, (c) 71, (t) 75
Litany, the great ... (t) 78
Local government, for ... P, (c) 27
Love, a prayer of (attributed to St. Francis) ... P, (c) 41
Lovely and of good report ... P, (t) 72
Lover of men, you are gracious ... P, (c) 92

Magistrates, bless the ... P, (t) 69
Mankind, future of ... P, (c) 33
[Mankind], vision of a new ... P, (c) 44
Married couples, for ... P, (c) 35
Martyrs and saints, all the ... T, (c) 47
Mary, the mother of our Lord ... T, (c) 47
Mayors of Cities, for ... P, (c) 27
Meals, grace at ... P, (c) 44, (t) 76
Means of grace ... T, (c) 46, (t) 77
Memorial days, on ... P, (c) 39, (t) 74
Mentally ill, for the ... P, (c) 37, (t) 73
Merciful and compassionate, ever ready to hear ... P, (t) 84
Mindful of the needs of others ... P, (c) 44, (t) 76
Ministers, good and faithful, raise up ... P, (c) 57
Ministry, a litany for the ... (c) 55
[Ministry], for the Ordained ... P, (c) 23, (t) 67
[Ministry], that in their vocation and ... P, (c) 93, (t) 93
[Ministry], the supply of candidates for ... P, (c) 23
Misery, you see all the ... P, (c) 94, (t) 94
Mission of the Church, a litany for the ... (c) 93
[Mission of the Church], for the ... P, (c) 21, (t) 66
[Mission of the Church] ... T, (c) 47
Monastic Orders, for ... P, (c) 24
Money, for the responsible use of ... P, (c) 32
Morning, in the ... P, (c) 42, (t) 75
Moses and all the prophets ... T, (c) 47
Mourn, for those who ... P, (c) 38, (t) 73
Mysteries of Christ, stewards of the ... P, (c) 57
Mystery of life, reverence before the ... P, (c) 33

Nation, for the ... T, (c) 48
[Nation] under your care, keep this ... P, (c) 26
[Nation], we commend this ... P, (c) 26, (t) 69
Nations, community of, our obligations in the ... P, (c) 26
[Nations], peace among the ... P, (c) 19, (t) 66
Nations of the earth, those who take counsel for ... P, (c) 93, (t) 93
Natural resources, for the conservation of ... P, (c) 33
Navy, for the ... P, (t) 84
Necessities before we ask, who knowest our ... P, (t) 88
Needs are known before we ask, to whom our ... P, (c) 89
Needy, minister in your name to the ... P, (c) 31, (t) 71
New things which had grown old are being made ... P, (c) 95, (t) 95
Night, our rest during the past ... P, (c) 42, (t) 75
[Night], protection through the coming ... P, (c) 42
Nurses, grant sympathy, skill to ... P, (c) 38

Old, none to care for them ... P, (c) 30
One Body and one Spirit ... P, (c) 22, (t) 67
One world, vision of ... T, (c) 49
Operation, for one about to undergo an ... P, (c) 37, (t) 73
Oppressed in the land, for the ... P, (c) 31
Oppression, no peace with ... P, (c) 28, (t) 69
[Oppression], teach us to eliminate ... P, (c) 31
Orders, for Monastic ... P, (c) 24

Pardon and peace (for the dead) ... P, (c) 39
Parents, bestow wisdom upon ... P, (c) 34
Parish family, for this ... P, (c) 22
Parklands, safeguard ... T, (c) 50
Patience in (under) their sufferings ... P, (c) 19, (t) 66
Peace among the nations ... P, (c) 19, (t) 66
[Peace] and unity of that heavenly City ... P, (c) 23
[Peace], domestic, restoration of ... T, (c) 49
[Peace], for negotiating ... T, (c) 48
[Peace], teach us to improve our ways of ... P, (c) 31
[Peace], that there may be (for our country) ... P, (t) 68
[Peace], for the restoration of ... T, (c) 49
[Peace], give them (troubled or bereaved) ... P, (c) 38, (t) 73
[Peace], guide our feet into the way of ... P, (c) 42, (t) 75
[Peace], I leave with you ... P, (c) 22, (t) 67
[Peace], kindle in the hearts of all men the true love of ... P, (c) 93, (t) 93
[Peace], make us instruments of your ... P, (c) 41
[Peace], to church, nation, and all mankind ... P, (c) 97

[Peace], to preach (mission of Church) ... P, (c) 21, (t) 67
[Peace], to your Church, nations, homes, hearts ... P, (c) 19
[Peace], within families ... P, (c) 34
Peaceable wisdom, guide with your ... P, (c) 19, (t) 66
Peacemakers, for ... T, (c) 49
People mindful of your favor ... P, (c) 25, (t) 68
Personal life, a litany for ... (c) 57
Petitions, promised to heed (hear) ... P, (c) 44, (t) 76
Physicians, grant wisdom, skill to (for hospitals) ... P, (c) 38
Plenteousness, fillest all things living with ... P, (t) 72
Poor, for the ... P, (c) 30, (t) 70
Poverty, teach us to eliminate ... P, (c) 30
Prayer, for the answering of ... P, (c) 44, (t) 76
Prayers, ever ready to hear ... P, (t) 84
[Prayers], of your people, accept the fervent ... P, (c) 92
Prejudice, teach us to eliminate ... P, (c) 30
Preserving our lives in perils ... T, (c) 49
President, for the (for sound government) ... P, (c) 26
[President] of the United States, for the ... P, (c) 26, (t) 69
[President] ... P, (t) 69
Presiding Bishop, bless N., our ... P, (c) 22
Prince of Peace ... P, (c) 20
Prisons and prisoners, for ... P, (c) 31
Protection of the law, equal ... P, (c) 31
Providence, blessings of thy merciful ... T, (t) 77
[Providence], tranquil operation of your .. P, (c) 95, (t) 95
Public opinion, for those who influence ... P, (c) 32
Pure and peaceable wisdom, guide with your ... P, (c) 93, (t) 93

Quiet confidence, for ... P, (c) 40, (t) 74

Race, human (future of mankind) ... P, (c) 33
Races and cultures, for the diversity of ... T, (c) 49
[Races] and nations of men, one family ... P, (c) 21
[Races] and tongues, people of many ... P, (c) 21
[Races], meeting-ground of (for cities) ... P, (c) 30
Rector, to choose a ... P, (c) 22
Regard not our sins but the faith of your Church ... P, (c) 22, (t) 67
Renew us this day (Sunday) through our worship ... P, (c) 41, (t) 75
Renewed, all things are being (for the Church) ... P, (c) 95, (t) 97
Representatives, guide ... P, (c) 26, (t) 69
Responsible use of money, for ... P, (c) 52
Rest with all your saints (for the dying or the dead) ... P, (c) 64

Resurrection to everlasting life (for those who mourn) ... P, (c) 38
Retreat, for a ... P, (c) 24
Returning and rest we shall be saved ... P, (c) 40, (t) 74
Reunite it, where it (Church) is divided ... P, (c) 20, (t) 66
Rich through your poverty ... P, (c) 24
Rights of all may be protected ... P, (c) 27

Sacraments, ministers of your Word and ... P, (c) 89
Sacraments may be faithfully administered ... P, (c) 22
St. Chrysostom, a prayer of ... P, (c) 86, (t) 87
St. Francis: a prayer of love ... P, (c) 41
Saints and faithful departed, for the ... T, (c) 47
Schools and colleges, for ... P, (c) 30, (t) 70
Self-acceptance, for ... P, (c) 41
Self-dedication, prayers of ... P, (c) 40, (t) 75
Self-mastery, for ... P, (c) 41
Seminaries, for ... P, (c) 30, (t) 70
Senators, guide ... P, (c) 30, (t) 70
Serenity to accept the things we cannot change ... P, (c) 41
Sermons, before ... P, (c) 43
Servants of others, that we may be the ... P, (c) 41
Service, for Christian ... P, (c) 31, (t) 71
[Service] is perfect freedom, whose ... P, (t) 83
[Service] of our country, those who have laid down their lives in the ... P, (c) 39, (t) 74
[Service], wholly dedicated to your ... P, (c) 40
Sheep of your own fold ... P, (c) 65
Shepherd of the sheep, the great ... (c) 46, (t) 76
Sick child, for a ... P, (c) 37, (t) 73
[Sick] persons, for ... P, (c) 37, (t) 72
Sickness, graciously pleased to deliver from ... T, (t) 78
Sinner of your own redeeming ... P, (c) 65
Social justice, for ... P, (c) 28, (t) 69
[Social justice], for the widening vision of ... T, (c) 49
[Social justice], struggles for ... P, (c) 28
Soil rich, make the ... P, (c) 33
Soldiers of our country, protect the ... P, (t) 84
Southwell Litany, the ... (c) 57
Space, for the exploration of ... P, (c) 33
Spirit, send us forth in the power of your ... P, (c) 44
[Spirit] and in truth, worship thee in ... P, (t) 76
[Spirit] of grace and of supplication ... P, (t) 76

[Spirit] of thy grace, the healthful ... P, (t) 67
Stewards of your bounty ... P, (c) 32, (t) 71
Still and know that you are God, be ... P, (c) 40, (t) 74
Suffering, give your blessing to all who work to prevent ... P, (c) 38
[Suffering], minister in your Name to ... P, (c) 31, (t) 71
[Suffering], you see all the ... P, (c) 94, (t) 94
Sufficient success upon earth ... P, (c) 55
Sunday, on ... P, (c) 41, (t) 75
Support us all the day long ... P, (c) 42, (t) 75
Supplication, to make our common ... P, (c) 86, (t) 87

Teach, bless all who ... P, (c) 30, (t) 70
Technology, show us how to transform ... P, (c) 30
Terror, for those who live in our land with ... P, (c) 31
Thanksgiving, a litany of ... (c) 53
[Thanksgiving], the General ... T, (c) 46, (t) 77
Those we love, for ... P, (c) 36, (t) 72
Travel, for safe ... T, (c) 51
[Travel] in other lands, for those who live and ... P, (c) 28
Travelers, for ... P, (c) 36
Trouble or bereavement, for a person in ... P, (c) 38, (t) 73
Trustfulness, for ... P, (c) 40, (t) 75
Truth and peace, from whom proceed all thoughts of ... P, (c) 93, (t) 93

Unemployed, for the ... P, (c) 29
Unity of that heavenly City ... P, (c) 23
[Unity] of the Church, for the ... P, (c) 22, (t) 67
[Unity] which is according to thy will ... P, (t) 67
Universe, you created the ... P, (c) 32
Universities, for ... P, (c) 30, (t) 70

Victory, eternal (for the dead) ... P, (c) 39, (t) 74
Victory, strength to have (Baptism) ... P, (c) 24
Vocation and ministry, that in their ... P, (c) 93, (t) 93
Vows of poverty, chastity, and obedience ... P, (c) 24

Water pure, make the ... P, (c) 33
Weather, deliver us from, the immoderate ... P, (t) 84
[Weather], give us seasonable P, (c) 29, (t) 70
Weekly remembrance of the glorious resurrection ... P, (c) 41, (t) 75
Welfare of our fellow man, to seek the .. P, (c) 28
When two or three are agreed together ... P, (c) 86, (t) 87
Wilderness, safeguard ... T, (c) 50

Witness, boldly bear ... P, (c) 23
Word may be truly preached, grant that your ... P, (c) 22
[Word] which we have heard this day ... P, (c) 44, (t) 76
Word and Sacraments, ministers of your ... P, (c) 89
Work, be present with your people where they ... P, (c) 29
[Work], for a right attitude toward ... P, (c) 32
[Work], for those whose work is difficult ... P, (c) 29
[Work] undertaken according to your will ... P, (c) 55
Worldly anxieties ... P, (c) 40, (t) 75
Worship, after ... P, (c) 44, (t) 76
[Worship], before ... P, (c) 42, (t) 76
[Worship], renew us this day (Sunday) through our ... P, (c) 41, (t) 75
Young persons, for ... P, (c) 35

PRAYER BOOK STUDIES 26: HOLY BAPTISM

A Form for Confirmation or the
Laying-On of Hands by the Bishop
with the Affirmation of Baptismal Vows

1973

PREFACE

The trial use of the rite of "Holy Baptism with the Laying-On of Hands" gave rise to a prolonged and intensive process of study and consultation. This process resulted in a significant consensus embodied in the two rites presented in this Study: "Holy Baptism" and "A Form for the Affirmation of Baptismal Vows with the Laying-On of Hands by the Bishop, also called Confirmation."

A brief outline of the process of consultation is given in Section I below. Section II contains a Statement of Agreed Positions reached in the course of the consultation. Section III is a chart showing in skeletal form the structure of the two rites. The texts of the two rites, presented separately, follow. A more detailed and elaborate discussion of some of the meanings of the two rites is published separately as a Supplement to this Study. It should be carefully studied as a necessary background to the understanding of the rites.

Historical Background

The combined rite of "Holy Baptism with the Laying-On of Hands"[1], prepared by the Standing Liturgical Commission in 1970, was authorized for trial use by the General Convention of that year under certain clearly stated conditions. These were as follows:

1. That the Baptismal Section of the same be authorized for trial use, subject to the direction and guidance of the Ordinary;
2. That children be admitted to Holy Communion before Confirmation, subject to the direction and guidance of the Ordinary;
3. That the Rite entitled, "Holy Baptism with the Laying-On of Hands", be authorized for trial use with a Bishop as the Officiant, provided that no children under the present age normal for confirmation shall receive the Laying-On of Hands during the trial-use period.[2]

The enabling resolution also provided that the Bishops should arrange a period of intensive study of and instruction in *Prayer Book Studies* 18 in their several Dioceses.

---

1. *Prayer Book Studies* 18, published by The Church Hymnal Corporation, New York, 1970. Reproduced in *Services for Trial Use* pp. 19-35, The Church Hymnal Corporation, New York, 1971.

2. These conditions are reproduced on p. 21 of *Services for Trial Use*.

As a result of this period of study and actual use, subject to the limitations cited above, numerous comments and suggestions were received and studied by the Drafting Committee on Christian Initiation[3]. The Committee prepared several major amendments of the rite, and these were subjected to careful scrutiny by the Standing Liturgical Commission and its consultants.

The whole question of Christian Initiation was considered at the Special Meeting of the House of Bishops in New Orleans, October 29—November 3, 1972[4]. Following this discussion, the House of Bishops requested its Theological and its Prayer Book Committees to meet in joint session with the Standing Liturgical Commission for the purpose of studying the proposals concerning Christian Initiation. The House of Bishops further requested "that there be issued, as a result of said joint meeting, a report or study document, to be submitted to the Bishops of the Church, both individually and collectively."[5]

The joint meeting took place in Dallas, Texas, on December 6—9, 1972. Two representatives of the General Synod Committee on Doctrine and Worship of the Anglican Church of Canada also took part in the discussions. A thorough exchange of views took place, and several positions were clearly defined. The joint meeting appointed an *ad hoc* committee to formulate these views in accordance with the wishes of the House of Bishops[6]. The present statement and the two rites which follow are the results of that consultation.

Statement of Agreed Positions

A. Concerning Baptism

1. There is one, and only one, unrepeatable act of Christian initiation, which makes a person a member of the Body of Christ.
2. The essential element of Christian initiation is baptism by water and the Spirit, in the Name of the Holy Trinity, in response to repentance and faith.

---

3. The Drafting Committee consists of the following: Rt. Rev. Robert B. Appleyard; Rt. Rev. Frederick B. Wolf; Rev. Lee Benefee; Rev. James Madison; Rev. Leonel L. Mitchell; Rev. Daniel Stevick; Rev. Thomas Talley; Mrs. Howard O. Bingley; Dr. Margaret Mead; Mr. Harrison Tillman; Rev. Bonnell Spencer, O.H.C., *Chairman*,

4. Report of the Special Meeting of the House of Bishops, New Orleans, Louisiana, October 29—November 3, 1972, p. 29.

5. For the full text of the Resolution moved by the Bishop of Louisiana and adopted by the House, see Report of the Special Meeting, p. 57.

6. The membership of the *ad hoc* Committee was as follows: Rt. Rev. John H. Burt; Rt. Rev. William F. Creighton; Rt. Rev. Richard S.M. Emrich; Rev. Robert W. Estill; Mrs. Richard L. Harbour; Rev. Massey H. Shepherd, Jr.; Rev. Bonnell Spencer, O.H.C.; Rt. Rev. Arthur A. Vogel; Rev. Canon Charles M. Guilbert, *Chairman*.

3. Christian initiation is normatively administered in a liturgical rite that also includes the laying-on of hands, consignation (with or without Chrism), prayer for the gift of the Holy Spirit, reception by the Christian community, joining the eucharistic fellowship, and commissioning for Christian mission. When the Bishop is present, it is expected that he will preside at the rite.

B. Concerning a post-baptismal Affirmation of Vows

1. An act and occasion for (more or less) mature personal acceptance of promises and affirmations made on one's behalf in infancy is pastorally and spiritually desirable.
2. Such an act and occasion must be voluntary; but it should be strongly encouraged as a normal component of Christian nurture, and not merely made available.
3. It is both appropriate and pastorally desirable that the affirmations should be received by a Bishop as representing the Diocese and the world-wide Church; and that the Bishop should recall the applicants to their Christian mission, and, by a laying-on of hands, transmit his blessing, with a prayer for the strengthening graces.
4. The rite embodying such affirmations should in no sense be understood as being a "completion of Holy Baptism", nor as being a condition precedent to admission to the Holy Communion, nor as conveying a special status of Church membership.
5. The occasion of the affirming of baptismal vows and obligations that were made by godparents on one's behalf in infancy is a significant and unrepeatable event. It is one's "Confirmation Day."
6. The rite itself, however, is suitable, and should be available, for other occasions in the lives of Christian people. For example, (1) when a person who has been baptized in some other fellowship of Christians wishes to become a member of The Episcopal Church, it is desirable and appropriate that this person be presented to the Bishop, as representing the world-wide episcopate, and that the new relationship be blessed with the laying-on of hands and a recommissioning to Christian service; and (2) when a person whose practice of the Christian life has become perfunctory, or has completely lapsed, awakes again to the call of Christ and desires to signalize his response publicly, and to receive a strengthening gift of the Spirit for renewal.

It is hoped that this statement of agreed positions will make clear what the rites are designed to accomplish. A more elaborate commentary on some of the meanings underlying the rites of Christian initiation has been prepared by three members of the Drafting Committee and is published separately under the signature of its principal author, the Rev. Dr. Daniel Stevik, as a *Supplement to Prayer Book Studies* 26. It deserves careful and thoughtful study by all who seek to understand the theological content of Christian initiation. The Standing Liturgical Commission commends it to all students of the meaning of Christian sacraments.

The Structure of the Rites

A chart showing the structure of the rites follows. It is not to be taken as a commentary or as a summary of rubrical directions and suggestions. Its purpose is to show at a glance the sequence of events in each rite and how the two rites may be used together or separately.

The Standing Liturgical Commission.

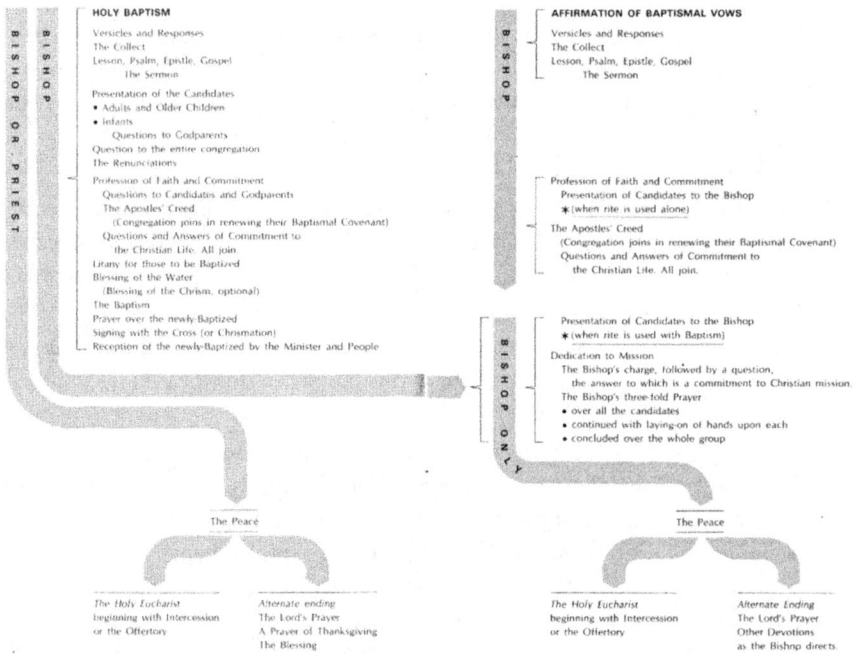

Concerning the Service

Holy Baptism is appropriately administered within the Eucharist as the chief service on a Sunday or other Feast.

When the Bishop is present, it is expected that he will preach the Word and, as the chief sacramental minister of the Diocese, will preside at Baptism and the Eucharist.

When the Bishop presides at Baptism, he officiates at the Presentation of the Candidates, blesses the water [and the oil] recites the prayer over the newly baptized, and signs them with the cross. He may himself baptize the Candidates or appoint other Ministers to do so.

In the absence of the Bishop, a Priest may conduct the whole service, except for the Blessing of the Oil. If the priest uses oil in signing the newly baptized, he must use oil previously blessed by the Bishop.

It is appropriate that the presiding Minister be assisted by other Priests and Deacons, if any are present, and by Lay Persons.

Each candidate for Holy Baptism must be sponsored by one or more baptized persons.

Sponsors of adults present their candidates to the Minister and thereby signify their endorsement of the candidates and their intention to support them, by prayer and example, in their Christian life. Sponsors of infants, commonly called Godparents, present their candidates, make promises in their own names, and also take vows on behalf of their candidates.

It is fitting that parents be included among the Godparents of their own children. Parents and Godparents are to be instructed in the meaning of Baptism, and in their duties to help the new Christians grow in the knowledge and love of God, and in their responsibilities as members of his Church.

Additional Directions and Suggestions will be found on pages 141 and 142.

Holy Baptism

A Psalm, Hymn, or Anthem may be sung during the entrance of the Ministers.

The Bishop or Priest says,

Blessed be God: Father, Son, and Holy Spirit.
And blessed be his Kingdom, now and for ever. Amen.

> *From Easter Day through the Day of Pentecost, in place of the above, he says*
>
> Alleluia! Christ is risen.
> *The Lord is risen indeed. Alleluia!*

There is one Body and one Spirit;
There is one hope in God's call to us;

One Lord, one Faith, one Baptism;
One God and Father of all.

The Lord be with you.
And also with you.

Let us pray.

At the principal service on a Sunday or other Feast, the Collect and Lessons are properly those of the Day. On other occasions, the following are used

Grant, O Lord, that all who are baptized into the death of Jesus Christ your Son may also live with him in the power of his resurrection; who lives and reigns with you in the unity of the Holy Spirit, one God, for ever and ever. *Amen.*

Lesson	*Epistle*	*Gospel*
Ezekiel 36:24-28	2 Corinthians 5:17-20 *or,* Romans 8:14-17 *or* Romans 6:3-5	Mark 1:9-11 *or* John 3:1-6 *or* Mark 10:13-16

THE SERMON
After the Sermon, the Ministers, the Candidates, and their Sponsors or Godparents may go to the font.

Presentation of the Candidates

Minister. Let the Candidates be presented.

Presentation of Adults and Older Children

When there are Candidates who are able to answer for themselves, they are presented individually by their Sponsors, using given names only.

Sponsor. I present __*Name*__ to receive the Sacrament of Baptism.

The Minister asks each Candidate as he or she is presented,

Do you desire to be baptized?

Candidate. I do.

Presentation of Infants

Then infants and children unable to answer for themselves are presented individually by their Parents and Godparents, using given names only.

Parents and Godparents. I present __*Name*__ to receive the Sacrament of Baptism.

When all have been presented, the Minister asks the Parents and Godparents:

Will you be responsible for seeing that this child is brought up in the Christian faith and life?

Parents and Godparents. I will, with God's help.

Minister. Will you by your prayers and witness help this child to grow into the full stature of Christ?

Parents and Godparents. I will, with God's help.

After the Presentation, the Minister addresses the congregation, saying,

Will all of you who witness these vows support these persons in their new life in Christ?

People. We will.

Then the Minister asks the following questions of the Candidates who can speak for themselves, and of the Parents and Godparents who speak on behalf of the infants:

Minister. Do you renounce Satan and all the powers of wickedness that rebel against God?

Answer. I renounce them.

Minister. Do you renounce all evil forces that exploit and destroy the creatures of God?

Answer. I renounce them.

Minister. Do you renounce all sinful desires that draw us away from the love of God?

Answer. I renounce them.

Profession of Faith and Commitment

Minister. Do you commit yourself to Christ as your Savior?

Answer. I do.

Minister. Do you put your whole trust in his grace and love?

Answer. I do.

Minister. Do you promise to follow and obey him as your Lord?

Answer. I do.

Minister. Do you desire to make your Profession of Faith in the words of the Church's baptismal Creed?

Answer. I do.

The Minister then addresses the congregation,

Let us all join with those who are now committing themselves to Christ, and renew our own baptismal covenant.

> *Instead of the foregoing, if there are persons ready to make a special Affirmation of their Baptismal Vows, the Bishop says to the congregation,*
>
> Dear friends, there are also present among us those who desire to make a special affirmation of their baptismal vows and to receive the laying-on of hands. Let us all join with them, and with those who are now committing themselves to Christ, and renew our own baptismal covenant.

Minister.	Do you believe in God the Father?
People.	I believe in God, the Father almighty, creator of heaven and earth.
Minister.	Do you believe in Jesus Christ, the Son of God?
People.	I believe in Jesus Christ, his only Son, our Lord. He was conceived by the power of the Holy Spirit and born of the Virgin Mary. He suffered under Pontius Pilate, was crucified, died, and was buried. He descended to the dead. On the third day he rose again. He ascended into heaven, and seated at the right hand of the Father. He will come again to judge the living and the dead.
Minister.	Do you believe in God the Holy Spirit?
People.	I believe in the Holy Spirit, the holy catholic Church, the communion of saints, the forgiveness of sins, the resurrection of the body, and the life everlasting.

Minister.	Will you continue in the apostles' teaching and fellowship, in the breaking of bread, and in prayers?
People.	I will, with God's help.
Minister.	Will you by word and example proclaim the Good News of God in Christ?
People.	I will, with God's help.
Minister.	Will you seek and serve Christ in all persons, loving your neighbor as yourself?
People.	I will, with God's help.
Minister.	Will you strive for justice and peace among all people, and respect the dignity of every human being?
People.	I will, with God's help.

The Minister then says to the congregation,

Let us pray for these persons who are to receive the sacrament of new birth.

A person appointed leads the following Litany:

Deliver them, O Lord, from the way of sin and death.Lord, hear our prayer.

Open their hearts to your grace and truth.
   Lord, hear our prayer.
Keep them in the faith and communion of your holy Church.
   Lord, hear our prayer.
Teach them to love others in the power of the Spirit.
   Lord, hear our prayer.
Send them into the world in witness to your love.
   Lord, hear our prayer.
Bring them to the fullness of your peace and glory.
   Lord, hear our prayer.

Blessing of the Water

The Bishop, or in his absence the Priest, blesses the water, first saying,

The Lord be with you.
And also with you.

Let us give thanks to the Lord our God.
It is right to give him thanks and praise.

We thank you, heavenly Father, for the gift of water. Over it the Holy Spirit moved in the beginning of creation. Through it you led the children of Israel out of their bondage in Egypt into the land of promise. In it your Son Jesus received the Baptism of John and was anointed by the Holy Spirit as the Messiah, the Christ who would lead us by his death and resurrection from the bondage of sin into everlasting life.

We thank you, heavenly Father, for the water of Baptism. In this water we are buried with Christ in his death. By it we share in his resurrection. Through it we are renewed by the Holy Spirit. Therefore, in joyful obedience to your Son, and looking for his coming again as Lord of all the nations, we bring into his fellowship those who believe in him and come to him, baptizing them in the Name of the Father, and of the Son, and of the Holy Spirit.

Now sanctify this water, we pray you, by the power of your Holy Spirit, that those who here are cleansed from sin and born again may continue for ever in the risen life of Jesus Christ our Savior; *Here he is to touch the water with his hand.*

To him, to you, and to the Holy Spirit, be all honor and glory, now and for ever. Amen.

Blessing of the Chrism

When the Bishop is present, he may bless oil of Chrism, saying,

Eternal Father, whose Son Jesus Christ was anointed by the Holy Spirit to be the servant of all, we pray you to consecrate this oil; that those who are sealed with it may share in the ministry of our great High Priest and King; who lives and reigns with you and the Holy Spirit, one God, for ever and ever. Amen. *Here he is to lay his hand on the vessel of oil*

The Baptism

Each Candidate is presented by name to the Minister, who then dips him in the water, or pours water upon him, saying,

<u>Name</u>, I BAPTIZE YOU IN THE NAME OF THE FATHER, AND OF THE SON, AND OF THE HOLY SPIRIT.

The People say, AMEN.

When all have been baptized, the Bishop, or in his absence the Priest, prays over them,

Let us pray.

Heavenly Father, we thank you that by water and the Holy Spirit you have bestowed upon these your servants the forgiveness of sin, and have raised them to the new life of grace. Sustain them, O Lord, with the riches of your Holy Spirit: give them an inquiring and discerning heart; the strength to will and to persevere; a spirit to know and to love you; and the gift of joy and wonder in all your works. *Amen.*

Then he places his hand on the person's head, marking on the forehead the sign of the Cross [using Chrism if desired], and saying to each one,

<u>Name</u>, child of God, inheritor of the Kingdom of heaven, by the water of Baptism you have been sealed by the Holy Spirit and marked as Christ's own for ever.

The Minister then greets the newly baptized person.

When all have been signed, the Minister presents the newly baptized to the congregation.

The Minister and People say,

We receive you into the household of God. Confess the faith of Christ crucified, proclaim his resurrection, and share with us in his eternal priesthood.

If the Form for the Affirmation of Baptismal Vows is not to follow, the Minister and People may now exchange the Peace with one another and the newly baptized.

The service then continues with the Intercession or with the Offertory of the Eucharist, followed by the Great Thanksgiving.

Those who have now been baptized may receive Holy Communion.

Affirmation of Baptismal Vows

When the Bishop is present, if there are any who desire to make a special Affirmation of Baptismal Vows, and have been duly prepared, they are now brought to the Bishop, and the persons appointed to present them say to him,

Father in God, I present these persons to you for blessing by the laying-on of hands.

The service then continues with the Dedication to Mission on page 145.

Alternative Ending

If there is no celebration of the Eucharist, the service continues with

THE LORD'S PRAYER

The Minister then says,

All praise and thanks to you, most merciful Father, for receiving us as your own children, for incorporating us into your holy Church, and for making us worthy to share in the inheritance of the saints in light; through Jesus Christ your Son our Lord, who lives and reigns with you and the Holy Spirit, one God, for ever and ever. *Amen.*

Alms may be received and presented, and the Minister may add other prayers, concluding with this Blessing:

Almighty God, the Father of our Lord Jesus Christ, from whom all fatherhood in heaven and earth is named, grant you to be strengthened with might by his Spirit. May Christ dwell in your hearts by faith, that you may be filled with all the fullness of God. *Amen.*

Conditional Baptism

If there is reasonable doubt that a person has been baptized with water In the Name of the Father, and of the Son, and of the Holy Spirit (which are the essential parts of Baptism), the person shall be baptized in the usual manner, but the form of words shall be,

IF YOU ARE NOT ALREADY BAPTIZED, *Name*, I BAPTIZE YOU IN THE NAME OF THE FATHER, AND OF THE SON, AND OF THE HOLY SPIRIT.

Emergency Baptism

In case of emergency, any baptized person may administer. Baptism according to this form.

Using the given name of the one to be baptized [if known] pour water on him, saying,

I BAPTIZE YOU IN THE NAME OF THE FATHER, AND OF THE SON, AND OF THE HOLY SPIRIT.

THE LORD'S PRAYER *is then said.*

Other prayers such as the following may be added.

Heavenly Father, we thank you that by water and the Holy Spirit you have bestowed upon this your servant the forgiveness of sins and have raised him to the new life of grace. Strengthen him, O Lord, with your presence; enfold him in the arms of your mercy, and keep him safe for ever. Amen.

A person so, baptized may receive Holy Communion.

The person who administers emergency Baptism should inform the Priest of the appropriate parish, so that the fact can be properly registered.

If the baptized person recovers, the Baptism should be recognized at a public administration of the sacrament, the person and his Godparents or Sponsor taking part in everything except the actual Baptism.

Additional Directions and Suggestions

Holy Baptism is especially appropriate on Easter Eve, the Day of Pentecost, the First Sunday after Epiphany, and on All Saints' Day or the Sunday after All Saints' Day. It is recommended that, as far as possible, Baptisms be reserved for these occasions, or when the Bishop is present.

The font is to be filled with clean water, either immediately before the service or before the Blessing of the Water.

When the Bishop is present, or on other occasions for sufficient reason, the Collect and one or more of the Lessons cited in the Baptismal Service may be substituted for the Proper of the Day.

In place of Ezekiel 36:24-28, any of the other Old Testament Lessons for the Easter Vigil (STU p. 524) may be used.[i]

Lay Persons may act as readers, and it is appropriate for Sponsors to be assigned this function. The Gospel is read by a Deacon or Priest.

The Nicene Creed is not used at this service.

---

[i] [Ed. Note: The alternate OT lessons on STU p. 524 are Genesis 1:1-2:2 (Creation); Genesis 22:1-18 (Sacrifice of Isaac); Exodus 14:15-15:1 (Giving of the Law); Isaiah 4:2-6 (God dwells on Zion); Isaiah 55:1-11 (Seek the Lord); Zephaniah 3:14-17, 19-20 (Sing aloud, Zion).]

Psalms, Canticles, or Hymns may be used after the Old Testament Lesson and after the Epistle; particularly suitable are Psalms 15, 23, 27, 42, 84, 87, 100, 122; and the First Song of Isaiah, and A Song to the Lamb. A suitable Psalm, Hymn, or Anthem may be sung when moving to or from the font. The Baptismal Litany may also be sung.

The Presentation of the Candidates shall normally take place at the font. If, however, the arrangement of the church building makes it difficult for the congregation to see the Ministers or to participate in the Profession of Faith, this part of the service may be performed in a more convenient place. And then, before or during the Litany (page 137), the Ministers, Candidates, and Sponsors go to the font for the Blessing of the Water.

When there are persons prepared to make the special Affirmation of Baptismal Vows in the presence of the Bishop, it is recommended that they stand together in some convenient place for the Profession of Faith and Commitment.

The Litany may be led by one of the Sponsors.

At the Blessing of the Water and at the Administration of Baptism, the Minister, whenever possible, should face the People across the font, and the Sponsors should be so grouped that the People may have a clear view of the action.

Other Bishops, Priests, or Deacons present may be appointed to assist in administering the Baptism of the Candidates.

After the Baptism a candle [which may be lighted from the Paschal Candle] may be given to the newly baptized or their Godparents.

When the Bishop is present, after all Candidates have been baptized, it is fitting that he go to the front of the congregation and that the newly baptized be brought to him there for the prayer he says over them and the signing with the Cross.

If there are many Candidates, the congregation may be seated during the administration of the baptisms and blessings. The Bishop may be seated for the signings and blessings.

The oblations of bread and wine at the Baptismal Eucharist may be brought forward by the newly baptized or their godparents. It is also fitting that the Sponsors receive Holy Communion with the newly baptized.

Baptized persons in good standing are eligible to receive Holy Communion.

A Form for Confirmation or the Laying-On of Hands by the Bishop with the Affirmation of Baptismal Vows

Concerning the Service

Holy Baptism is full initiation by water and the Holy Spirit into Christ's body the Church. The bond which God establishes in Baptism is indissoluble.

In the course of their Christian development, baptized members of the Church are expected, as a normal component of their Christian nurture, to reaffirm their baptismal promise in the presence of the Bishop. Such Affirmations should be made by:

- *Those who are ready, and have been duly prepared, to make a mature public affirmation of their faith and commitment to the responsibilities of their Baptism;*
- *Those who wish to return to the Christian life and mission after having neglected or abandoned it;*
- *Those who have come into the Bishop's jurisdiction from another Church.*

The first part of this Service, preceding the Dedication to Mission on page 145, is to be omitted when the Affirmation of Vows takes place within the context of the Service of Holy Baptism.

A Form for Confirmation or the Laying-On of Hands by the Bishop with the Affirmation of Baptismal Vows

When a Bishop is present with a congregation, it is desirable that he preside at the administration of Holy Baptism. But if there is no Baptism, and if there are those who have been prepared to make a special Affirmation of their Baptismal Vows, the service begins as follows:

A Psalm, Hymn, or Anthem may be sung during the entrance of the Ministers.

The Bishop says,

Blessed be God: Father, Son, and Holy Spirit.
And blessed be his Kingdom, now and for ever. Amen.

> *From Easter Day through the Day of Pentecost, in place of the above, he says*
>
> Alleluia! Christ is risen.
> *The Lord is risen indeed. Alleluia!*

There is one Body and one Spirit;
There is one hope in God's call to us;

One Lord, one Faith, one Baptism;
One God and Father of all.

The Lord be with you
And also with you.

Let us pray.

At the principal service on a Sunday or other Feast, the Collect and Lessons are properly those of the Day. On other occasions, the following are used:

Almighty God, grant that we who have turned from the old life of sin by our Baptism into the death and resurrection of your Son Jesus Christ, may be renewed in your Holy Spirit, and live in righteousness and true holiness; through Jesus Christ our Lord, who now lives and reigns with you in the unity of the Holy Spirit, one God, for ever and ever. *Amen.*

Lesson	*Epistle*	*Gospel*
Jeremiah 31:31-34	Ephesians 4:7, 11-16	John 14:15-21

THE SERMON

Profession of Faith and Commitment

After the Sermon, those who desire to make a special Affirmation of their Baptismal Vows, and have been duly prepared, take their places before the Bishop, together with those who are to present them.

The Presenters address the Bishop,

Father in God, I present to you these persons for blessing by the laying-on of hands.

The Bishop says to those presented,

Do you desire to make your Profession of Faith in the words of the Church's baptismal Creed?

Answer. I do.

The Bishop then says to the congregation,

Dear friends, let us all join with these persons in renewing our own baptismal covenant.

Bishop. Do you believe in God the Father?

People. I believe in God, the Father almighty,
 creator of heaven and earth.

Bishop. Do you believe in Jesus Christ, the Son of God?

People.   I believe in Jesus Christ, his only Son, our Lord.
  He was conceived by the power of the Holy Spirit
  and born of the Virgin Mary.
  He suffered under Pontius Pilate,
  was crucified, died, and was buried.
  He descended to the dead.
  On the third day he rose again.
  He ascended into heaven,
  and seated at the right hand of the Father.
  He will come again to judge the living and the dead.

Bishop.   Do you believe in God the Holy Spirit?

People.   I believe in the Holy Spirit,
  the holy catholic Church,
  the communion of saints,
  the forgiveness of sins,
  the resurrection of the body,
  and the life everlasting.

Bishop.   Will you continue in the apostles' teaching and fellowship, in the breaking of bread, and in prayers?

People.   I will, with God's help.

Bishop.   Will you by word and example proclaim the Good News of God in Christ?

People.   I will, with God's help.

Bishop.   Will you seek and serve Christ in all persons, loving your neighbor as yourself?

People.   I will, with God's help.

Bishop.   Will you strive for justice and peace among all people, and respect the dignity of every human being?

People.   I will, with God's help.

Dedication to Mission

Then the Bishop addresses those who have been presented for the laying-on of hands:

You have joined with us in renewing the covenant of Baptism. You have recognized that Christ has called his people to be his ambassadors in the world. Do you here renew your individual commitment to proclaim by word and deed his message of reconciliation, hope, and love?

Answer. I do. With God's help, I will follow Jesus Christ as my Savior and Lord, and I will work and pray and give for the spread of his kingdom.

The Bishop says this Prayer over the entire group to be blessed:

Almighty God, we thank you that by the Cross of your Son Jesus Christ you have overcome sin and brought us to yourself, and by the sealing of your Holy Spirit have bound us to your service. Renew in these your servants the covenant you made with them and all your people, and send them in the power of that Spirit to perform the tasks you set for them.

The Bishop lays his hand on the head of each person and continues,

Strengthen your servant, _Name,_ with the riches of your Holy Spirit; sustain him and empower him for your service.

When all have been commissioned, the Bishop continues, saying,

Defend, O Lord, these your servants with your heavenly grace that they may continue yours for ever; and daily increase in your Holy Spirit more and more, until they come to your everlasting kingdom.

The People respond to the Bishop's Prayer, saying,

Amen.

The Bishop and People exchange the Peace.

Then, if Baptism has been administered, the service proceeds either with the Intercession or with the Offertory of the Eucharist, followed by the Great Thanksgiving, at which the Bishop should be the principal celebrant. If, however, there has been no Baptism, the service continues with the Intercession.

When there has been no Baptism, the Bishop may bless oil of Chrism for use at subsequent Baptisms, using the prayer on page 138 of the service of Holy Baptism.

Alternative Ending

If there is no celebration of the Eucharist, the service continues with

THE LORD'S PRAYER

and such other devotions as the Bishop may direct.

SUPPLEMENT TO PRAYER BOOK STUDIES 26: HOLY BAPTISM

A Form for the Affirmation
of Baptismal Vows
with the Laying-On of Hands
by the Bishop
also called
Confirmation

prepared for
The Standing Liturgical Commission by

Daniel B. Stevick

1973

FOREWORD

Prayer Book Studies 26 is published in two parts. The first contains the text of the rite of "Holy Baptism together with A Form for the Affirmation of Baptismal Vows with the Laying-On of Hands by the Bishop also called Confirmation." It also contains the Statement of Agreed Positions on Baptism and on a post-baptismal Affirmation of Vows. Both the rites and the Statement of Agreed Positions represent a significant consensus reached after prolonged and detailed consultations.

The whole question of Christian Initiation was discussed by the House of Bishops at its Special Meeting in New Orleans, Louisiana, October 29-November 3, 1972. As a result of this discussion, a joint meeting of the Standing Liturgical Commission and the Prayer Book and Theological Committees of the House of Bishops was held at Dallas, Texas, on December 6-9, 1972, and the joint meeting appointed an ad hoc committee which worked out the Statement of Agreed Positions.

Concurrently with the consultations referred to above, the Drafting Committee on Christian Initiation was revising its drafts of the rites and was working on a more elaborate background study on some of the meanings underlying the rites of Christian initiation. The Commission read the draft study in detail and with deep appreciation of its insights and scholarship. The Commission decided, however, to publish it not as its own official rationale or statement of position, but under the name of its principal author, the Rev. Dr. Daniel B. Stevick, as a valuable background paper and commentary on the rites it has prepared. Dr. Stevick's paper is the present Supplement to *Prayer Book Studies* 26.

This course of action, the Commission felt, would give Dr. Stevick the opportunity to state his own views freely, and without the necessity of qualifying or adjusting them in any way in order to meet other points of view represented on the Commission. It would also avoid any possible confusion between the points of view expressed in the Statement of Agreed Positions and the views set forth in the present essay. The Commission desires to place on record its gratitude to Dr. Stevick, and to all who assisted him, for this important study. The Commission hopes that this work will contribute significantly to the thinking of the Church as it considers the rites set forth in *Prayer Book Studies* 26.

—The Standing Liturgical Commission

AUTHOR'S PREFACE

The services in *Prayer Book Studies* 26, unlike those in previous booklets of the series, are commented upon in a signed essay. That being the case, perhaps the author may step out from the wings for a prefatory note and some acknowledgments.

This essay was originally written at the request of the Chairman of the Drafting Committee on Christian Initiation, the Rev. Bonnell Spencer, O.H.C. It was felt that a rather full explanation was called for at this point to give an overview of some of the issues that confront the doctrine and administration of Christian initiation in today's Church. The resulting draft was too long (and doubtless too idiosyncratic) to allow the Liturgical Commission to make it its own, and issue it under its own signature, as some other introductory material has been issued. The Commission, after a careful reading, has commended it as an introduction to the thinking that produced the rites in Prayer Book Studies 26 and as a study guide to current discussion of Christian initiation. But it is not the Commission's official account of the rites being proposed.

Anglican rites have characteristically stood as vehicles of the liturgical actions of the Church without any official, binding, definitive rationale. The tradition of liturgies and the tradition of explanation of liturgies have been distinct. The two interact, of course, and especially so at times when liturgies are undergoing change. But the two are not identical. If the initiation rites of *Prayer Book Studies* 26 commend themselves to the Church, they may well be seen in other contexts, and may receive other and better explanations than the one which accompanies their publication. If this essay can contribute to the depth and sophistication with which Christian Initiation is discussed, it will have done its task.

Anyone familiar with any of the kinds of material dealt with here will recognize how much more might be said at every point. Little in the essay is original, and nothing is argued exhaustively. Yet it seemed important to bring together theological, historical, liturgical, pastoral, and strategic considerations. The interdisciplinary character of this account may suggest the many-sidedness of the issues of Christian initiation in the concrete life of the church.

As this study went through its revisions, useful suggestions were made by members of the Drafting Committee on Christian Initiation and by members of the Liturgical Commission. Special mention should be made of two committee members, the Rev. Dr. Leonel L. Mitchell and the Rev. Dr. Thomas I. Talley, who gave generous help at many points in the writing, but whose learning and care in statement were particularly valuable in the historical material. The general outline and argument and all of the remaining defects are my own.

—Daniel B. Stevick

Introductory

The rites of Christian Initiation have classically been three: Baptism, Confirmation, and first Communion. These rites are closely bound up with one another, with the Gospel itself, with the shared life of the Church, and with individual Christian identity. Yet, important as they are, these three classic actions have not been constant. Over the centuries, they have been variously interpreted, variously combined, and variously administered. They have had fully as complicated a history as has the Eucharist, and one that has been given less attention.

The Episcopal Church's pattern for becoming a Christian, not greatly different from the pattern of many other Western Churches, has been a two-stage rite. At birth a child of the Christian community is baptized. The baptized child is regarded as a member of the Church and is nurtured as such. He is granted a significant, if still partial share in the Church's life. At a later time, after he has developed a capacity for understanding and has received some teaching, the child is confirmed by the bishop and admitted to communion. This has been the basic pattern for which the liturgical texts are written. The pattern is adapted as necessary to suit the different circumstances of persons who come to Christian faith as adults, or who come as baptized Christians to the Episcopal Church from another obedience.

In recent generations, dissatisfaction has been expressed in Anglicanism and in many other parts of the Christian community with the accustomed rites of becoming a Christian. The issues raised are of several kinds. Liturgical and theological clarity are obscured when rites closely united in meaning are observed in two widely-separated stages. As the historical record is more adequately filled out, it is clear that rites largely shaped in the sixteenth century cannot, with respect to certain important features, be identified with customs of the early Christian centuries - a disquieting consideration for a communion which has taken the New Testament and the early Church as a norm for teaching and practice. The two-stage pattern seems to assume, for its best operation, social conditions and ways of personal development which cannot be taken for granted today.

Rather generally it is felt that Christian initiation has become a thing of reduced significance. Rites which should stand for an original and powerful apprehension of the reality of God have become perfunctory and casual. Some reform movements have sought to make the existing ritual patterns workable. Of course, pastoral diligence is always desirable, but uneasiness has increasingly come to focus on the adequacy of the accustomed ritual pattern itself.

We are now in a period of deep cultural change. History - and, as the community of faith sees it, the Lord of history — is asking for serious rethinking of the Church's own identity and its relation to its society. A kind of death and resurrection, a process with which the Church should be familiar and which it should not fear, is taking place. Institutional and ritual forms are feeling the pressure of new demands. Old truths are being repossessed; continuities are being re-emphasized; essential and non-essential elements of the liturgical inheritance are being disentangled. New adaptations, recognizing unprecedented factors present in today's world, are being tried. It would be strange if something as basic to the Christian community and life as Baptism were unaffected by such upheavals. And of course it is not. In many churches and in many parts of Anglicanism, modifications of traditional rites of initiation are being discussed, proposed, and introduced.

The essay which follows provides a general introduction to some current thinking about Christian initiation. The essay begins with some theological affirmations concerning Christian initiation, for any altered practice must commend itself by its rootage in the basic meanings of this sacrament of the Gospel. A historical sketch follows which emphasizes the variety in the practice of Christian initiation, and the specific history which has given the Episcopal Church its initiatory customs. A brief analysis of the contemporary situation of the Christian community in Western culture identifies some factors which are raising problems for inherited practices and understandings. Some of the specific issues which gather around Baptism, around Confirmation, and around first Communion, are then examined. Finally, some directions for change are indicated, leading to a running commentary on the rite of *Prayer Book Studies* 26. A bibliography suggests resources for further inquiry.

Some Basic Theological Meanings

Baptism is a sacrament of beginnings, of newness, of grace, of a fresh start within history and in the depths of existence. It is the beginning of life in Christ and his people. It is the sign of the new life which is always coming into being within the Church. It is the Christian Gospel in action. Baptism is the ritual side of the way by which world passes over into church and church reaches into the world.

Baptism signifies and conveys that one great redemptive reality which centers in Jesus Christ. His coming, his life of obedience and self-giving, his death and resurrection, were not only his own individual achievement. In them he was representative man, the one man for all men. He graciously identified himself with the "many." He is the inauguration of a new humanity, the "first fruits" of mankind renewed after the intention of the Creator. Christ's work is pictured in the New Testament as a "general baptism", as the world's true washing, the birth of a new creation, the overcoming of darkness by light, the breaking of the powers of bondage. Through Christ the new age of forgiveness and life has dawned within the old age of sin and dying.

The new reality which has come in Christ calls into being a community of response. The Church is set as a sign of the new thing which has come to be in Christ, and which is coming to be. It is a community of lives sharing in one another, as together they share in the life of their common Lord. It is the fellowship united with God in Christ and available to him for his work in the world.

Baptism is a death and resurrection which brings a repenting and believing person within that transformed life whose manifestation is the Church. It is the sacramental link between the individual and the redemption which Christ has won for all men. Baptism is the step by which a person leaves the old age - its style and power - and enters the new. For the person who enters, this step is his cleansing, his rebirth. Archbishop Ramsey once put the matter this way: "As Christ is baptized into man's death, so men shall bebaptized into His; and, as He loses His life to find it in the Father, so men may by a veritable death find a life whose center is in Christ and the brethren."[1]

The meanings of Baptism, such as washing, death and resurrection, new birth, child of God, are obviously expressed in symbolic speech. But no other kind of words is available for expressing ultimate meanings. Images are drawn from the deepest reaches of man's experience: they are, at the same time, our principal terms for capturing the disclosure of God. The encounter of God and man creates and renews great basic images; the images can evoke and inform the recognition of God.

It is apparent that the church's account of Baptism does not use peripheral symbols. The terms in which the church speaks of Baptism are the same terms as those in which it speaks of the saving Mystery in which its own life is constituted. In terms of the action of God, Baptism signifies and imparts the outreaching love of the Father, restoring persons to relation with himself. It unites persons with Christ the Redeemer, and places them within the redemption-bearing community, his Body. It is the seal in the Holy Spirit of the new life, present and to come. In terms of the human response, Baptism enacts and shapes the entry on the life of faith, obedience, and expectation. It is the sacrament of conversion, expressing a new mind, a re-direction, the rejection of the tyranny of sin and the commitment to righteousness. It is the inauguration of a life renewed and set free. All of Christian life—its beginning and its end, now and forever—is related to the life of God in a bond that is not broken.

No liturgical form and no pastoral practice can capture so large a meaning. The best rites are little more than hints. Yet Christ has been pleased to minister

---

1. Ramsey, A.M., *The Gospel and the Catholic Church*, Longmans, London: 1956, 2nd ed., p. 27.

himself, graciously and fully, through liturgies and customs that seem thin and inadequate. Emergency conditions have sometimes restricted to a minimum the words and actions of baptisms which are nevertheless acknowledged to be true sacraments. Yet, even though under necessity very little may be enough, the Church cannot legitimately ask, when it fashions its rites, how little can safely be done. On the highest theological grounds, a great Gospel requires the Church to give serious attention to adequate forms for liturgy.

A Sketch of Historical Development

In order to form a responsible judgment of what may be expected of us in the present moment, it is necessary to have some awareness of the past. The accustomed rites of Christian, initiation have a long history - a record impressive both for its continuity and for its variety.

A. The New Testament

The Church has been a baptizing community from its beginning. The first Christian sermon closed with the plea "Repent and be baptized every one of you in the name of Jesus Christ for the forgiveness of sins, and you shall receive the gift of the Holy Spirit." (Acts 2:38.) Christian baptism probably, but not quite certainly, found a model in Jewish proselyte baptism, and it obviously stood in continuity with the ministry of Iohn the Baptist. Indeed, it drew on some of the deepest and oldest religious instincts of the race. But it claimed a crucial originality. It was, on the Church's account of the matter, a rite grounded in the authority over heaven and earth given to the risen, living Christ (Matt. 28:18-20). It was Baptism in his Name and into his life-through-death.

References to Baptism are frequent in the New Testament, but they supply little detail about the manner of the rite. Acts emphasizes that Baptism was a response to the word and a witness to faith, "They that received his word were baptized" (Acts 2:41).[2] Sometimes evidence of the Holy Spirit came before, or at Baptism, as though a missionary breakthrough were being validated by a new Pentecost.[3] Sometimes a manifestation of the Spirit followed baptism, perhaps as a witness that, through the apostles' laying-on of hands, new Christians were

---

2. Passages which link baptism with the Word and with belief or hearing are gathered in Flemington, W.F., *The New Testament Doctrine of Baptism*, S.P.C.K., London: 1957, p. 49. Flemington summarizes that baptism "might be called an embodiment of the *kerygma*."

3. See esp. Acts 10:44-48, in which the Holy Spirit comes upon Cornelius and others when they have heard Peter's preaching. The apostle decides that baptism cannot but follow this initiative of the Spirit. Note the implied reference to Pentecost in the words "These people who have received the Holy Spirit, just as we have."

brought into the unity and the full life of the Christian fellowship.[4] Often, however, most strikingly, perhaps, in the accounts of Paul's baptism, the evidence of the Spirit and the ministry of the apostles are not mentioned at all. The term "baptism" — the washing, the bath — stood alone. In New Testament practice, as soon as there was evidence of belief, water (apparently quite common water) was sought, and the convert was baptized. The new reality had manifested itself, and its sign need not be delayed.

If we ask whether or not "infant Baptism" was the practice of the primitive Church, we probably put the wrong question. The New Testament does not speak of "infant Baptism," but there are strong suggestions of what might be termed "family baptism."[5] Apparently Christian thinking followed Jewish thinking in regarding a household as a unity. When the head of the household became a Christian, it was inconceivable that all the members of the household would not enter the new life in Christ together. In general, however, the early Church was a missionary community, and the normal subject of baptism was the adult convert. The place of children was derivative.

B. The Early Church

Within a short time, the rites of Christian Initiation took on greater formalization and complexity. The basic meanings were ritually enacted. New features were added as pastoral and evangelistic strategy seemed to require.

After the Church had moved into a predominantly gentile society, there developed a period of teaching, probation, and limited membership known as catechumenate, prefixed to Baptism. This catechumenate may have had roots in the first century, and by the third century, it was a well-established practice. The period of teaching extended perhaps as long as three years. A catechumen might have to change his employment, for in the ancient world many kinds of work involved some acquiescence in idolatry or immoral practices. The teaching of the catechumens appears to have been heavily ethical, stressing such matters as truthfuhiess, faithfulness in marriage, and the peril of idols.

---

4. See esp. Acts 8:15-17. The apostles "came down from Jerusalem." The central point of the passage seems to be the link of a new Christian community in schismatic Jewish territory with the parent Christian community in Jerusalem.

The material in Acts is notoriously difficult. No consistent pattern underlies primitive initiatory practice. The narrative is an account of missionary expansion; we ask questions about institutional and sacramental matters which the author was interested in only incidentally. Some illuminating comments on the variety of baptismal patterns in Acts can be found in Oulton, J.E.L. "The Holy Spirit, Baptism and Laying on of Hands in Acts," in *The Expository Times*, LXVl (1955), pp. 236-240, and in Williams, C.S.C., *The Acts of the Apostles*, A.&C. Black, London: 1957, Appendix 3 "The Giving of the Spirit."

5. I Cor. 1:16, Acts 16:17, 33, 18:8. See the remarks of J. Jeremias on "The *Oikos* Formula" in *Infant Baptism In the First Four Centuries*, Westminster Press, Philadelphia: 1962, pp. 19-24.

Most baptisms took place at Easter; hence, baptismal themes would be enacted against an interpreting background of Jesus' death and resurrection, and of Passover motifs from the Old Testament. Baptism was seen as the entry into the great Paschal Mystery which gathered up the central redemptive themes of the faith. The great enslavement to sin was broken. The true Passover had been sacrificed. A baptized person came through the Red Sea into a new pilgrimage, with a new covenant people, moving towards a promised land, of which sacramental life was a foretaste.

The initiatory rite was quietly dramatic. After a period of preparation and an all night vigil of instruction and prayer, those to be baptized were brought early on Easter morning to the water (originally outdoors, but later to a baptistery located apart from the main eucharistic room). They would lay aside all clothing and ornaments and be led by deacons or deaconesses into the water. There, each candidate would renounce his pagan loyalties— "Satan, his works and his pomp." He would then be asked three questions, corresponding to the three sections of what came to be the Apostles' Creed: "Do you believe in God, the Father Almighty? . . ." As he replied "I believe" to each question, he would be immersed. Often this part of the rite was led by presbyters. Children who could not answer for themselves were baptized before the others in the family, and sponsors answered for them. The newly baptized persons emerged from the font and were anointed; they reclothed themselves (later in the era they were given white garments) and, in some places, received a signing with the cross, a laying-on of hands, or a second anointing by the Bishop (customs differed widely). They were then conducted to the eucharistic assembly, where, for the first time, they shared in the kiss of peace, made their own offering of bread and wine, and received the Body and Blood of Christ.

This combination of ceremonies varied from region to region. The Roman Church had two anointings after baptism, one performed by a presbyter and the other by a Bishop. The large and important Syrian Church had no post-baptismal anointing at all, and it can be argued that the anointing it did have before baptism was preparatory in character.[6]

The rites were elaborated in the course of time. The ceremony of enrolling as a catechumen became rather full. A special service late in the catechumenate imparted the terms of the Creed to the learners. Austerities and exorcisms to expel evil spirits became important preparatory rituals. A prayer, often lengthy and poetic, of blessing the font became a conspicuous feature of the baptismal liturgies. The brief "formula of baptism", which was apparently at first a peculiarity of the Syrian Church, eventually replaced the interrogatory use of the

---

6. The material for tracing the variety of early practice can be found in Whitaker, E.C., *Documents of the Baptismal Liturgy*, 2nd ed., S.P.C.K., London; 1970. Whitaker's introductory essay on the Syrian Church (pp. xiii-xxii) is informative, but some scholars question some of his opinions. See also Mitchell, L.L., *Baptismal Anointing*, S.P.C.K., London: 1966.

Creed at the moment of baptism. Instructions on the meaning of the sacraments were given in the days after Easter to the new initiates. Indeed, the character of the pre-Easter and post-Easter seasons of the church year was shaped by their relation to Christian Initiation. But, with changes and enlargements, the main sequence of actions remained clear and straightforward.

The early liturgies of initiation gave form to actual inward processes of leaving paganism and entering the community in Christ. The significant words of the rites, the expressive ceremonies, and the interpretive explanations would doubtless all have been remembered by the adults who had experienced them as parts of one decisive moment - a watershed in each one's own experience, a putting away of one way of life and an entry on another.

It is impossible to say at what point most baptisms came to be of children born to Christian parents. Doubtless the Church moved into this "second generation" situation at different times in different places. But "in the great centers of the West there were probably few adults left to be baptized by the year 500."[7]

Two theological tendencies were at work in the early Church which had differing effects on baptismal practice. One was the rather moralistic view that baptism cleansed only from sins committed prior to baptism. Baptism was thought of as an absolution, largely retroactive in efficacy — hence, the later its administration, the better. This teaching removed the urgency from infant Baptism. In fact, fear of post-baptismal sin led, in the third century and following, to the postponement of baptism even in instances of people born to devout parents.[8] Many statements from the period contain exhortations to adults who have postponed baptism until late in life to postpone it no longer. The other tendency, which proved more powerful and lasting, was the growing definition of original sin. Augustine, influenced by his own twice-born experience and by his conflict with Pelagius, became convinced that guilt is inherited by all persons by their descent from Adam. It is evident that Augustine argued, at least in part, from church practice to doctrine. He reasoned that Baptism is for the forgiveness of sins; the Church administers Baptism to infants; therefore infants must, in some sense, have sinned.[9] Augustine's doctrine that Baptism cleansed from inherited guilt reinforced the practice of baptizing children as early as possible. Until fairly

---

7. Whitaker, E.C., *The Baptismal Liturgy*, The Faith Press, London: 1968, p. 38.

8. See Jeremias, *op. cit.*, pp. 87-91 and Wiles, M.F. "One Baptism for the Remission of Sins," in *The Church Quarterly Review*, CLXV (1964), pp. 59-66.

9. Augustine's mental processes can be observed in the early part of Book 10 "On the Merits and Forgiveness of Sins, and on the Baptism of Infants." See the chapters on Augustine in Williams, N.P., *The Ideas of the Fall and Original Sin*, Longmans, London: 1929.

Augustine depended on the Latin Bible which contained a crucial mistranslation of Romans 5:12. The final phrase reads "*because* all sinned." The Latin has "*in whom* all sinned." St. Paul meant: "Because (as a matter of record) all (as they had opportunity and competence) sinned (consented to the Adamic condition)." Augustine read it as: "In whom (in solidarity with Adam, the first parent) all (as a matter of inherited condition) sinned."

modern times, Augustine's teaching (often reduced to little more than a superstition) formed at least one important background factor in the common rationale in the West for the practice of infant Baptism.

The change to infant Baptism brought no changes in the liturgies. The forms that had introduced adult converts into the church continued to be used, but for a markedly different function. The service of making a catechumen was moved to the church door as a preamble to baptism proper. Responses, renunciations, and commitments were made entirely by others in the name of the child. The liturgical forms were compressed into a rite of perhaps a half-hour's duration. Yet the same words and actions were used, and the same theological account of their meaning was given, as when the initiatory process had occupied an adult convert for months or years.

C. Adaptation I: The Delegation of Ministries

The Christian movement began in the centers of population, and Bishops were located in cities. But as churches took responsibility for evangelizing outlying areas, Christian congregations, with resident presbyters, grew up which were dependent on the urban center and its chief pastor but which were at some distance from the see city. Increasingly, the full sacramental life which had been exercised by or under the presidency of the Bishop came to be claimed and exercised by presbyters in local parishes. The continuation of an initiatory rite in which bishops, priests, and deacons took part together became particularly difficult.

Outside the immediate sphere of influence of the Roman Church, the initiatory rite in its unity was left as the prerogative of the local priest. This pattern is known today largely as the practice of the Eastern churches, but it was for a time also the practice of large portions of the West. The right to administer Christian Initiation in its entirety was exercised by presbyters in Spain and in parts of France and in North Italy.

The prevalence in the West of presbyteral administration of both Baptism and the post-baptismal rites is not as widely recognized as it should be. But the evidence is abundant. A brief selection may suggest the character of the material:

For Spain, the important text, the *Liber Ordinum*, gives directions concerning the newly baptized infant: "The priest anoints him with chrism, making the sign of the cross on his forehead alone. . . . Then he lays his hand upon him."[10] The Council of Elvira (305 A.D.) legislated that persons baptized by a layman (Canon 38), or a deacon (Canon 77), should be brought to a Bishop to be confirmed. Persons baptized by a presbyter are not mentioned as being under a similar requirement.[11] A scholar who has recently surveyed the evidence summarizes

---

10. Whitaker, *Documents*, p. 121.
11. *ibid.*, p. 222f.

his findings for seventh century Spain on presbyteral "perfecting": "I can only conclude, that there were episcopal baptisms, baptisms administered by presbyters (and *chorepiscopi?*) at the command of, sometimes in the absence of, the bishop, and presbyteral baptisms *per se*; that oil was used, sometimes twice, sometimes perhaps together with the water poured that . . . the minister's hand was imposed and the sign of the cross often (but not necessarily) traced on the forehead. . . . I can only think that any baptism by any minister, given regularly and attested, was accepted as complete and sufficient."[12]

For Gaul, the *Missale Gothicum*, a Gallican sacramentary from about 700 A.D., contains, in the priest's rite of baptism, a direction and prayer for the post-baptismal anointing. Other evidence is consistent with this document. Dr. L.L. Mitchell comments: "In sum, none of the Gallican sacralmentaries includes a rite of episcopal confirmation, nor have we any evidence requiring us to assume that such a rite was customarily added to the extant baptismal rites, nor that the administration of the single Gallican post-baptismal anointing was confined to bishops."[13]

For Northern Italy, the evidence contains a rite (in the Ambrosian Manual) with a post-baptismal anointing by a priest, while the bishop is present, and a rite (described by Beroldus in the twelfth century) with a post-baptismal episcopal anointing. Evidently the two should be taken as equivalent.[14]

By allowing the presbyter, when necessary, to be the minister of all parts of Christian initiation, the actions of water baptism, anointing (or other form of post-baptismal rite), and first communion remained parts of a single event. There were changes from the customs of antiquity. All these actions came to be administered to infants. Even though the unified rite was kept, the link with the Paschal season was eventually lost; baptisms came to depend on when a child was born, not on when Christ had died and risen. The Bishop (today in the East generally the Patriarch) participates by the token of the chrism which he blesses for the baptismal anointing. This pattern of initiation was an adaptation, made to deal with social and ecclesiastical developments. It once commended itself as a good adaptation throughout many parts of the Christian community, East and West. It has persisted as the initiatory way in the East. It provides an alternative pattern by which to examine the very different line of development of which Western churches are heir.

---

12. Akeley, T.C., *Christian Initiation in Spain c. 300-1100*, Darton, Longman and Todd, London: 1967, p. 67f. See also Mitchell, *op. cit.*, pp. 131-143.

13. Mitchell, *op. cit.*, p. 125.

14. Whitaker, *Documents*, ch. 10 and Mitchell, *op. cit.*, pp. 143-154. The best sources for investigating these developments from the early initiatory rites are Dr. Mitchell's book and Fisher, J.D.C., *Christian Initiation: Baptism in the Medieval West*, S.P.C.K., London: 1965. Canon Fisher devotes full chapters to Spain, Gaul, Northern Italy, and the British Isles. Goodson, Mercer L., "What About Confirmation by Priest?" in *The St. Luke's Journal* XVI (1972), pp. 72-80, gives a digest of information largely from Fisher. A short, valuable Roman study is Rodriguez, Antonio Mostaza,"The Minister of Confirmation," in *Concilium*, Vol. 38, pp. 28-36.

D. Adaptation II: The Division of the Rite

In much of the West, by a gradual process, another pattern came to prevail. The unity of the initiatory rite was broken up. Its parts came to be observed at different times and by different ministers. Actions which had been moments within a unified ritual became, in effect, separate services.

Even in the pre-Constantinian church, disciplinary conflicts over schismatic baptism had suggested an independent identity for an episcopal laying-on of hands. Differing provincial customs had grown up in North Africa and in Rome for the reconciliation to the Church of those who had been baptized in schismatic groups. Cyprian, arguing from local African tradition and from his own theology of the Church, held that persons baptized, in schism had not been truly baptized at all; the whole initiatory ritual needed to be repeated. But the Roman community upheld a different practice. True Baptism belonged to the Name, not to the administering group. But Baptism could only become efficacious within the true catholic community. By Roman custom, schismatics, on their reconciliation, did not have their baptism repeated, provided it had been formally correct. The bishop's laying-on of hands, however, was used as a gesture of unity and pardon. This practice gave one step of the baptismal rites a meaning apart from the rest.

The Church at Rome was especially conservative in keeping the Bishop's prerogative as the minister of a required baptismal anointing. Dioceses in central Italy were small, and most people could visit the Bishop's church easily. Many persons were brought into the Christian community at initiation ceremonies held at Easter and Pentecost, presided over by the Bishop. Where the local priest became the normal minister of water baptism and the presbyteral anointing, the rite of initiation was regarded as incomplete without the Bishop's anointing. As soon as the baptized child and the Bishop could be brought together, the Bishop "perfected" the baptism. For many centuries, in the vicinity of Rome, this pattern seems to have worked well. Most persons received episcopal chrismation, and not much time elapsed between the two stages of initiation.

In time, the Roman practice was extended more widely to the West, but not without difficulty. A few items in this development (most of them the subject of complicated scholarly discussion) can be noted:

Jerome acknowledged that "it is the custom of the church that the Bishop should rush about to those who have been baptized by presbyters and deacons far from the larger cities, to invoke the Holy Spirit upon them by the laying on of hands."[15] This is an early reference to Bishops visiting to administer their own part of Christian initiation to those who lacked it. Jerome characteristically

---

15. *Dialogue Against the Luciferians*, ch. 9, written about 379 A.D., in the East, but presumably reflecting Western custom.

argued that the Bishop is the minister of this laying-on of hands, not by a law of necessity, but as a matter of order and dignity.

In a letter to Decentius of Gubbio (416 A.D.), Pope Innocent I decreed that consignation of baptized infants should be only by the Bishop, for this specific ministry belongs only to those in "the highest rank of the pontificate." A presbyter might anoint the baptized with chrism (blessed by the Bishop) whether the Bishop were present or not, but only the Bishop might sign the baptized on the forehead.

Gregory the Great wrote an illuminating sequence of letters in 593 A.D. to the troublesome Archbishop of Sardinia. In the first, Gregory said that presbyters may anoint newly baptized persons on the breast, but anointing on the forehead is reserved for the Bishop. This regulation evidently went against long-standing local custom and caused offense. In a later letter, Gregory, with his usual statesmanship, allowed presbyters (where a Bishop could not be present) to anoint the forehead of persons newly baptized.[16]

At the end of the era of the Church Fathers, the Roman custom was a minority practice in the Christian community. It was not even in use throughout the Roman province. In the city of Rome, however, its use allowed the rites of initiation to be observed as a ritual unity, with the Bishop (whose personal participation had become exceptional elsewhere) taking his part as minister of the post-baptismal chrismation.

The eighth century reforms under Charlemagne moved strongly towards standardization of practice in the West. The Roman service books were introduced into Gaul and Germany, and ultimately more widely throughout Europe. Episcopal confirmation was introduced in places that had not known it. In Northern Europe, dioceses were large, and travel was difficult. Bishops could not visit congregations readily, and few people could come to the see city. In some places, "baptismal churches" were designated in decentralized areas of the diocese, and Christian initiation might be administered there at appointed seasons by authorized ministers. But the Roman pattern, reserving the second post-baptismal chrismation to the Bishop, represented an ideal for which adequate conditions did not exist. As a result, where Confirmation was not actually neglected, the parts of the initiatory rite grew apart. Not all bishops were diligent about confirming, and not all parents were diligent about having children confirmed. Moreover, Confirmation, unlike Baptism, was not regarded as necessary for salvation. As a result, when Confirmation was observed, it came at a stage of life somewhat later than infancy.

Legislation in the next few centuries seems designed to place Confirmation as close to Baptism as possible. But such laws witness to problems of neglect and delay. An English canon from 960 A.D. gives a sense of the period: "We teach

---

16. Letters IV.9 and 26.

that each priest perform baptism as soon as it is required. And then let him enjoin his parish that each infant be baptised within thirty-seven days, and that no one too long remain unbishopped."[17] A widely promulgated rule required parents to bring children to the Bishop for Confirmation whenever the Bishop came within seven miles. In local regulations, Confirmation was required at various ages, ranging from one to seven years.[18]

By the thirteenth century, seven years was coming to be regarded as a minimum, rather than a maximum age. With this acceptance of a separation in time, some expectation grew up that instruction would have taken place before Confirmation.[19]

In the Middle Ages, many persons were baptized and communicants, confirmation having been bypassed. In 1281 Archbishop Peckham issued a canon (best remembered because, through the Sarum *Manual*, it became the "confirmation rubric" in the Prayer Books) requiring that Confirmation be the prerequisite to receiving communion. His aim was to rescue Confirmation from the "damnable negligence" into which it had fallen. Yet the rite continued to be administered carelessly. One scholar summarizes, "Gradually but inevitably, Confirmation in the West became the privilege of the few rather than the obligation of the many."[20]

As the divided rite became the usual practice, theologians provided it withan attractive rationale. St. Thomas taught that baptism made one a member of Christ and the Church and gave him the Holy Spirit. Confirmation he described (using phrases introduced into the tradition and perpetuated by his predecessors) as an "augmentation" of grace, giving further gifts of the Spirit appropriate to spiritual combat.[21] This two-stage initiation he related to a scheme of human development; the sacramental system provides means of grace suited to the needs of life. Baptism is the church's way of meeting birth. Confirmation belongsto growth, to advancement to spiritual perfection (not necessarily related to chronological age),

---

17. Johnson, *English Canons* (1850 ed.), vol. l, p. 415.

18. JFisher, *op. cit.*, pp. 120-140. See also the article, Lockton, W. "The Age for Confirmation," *The Church Quarterly Review*, 100 (1925), pp. 27-64. The article is somewhat out of date, but it contains a great deal of fascinating information not readily located elsewhere.

19. The factors cited here in the text are only part of the complex story of the disintegration of the Christian initiation rite in the Medieval West. The fullest account is in Fisher's book already cited. Canon Fisher has given a summary in his chapte "History and Theology" in Perry, M. (ed.), *Crisis for Confirmation*, S.C.M., London: 1967.

20. West, Edward N. "The Rites of Initiation in the Early Church," in Cully, K. (ed.), *Confirmation: History, Doctrine, and Practice*, Seabury, New York: 1962,p.13.

21. *S.T.*, III, q. 72, esp. a. 1 and 5-7, and q. 65, a. 1. The crucial phrases by which St. Thomas explains the distinctive meaning of Confirmation came to him by way of (to abbreviate) Peter Lombard, Gratian, the Forged Decretals (where words are wrongly attributed to a Pope Melchiades) and perhaps ultimately Faustus of Rietz.

and to struggle with spiritual enemies. "Confirmation is to Baptism as growth to birth." Thus, the practice of the late Middle Ages (which was not known to be the development that, in fact, it was) was made the basis for the characteristic Western doctrine of Confirmation.

E. The Churches of the Reformation

The major Reformers assumed and defended the practice of infant baptism. Indeed, the continuity of baptismal teaching and practice at the Reformation is remarkable for a time of much discontinuity. Luther was thankful that baptism had, over the centuries, remained relatively uncorrupted.[22] The baptismal liturgies of the Reformation adapted the rites to correspond more closely with the actualities of infant Baptism, which was the universal practice.[23]

Lutherans and Calvinists had no similar attachment to Confirmation. In both traditions, the rite as it had been practiced in Catholicism was attacked immoderately.[24] It was regarded as an invented sacrament. Since it was administered by the Bishop, it was regarded as pretending to a superiority over Baptism. The Reformed tradition had a general distaste for the involvement of material things — in this case chrism — in Christian worship.

Yet the Reformers felt the pastoral and theological need for what John Calvin called "a catechetical exercise, in which children or youths (would) deliver an account of their faith in the presence of the Church."[25] This concern for adult ratification as the complement of infant Baptism lay deep in the Reformation impulse. It can be traced to Wycliffe and to the Bohemian Brethren, followers of John Huss. Luther himself provided no liturgical text for Confirmation, though within his own lifetime some of his followers did.[26] Catechisms were written, and clergymen added teaching to their accepted duties. Confirmation, administered by local presbyters, became widely used as the occasion on which an instructed young Christian, who had been baptized in infancy, makes a public witness to his faith and accepts the duties and privileges of adult church membership. The conscious elements of catechesis and commitment which in the early Church had gathered around Baptism and which had been lost in the Middle Ages, were restored in the churches of the Reformation — but gathered now around an adolescent rite of Confirmation and First Communion.

---

22. Comments on Baptism in "The Babylonian Captivity of the Church."
23. See Fisher, J.D.C., *Christian Initiation: The Reformation Period*, S.P.C.K., London: 1970.
24. *ibid.*, sections 33 and 51.
25. *ibid.*, p. 258.
26. Repp, Arthur C., *Confirmation in the Lutheran Tradition*, Concordia, St. Louis; 1964, describes stages of development in Lutheran thinking about Confirmation.

From the sixteenth century, some varieties of Protestant thought and practice rejected infant Baptism. They could not credit the application of meanings formed around the primitive Church's baptism of converts to a rite in which there was no conversion or personal expression of faith. Children of Christian parents were only baptized when, having reached years of accountability, they were able to present themselves and be received into the Church "on profession of faith."[27]

F. Anglicanism

The English Reformation kept the two-stage pattern of Christian initiation. Baptism was considered a rite of full initiation into Christ and his Church, administered to infants by the local priest; in it the Holy Spirit was given. Confirmation remained the Bishop's prerogative. It was regarded as an additional rite in which the Holy Spirit was "increased" for strength for a more mature Christian witness. A catechism was printed between the baptism service and the confirmation service in the Prayer Books. In the interest of "edification", before a person should be regarded as eligible for Confirmation, he should be able to say the Creed, the Lord's Prayer, and the Ten Commandments in English, and be able to answer questions from the catechism. The intention of Confirmation was stated in an opening rubric: "Because that when children come to the years of discretion and have learned what their godfathers and godmothers promised for them in Baptism, they may themselves with their own mouth, and with their own consent, openly before the Church ratify and confess the same, and also promise that by the grace of God they will evermore endeavor themselves faithfully to observe and keep such things as they by their own mouth and confession have assented unto."[28] "Years of discretion" was not a phrase uniformly understood, but much evidence points to its having been regarded in the sixteenth century as about the age of twelve.[29]

In the Prayer Book revision of 1662 a service of adult baptism, adapted from the infant baptism rite, was provided for the first time. Since the disruptions of the seventeenth century, many people, through neglect, necessity, or conscientious scruple, had not been baptized in infancy. The same revision brought the personal "ratification" of baptismal vows from an introductory explanation into the action of the confirmation rite itself.

The practice of the Church of England has been uneven since the seventeenth century. Parish clergy administered Baptism quite faithfully. Many

---

27. See Gilmore, A. (ed.), *Christian Baptism*, Judson Press, Philadelphia: 1959; Beasley-Murray, G.R., *Baptism in the New Testament*, Macmillan, London: 1963; and the same author's *Baptism Today and Tomorrow*, St. Martin's Press, New York: 1966.

28. Rubric of the 1549 Prayer Book, repeated in 1552 and 1661.

29. See Lockton, *art. cit.*, pp. 54-64.

seventeenth and eighteenth century Bishops did their best as ministers of Confirmation. But the numbers of people were large, travel was difficult, and there were no assisting Bishops. Thus there was little opportunity to personalize the rite; large groups were sometimes confirmed *en masse*. Other Bishops carried out their pastoral duties carelessly; some never visited their dioceses. The low point in confirmation practice seems to have come in the late eighteenth century.[30]

Both the Evangelical Movement and the Oxford Movement took Confirmation seriously; Evangelicals, because it stressed teaching and inward experience; Tractarians, because it represented an ancient ministry of the Bishop. The model for the modern parochial visit of the Bishop for the Confirmation of a well-prepared class seems to have been provided by the nineteenth century Bishop of Oxford, Samuel Wilberforce.[31]

In the Episcopal Church in the colonial period, there were no Bishops, and except for persons who had received Confirmation from English bishops, members were admitted to Communion Without being confirmed — desire for Confirmation sufficed. For a time after the episcopate had been secured, dioceses were entire states, and Bishops were rectors of large parishes. Episcopal visitations for confirmation were irregular. But as the Church expanded westward under missionary Bishops such as Hobart, the pastoral oversight of a Father in God came to be part of the earliest experienceof most congregations. The comfortable doctrine of the ubiquity of Bishops was made possible by the introduction of modern means of transportation.

This historical sketch will have suggested that modern baptismal customs and understandings have had a long and varied history. The "one baptism" has been adapted widely over the centuries as changing situations have seemed to require.

It is striking how often in this process of adaptation the forms of Christian initiation were shaped by extrinsic forces. Augustine derived his theology from current church custom, and defended it by a critical misreading of St. Paul; St. Thomas' doctrine of Confirmation reflected the practice of confirming at a moment of life subsequent to baptism. The Roman view that the Bishop should retain the right to confirm prevailed in the West by a process that had little to do with the merits of the issue. The size of dioceses in Northern Europe brought non-theological and non-liturgical problems to the administration of Christian initiation. The rites of the sixteenth century Reformation and Counter Reformation were shaped without the historical data as to how initiatory practice had developed.

---

30. See Ollard, S.L., "Confirmation in the Anglican Communion," in *Confirmation*, Vol. I, S.P.C.K., London: 1926, pp. 176-223.

31. See *ib.*, p. 220. Bishop Wilberforce's confirmation "set a standard which was gradually followed in other dioceses until it became, as it now is, thenormal use."

Pragmatic, disciplinary, and polemic considerations have dominated the history of Christian initiation. Few new departures have stemmed from a fresh insight into the meaning of becoming a Christian. Rites of Christian initiation for today ought to have behind them an appreciative and critical review of the historical process which has brought us where we are. But we do not need another improvisation now. We need, within our specific historicisituation, a renewed apprehension of the meaning of this basic sacrament of redemption, community, faith, and life. Liturgical integrity requires, above all else, rites fashioned under the informing criterion of the Gospel they enact.

The Situation Now: The Breakdown of "Christendom"

The situation in which we are living seems to be calling familiar rites and meanings into question. Customs, teaching, and ritual, which once commended themselves as self-validating, functional, and life-supporting, no longer seem fully appropriate. It is worth some effort to discover why the Anglican pattern of initiation rites, largely unchanged for four centuries, is under question in the mid-twentieth century.

Part of the source of the questions comes from the altered relation between the Christian community and Western society. Ritual must provide focus points for life as we actually experience it. When the Church is fairly well adjusted to a society and its ways—and this adjustment may involve many sustained tensions—the Church's practice and its expectations for its members seem believable and livable. One's inner awareness confirms institutional pattern and doctrine.

But when changes throw the Church's relation to its society out of adjustment, old rites and ways can seem arbitrary: forms to be gone through, but with their meaning deeply qualified. In a period of change, there is certain to be a great deal of widely-felt frustration. A large diversified community, groping towards a new adjustment, can seldom be graceful and confident. Things which used to work, and teachings which used to be convincing, are felt to be problematic. Something has gone wrong, and there is a tendency to blame oneself, or to blame the system.

Christian initiation has been the way in which, at least since the sixteenth century, the Church has sought to interpret the two crises of being born and of growing up. To a great extent the Christian Church has provided the culture with its rites of passage: rites of marriage and burial, as well as of birth and puberty. Being bornand growing up are physiological, biological, events. But their meaning is socially determined. Theyare looked at and handled differently in different parts of the world, and their meaning within, any culture may undergo change. In our time, we are going through adeep, pervasive, upheaval which is shaking the social conditions to which the forms of religious life have related.

At the same time, the Christian community is seeking, out of its own resources, a more independent basis for its life. If it has become over-identified with a cultural moment, it can only be true to itself by criticising by its own Gospel, that over-identification.

These changes are often described as the breakdown of "Christendom." The term refers to the positive accommodation between Christianity and the organized life of Western culture which has prevailed, with changing forms but with important continuities, from the fourth century through late antiquity, the Middle Ages, and the Renaissance. Societies were taken to be Christian people. Some favored status, official or informal, was accorded to Christian leaders and institutions. Throughout the society, there was wide acceptance, even among persons whose own faith was nominal or non-existent, of the Christian myth, teachings, forms of piety, and ethics. This relationship has had great strengths and great weaknesses. Christian culture is too complex, and we are too close to it, for a just evaluation to be possible.

But the important fact with respect to it is that, at least within the last three centuries, this "Constantinian" arrangement has been crumbling. The West is by now deeply secularized; major decisions, personal and national, are made without reference to Christian revelation, faith, or ethical sanctions. Other authorities, other motivations, other criteria, now move and control. The modern West is post-Constantinian.

The Church, where it insists on retaining ecclesial integrity, is forced into a kind of isolation. Life-in-society and life-in-the-Church are not parts of an experienced continuity. Being a good member of the society does not necessarily support being a good Christian. Being a good Christian may set one against society at crucial points. Individual decision is demanded. A Christian identity is a more specifically religious, and a less conventionally social, thing. Karl Rahner has observed that in the modern situation — he calls it the "diaspora" — "Christianity ceases to be a religion of growth and becomes a religion of choice."[32]

The disintegration of Christendom is uneven. In some places it is very far advanced. In other places, aspects of the old relationships may still be an important spiritual and social reality. In many places, its residual forms seem like empty houses in which no one is living. Judgments in the matter may well differ. But forms of Christendom, where they endure at all, can only be accepted at face value at the risk of underestimating the actual de-Christianization of Western society.

Christian baptism is a border rite. It marks the boundary between Church and not-Church. A change in the relationships between Church and society is certain to change the sense of the appropriateness of baptismal rites, as it is

---

32. Rahner, Karl, "A Theological Interpretation of the Position of Christians in the Modern World," in *Mission and Grace: Essays on Pastoral Theology*, Sheed and Ward, London: 1963, Vol. I, p. 34.

certain to change the experience patterns to which those rites must refer. In one situation, Christian initiation may stress continuity between being a socialized person and being a Christian; in another situation it may stress discontinuity. At one moment the Church may want to identify closely with its culture, at another it may want to be sharply distinct.[33] These matters put pressure on the theology, practice, and forms of Baptism.

There is a general recognition in our time that the breakdown of Christendom is an opportunity, not a loss. Old assumptions are being shaken; innovation is required. But the death of an old, and a coming to birth of a new, is a kind of *kairos*—a moment in which God moves in history to challenge, demand, call, and promise. There is danger in carrying the assumptions, practices, and understandings, from Christendom into an era of post-Christendom, without questioning and re-evaluation.

Where Questions are Being Felt: (1) Infant Baptism

This essay began with the observation that the rites of Christian initiation are classically three: Baptism, Confirmation, and First Communion. Much of the questioning and the call for ritual reshaping has come to focus on Confirmation—the rite which, now that the three have become distinct, has emerged with the most uncertain theology, and, as a second stage of initiation generally administered to adolescents, with the most doubtful pastoral value. But these three rites of initiation are separated moments of an original unity. Despite their long standing division in the West, they remain so interrelated, that serious questions about any one of them affect thinking about the other two. Confirmation is bound up with the theology and administration of baptism and of first communion. Any reconsideration must take into account each of the three and the unity among them.

The new situation of the church, as sketched in the foregoing section, is posing questions for all of the now separated parts of the initiatory ritual. The following sections of this essay will consider in sequence the points at which issues are emerging in the fragmented parts of Christian Initiation.

One of the basic questions which is being newly raised is "Who is a proper subject for Christian baptism?" Old answers no longer pass unexamined.

Any investigation of the matter must consider the present situation of the Church in American society. But most of the fundamental patterns of church practice show signs of their derivation from sixteenth century Europe. Little

---

33. Walter Ullmann in *The Individual and Society in the Middle Ages*, Methuen, London: 1967, pp. 7ff., has an analysis of the way in which the understanding of baptism in the Middle Ages was adapted to imply citizenship. The rite which conferred personhood in the Church also brought one into the public order and made one subject to its laws. The universal Church was also the universal political order.

critical thinking on infant baptism and adolescent confirmation has originated in the Episcopal Church. The topic, by contrast, has been very preoccupying in the Church of England, where the rootage of the Anglican heritage in a State Church is evident.

The leaders of the English Reformation assumed that to be a Christian and to be a citizen were both normal parts of an Englishman's inheritance. The English Church and the English Commonwealth were the same community called by different names and seen from different perspectives. The Prayer Book contained no service of adult baptism from 1549 until 1661. It was assumed that a child would grow to understanding and competence in the religious community much as he did in the political community. This assumption was shared, of course, by much of continental Reformed and Catholic thought: it was an extension of Medieval Christendom.

The intention to shape a Christian nation unified by a single Church may have represented a great dream. But it never worked. Religious pluralism was a fact of English society from Tudor times. It was slowly recognized in law and in terms of social privilege from the seventeenth through the nineteenth centuries. Yet the traditional place which the Church has held in English society continues to be reflected in the staggering pastoral problems over Christian initiation. It remains a widespread practice to have children baptized "C. of E.", even though nothing will be done about these baptisms later. It is a kind of claim that parents feel they can make on the Church, which many incumbents do not feel they have a right to refuse. The result of years of such practice is that something like 55 per cent of the English population is baptized in the Church of England, while only about 6 per cent of those eligible make Easter Communions.[34] Such statistics indicate the seriousness of the problem which has come to be known as "indiscriminate baptism." More than one attitude towards it is possible for conscientious clergy. Yet many have become persuaded that for the Church to continue to encourage this widespread but meaningless practice cheapens one of the Gospel sacraments and lowers regard for the Church.

Similar questions are being raised in other European countries, in which similar disproportion prevails, and similar state churches are wondering what their pastoral responsibility is.

The American situation is not identical. All American churches are voluntary associations. Yet related factors apply. The Episcopal Church has stood for

---

34. Figures of this kind are available in many places. A recent summary is in Wilson, Bryan, *Religion in Secular Society: A Sociological Comment*, Penguin Books, Baltimore: 1969, ch. 1.

One writer recently commented on the English situation that the lapsed baptized person or apostat "is not a freak on whom it would be artificial to focus attention.... He is statistically the standard case, by an overwhelming majority of at least 10 to 1." Kidner, D. "The Meaning and Efficacy of Baptism," in *Theology*, LXVIII, 1965, p. 468.

high social status in many communities. Perhaps for this reason many persons who turn to it for little else, turn to it for rites which represent socially accepted rites of passage. Whether the Episcopal Church has a higher proportion of such loosely attached members than most other churches would be a difficult and doubtless an unprofitable inquiry; But the factor is large enough so that clergymen often wonder about their duty. When they are approached by a family which is remotely connected with the parish but which seeks baptism for a child, they ask how they can avoid adding to the number of nominal members, and whether they would be doing the child, the family, or the Church, any good by consenting to the baptism unless the parents accept some commitment and responsibility.[35]

Such considerations deal only with howv infant Baptism can be responsibly administered. But questions are increasingly raised as to whether or not it is possible to practice infant Baptism responsibly at all. In the individualism of the modern world and of American society, many adults ask how much they can honestly promise in the name of an infant in so personal a matter as ultimate religious faith and loyalty. Increasingly, there are indications that young persons, for their part, question the extent to which they are bound by solemn commitments that were made in their name without their consent.

Further, the theology of infant Baptism is less secure than is sometimes realized. The most common rationale now given seems to be that infant Baptism witnesses to God's initiative. He loves us when we are helpless; his grace depends on nothing within us he acts to place us within his family apart from any achievement of ours. This is a powerful theological idea, and these are things we would want to say about a Christian child. But are they aspects of the Christian message that are inherent in the rite of Baptism? The motif of prevenience is a new theological account of infant Baptism; it has no history prior to the modern era. It is much more directly derived from the Christian Gospel than was the Augustinian idea which gave urgency to infant Baptism until recent generations. But it might be argued that it is, no less than the Augustinian theory, an *ex post facto* theological account which grew up to support an existing Church practice.

Despite such arguments as these, there are still good reasons for infant Baptism. A child of a devout family has dealings with God from the time he is born. Baptism is a witness to the actuality of God's love in the life of that child, as it reaches him in care and acceptance through the parents in the Church. He knows God before he knows what to call him. Infant Baptism expresses the deep continuity of human generations. What parents regard as of ultimate value for life for

---

35. The pastoral crisis in Christian initiation in the Episcopal Church is most often put in terms of "loss of confirmands." At least half of those who are confirmed soon come to take no significant part in the life of the Church. See ch. 1, "Tell It Like It Is" in *Confirmation Crisis*, Seabury Press, New York: 1968.

theirchildren, they do not, because they cannot, withhold until the child can make up his own mind on the matter. The family is a divinely ordained unit in creation and redemption. The impossibility of articulate faith on the part of the one being baptized, does not mean that infant Baptism is devoid of faith. It is an occasion full of faith; a child is carried by the living faith of the Church. Every pastoral effort to make infant Baptism a family-in-the-Church occasion, speaking of redemption, rather than a family-in-the-community occasion, speaking of respectability, has helped to bring out the inherent evangelical seriousness of the rite.

Yet such reasons as these are not likely to commend themselves equally to everyone. Even among practising Christian parents in the churches which have traditionally practised infant Baptism, it may not seem appropriate to bring children to Baptism. Where the arguments for infant Baptism seem less than fully compelling, other possibilities are likely to be sought.

Many parts of the Christian community have been wrestling with this issue for some time. Several Church of England, Roman Catholic, and Lutheran studies have questioned infant Baptism — or at least its abuse.[36] Some writers propose a service of naming, blessing, and admission to the catechumenate for infants. Baptism itself would be a later and a different thing. Such questioning and such proposals are part of the ecumenical conversation on the meaning of initiatory rites in a post-Christian society. A Lutheran writer recently argued: "Since infant Baptism inevitably ties the church more closely to the culture, while adult Baptism establishes a break with the culture, the Church should baptize infants when it is attempting to penetrate a culture in the post-missionary situation, and become more reluctant to do so when it is attempting to re-establish its transcendence of culture after capitulating to it."[37]

All of the factors which have raised this issue urgently elsewhere are also present within the Episcopal Church. As the churches of the West move beyond what has been described above as "Christendom," it cannot be assumed that influences from a Christianized society will be present to fill out the promise of infant Baptism or to excuse lax administration. It may seem necessary to give more emphasis to adult decision.

Yet few people seem to want or expect a wholesale abandonment of infant Baptism. A shift to the obvious alternative — the baptism on an adult basis of children of Christian parents — would solve little, for the churches which

---

36. For a few items among many, see the appropriate passages in Moss, Basil S. (ed.), *Crisis for Baptism*, S.C.M., London: 1965; Saunders, George "A Service of Dedication of a Child," in *Theology* XLV, 1962, pp. 501-503 and the correspondence in subsequent issues; Cryer, Neville, *By What Rite? Infant Baptism in a Missionary Situation*, Mowbray, London: 1969; Redmond, Richard X. "Infant Baptism: History and Pastoral Problems," in *Theological Studies* 30, 1969, pp. 79-89; Jenson, Robert "On Infant Baptism," in *Dialog* 8, 1969, pp. 214-217.

37. Jenson, *op. cit.*, p. 216.

practice "believer's Baptism" are experiencing with their own children the same questions over the right age for Baptism as other churches have over the right age for Confirmation. Where "believer's Baptism" is the prevailing pattern in a community, the adult decision it requires becomes quite predictable. Life tends to follow art, and where conversion leading to Baptism is expected of children or young people, the appropriate experience occurs at about the anticipated age. It remains so much under the control of the elder generation and the internalized community pattern, that it is only questionably adult in character.

Each system looks best as critic of the abuses of the other. Each tends towards abuse when it is alone and unchallenged. Those who contend for believer's Baptism seek to make the New Testament and the "first generation" initiatory pattern normative. But this aim becomes associated with an individualistic, sectarian ecclesiology, and with some effort to manipulate Christian experience. Those who uphold infant Baptism ask whether the "first generation" is not always the one exceptional generation, and whether it can provide a model for the initiatory practice of all succeeding generations. The infant children of a Christian convert do not start where the convert himself did, and should their sacramental initiation follow a pattern identical with the parent's? The direct appeal to the New Testament seems to ignore history. The practice of including children within the baptized community encourages an organic view of the Church, and that is certainly faithful to the theology of the New Testament. But emphasis on social continuity risks losing the constant judgment of the "first generation" over every subsequent generation. It assumes that influences in the family, church, and community will shape persons into conscious faith, as in fact they often still do. But this ritual pattern is ill prepared to adjust when such influences are generally ineffective or non existent. Adult decision and commitment have been inadequately incorporated into the theology, catechetics, and liturgy, of becoming a Christian.[38]

Hitherto each system has been used within a given church body exclusively. The thing that has not been tried is for the positive side of the polemics of each pattern to be recognized, and for the two systems to be permissible and responsible usages within a single ecclesiastical unity. It may be that something of the kind is emerging now. Such a mixture would bring about practical problems; local, personal, and situational decisions would have to be made, for which probably few persons are prepared. Yet it may be that the specific meaning and vocation of adult Baptism and of infant Baptism within the Christian fellowship would be enhanced, if both were real possibilities and were common enough in practice to have to endure the corrective of one another.

---

38. Matters of this kind are discussed with honesty and ecumenical spirit in Baillie, John, *Baptism and Conversion*, Scribners, New York: 1963; and Carr, Warren, *Baptism: Conscience and Clue for the Church*, Holt, Rinehart and Winston, New York: 1964. The material in Carr's book has been given less attention than it merits.

In sum, the two-stage initiatory rite of the modern West has developed as it has, on the assumption that a first stage would be infant Baptism. A second stage dealt with sacramental and catechetical matters that infant Baptism did not include. It is impossible to say just how the practice of Christian initiation will develop. But it would be unwise to shape rites for the future that were built as though a first stage, infant Baptism as it has been known, were going on unquestioned. New rites should allow for the persistence of this ancient and valued custom. But rites should not be so attached to this practice that where it is not done, alternative ways of administering Christian initiation seem exceptional and awkward.

Where Questions are Being Felt: (2) Confirmation

Throughout its history, Anglicanism has lacked clarity about the meaning and function of confirmation. A number of different points of view have been articulated. Since the late nineteenth century a large literature has grown up debating the relation of Baptism to Confirmation. Indeed, this preoccupation has kept Anglican writers from saying much of importance on the meaning of Baptism itself. Dissatisfaction with existing theory and practice was summarized recently this way: "A number of ill-assorted matters are packaged together in the grab-bag that we call Confirmation. There is the concept that Confirmation is the fulfillment of the commitment of Holy Baptism. There is the imagery of the reception of the seven-fold gifts of the Holy Spirit symbolized by the laying-on of hands. There is the practical use of the service of Confirmation as a discipline of admission to the Holy Communion. Finally, this is all made the occasion of an episcopal visitation to the congregation and a church. These unlikely matters are intertwined in utter theological and practical confusion."[39]

Confirmation seems to involve at least three kinds of issues: (1) those arising out of the mixture of meanings and functions that have been brought together in Confirmation as we have known it; (2) those arising out of the theological relation of a second stage of Christian initiation to a first stage, and of this two-stage process to the reality of life in Christ; and (3) the practical problem of how to administer a second stage of Christian initiation at a moment of life when it can have its intended meaning. The following sections of this essay will consider these issues in sequence.

---

39. Warnecke, Frederick J. "A Bishop Proposes," in *Confirmation Crisis*, p. 136. Bishop Warnecke might have added that the same overburdened rite also admits baptized persons from non-episcopal church bodies.

A. The Inherent Instability of the Anglican Pattern

The historical sketch in a previous section of this essay has indicated that Confirmation as it has been practiced in Anglicanism has brought together actions, functions, and interpreting doctrines from different sources. A new and largely unprecedented unity was created.

Two principal themes and sources are distinguishable: (1) One line of ancestry of Confirmation is the post-baptismal blessing, which traces to the early Church. As has been observed above, this rite took many forms, but in the early Church, it was always continuous with Baptism itself. But by the later Middle Ages in the West, it had become part of a second stage of initiation. (2) Another line of ancestry came from the Reformation. It is the ratification of baptismal promises. This function had no ritual continuity with the early Church. Of course, the early Christians did teach candidates before Baptism, and persons being baptized professed their faith. But the transfer of these features of initiation to Confirmation, as a second and later stage of initiation, has commended itself in many of the churches of the modern West as a way of dealing with what had come to be felt as the psychological incompleteness of infant Baptism. One rite was sacramental, the other catechetical. One derived from the liturgy of becoming a Christian; the other was something done by a Christian at a certain stage of his maturation. One signified the Holy Spirit, the other the renewal of promises made at an earlier rite in one's behalf. One emphasized what God does, the other what man does.

One reason for the chronic uncertainty about Confirmation in Anglicanism is traceable to this mixed ancestry. Some Anglicans see Confirmation in the context of one of its antecedent sources; some interpret it through another. In general, it can be said that persons who approach Confirmation from liturgical and patristic studies regard the early sacramental tradition as normative, and they seek its restoration. Others who approach Confirmation with issues of education and nurture in mind, take the catechetical side as describing what confirmation really is, and they would like to adapt ritual to support something that has become a practical necessity. Each side tries to do some justice to the thing that is important to the other, but such efforts tend to be unconvincing. Both use the term "confirmation" for the important observance they describe, but it would be difficult to demonstrate that they are talking about the same thing. In Anglican treatments of Confirmation, the contradiction can be observed within the covers of a single work. In the symposium volumes of half a century ago, *Confirmation: or the Laying on of Hands*,[40] the historical and doctrinal material of Volume I, much of it still of considerable value, describes largely the development and meaning of the ancient sacramental rite. In Volume II, the practical essays now very dated, deal with catechetical matters of education for intelligent religious commitment. The same observation

---

40. S.P.C.K., London: 1926. No editor was listed for this work.

could be made of the a material in the volume edited a few years ago by Kendig B. Cully called *Confirmation: History, Doctrine and Practice*.[41] The historians and theologians deal with one agenda, the Christian educators with another. Recent work in the Church of England demonstrates the same duality. Some authors argue liturgical and historical matters from early and medieval sacramentary and ordo texts, with little recognition of what the Reformed inheritance has meant in the teaching and ethos of the Church of England.[42] By contrast, the recent report, *Christian Initiation: Birth and Growth in the Christian Society*,[43] treats Confirmation largely in the context of developmental and educational concerns. Each side looks at the history and function of Confirmation differently, and criticizes the present administration of the rite by different criteria. What each seeks by way of remedy is different. The two estimates of the past and present, and thetwo lines of hope for the future, are not necessarily irreconcilable. But before true common ground can be discovered, it may be necessary to ask whether or not all the parties to the discussion of Confirmation are talking about the same thing.

Each of the ingredients in Anglican Confirmation deserves a closer look:

(1) The first, the post-baptismal rite from the ancient Church, began as an enacted explication of some of the meaning of entry into Christ and his people. Christian baptismal practice was doubtless influenced by customs in the ancient world which regarded washing with water and anointing with oil as normal parts of a bath.[44] In the rich biblical imagery which surrounded the ritual of the early Church, an anointing with chrism was likely to suggest the Holy Spirit. In addition, many of the church Fathers explain this post-baptismal rite as speaking of Christ, the Anointed One. Cyril of Jerusalem even says of those who had recently been baptized and anointed, "Now you were made christs (christoi)."[45]

It is difficult to trace these post-baptismal rites from antiquity into the present. One cannot be certain what part of an ancient practice is to be taken as the equivalent of a later custom. As Charles Davis has put it: "From the point of view of ritual, Confirmation has not remained identical with itself. Christian initiation soon included several post-baptismal rites. Which is to be taken as the essential rite of Confirmation? It is not an easy question to answer, and history shows that now one rite, now another, was regarded as the essential part."[46].

---

41. Seabury Press, New York: 1962.

42. For instance Pocknee, C., *Water and the Spirit*, Darton, Longman, and Todd, London: 1967.

43. Church of England Board of Education: 1971.

44. See the material in the section on "Pagan and Secular Use of Oil", inMitchell, *op. cit.*, pp. 25-29.

45. *Mystagogical Cathecheses*, lll. 1f., *Migne's Patrologia Graeca* XXXIII, col. 1088A. St. Cyril of Jerusalem, *Lectures on Christian Sacraments* (F.L. Cross, Tr.), S.P.C.K., London, 1951 p. 63.

46. Davis, Charles, *Sacraments of Initiation: Baptism and Confirmation*, Sheed and Ward, New York: 1964, p. 107.

But historical inquiry must focus on Rome, the source of the Anglican ritual inheritance. It has been noted above that Rome had certain peculiarities. But more detail here may show how difficult the issues are. If the early third century account by Hippolytus can be taken to represent Roman ways, initiation there involved an anointing immediately before Baptism (apparently regarded as a final exorcism) and two immediately after it. The first of these later anointings was given as the initiate emerged from the water. A presbyter anointed him with an "Oil of Thanksgiving" blessed earlier in the rite; and doubtless the whole body was anointed. The second anointing was given by the Bishop at the time the initiate, now reclothed, came to the eucharistic room where the community was already assembled. The Bishop placed his hand on the head of each and offered a prayer referring to the Holy Spirit. (Some editors read these texts as a prayer for the giving of the Spirit; others read them as acknowledging that the Spirit has been given in Baptism and as asking for grace.)[47] He then anointed the head of each with consecrated oil, sealed him on the forehead, and gave him the kiss of peace.

Was this Bishop's anointing constitutive of the rite, and the priest's anointing preparatory and transitional? Or was the Bishop's anointing a token public continuation and acceptance of the anointing which had already been made in a darkened, private setting by the priest?

Such questions are probably unanswerable today. If they were asked of the persons who shaped the early rites, they would probably be unintelligible. Hippolytus' rite is striking for its use of many ministers serving complementary functions. In Rome (and eventually throughout the West, as Roman ways came to dominate), the presbyter's post-baptismal anointing became reduced in importance. The anointing by the Bishop was continued. It was subject to the separate development, the practical difficulties, and the imposed interpretation we have noted above.

In its early history, the post-baptismal anointing was part of a coherent sequence of actions within a unified initiatory ritual. In that setting it had a meaning and function as part of the enacted *kerygma* of Christian initiation. Apart from that setting, the functions and meanings that are assigned to this rite seem arbitrary. Can a portion of a unified initiatory ritual become detached and be the center of a true development of enriched, latent meanings? Or is it inevitable that such a rite will only seem reduced or problematic when it exists apart from the setting in which it emerged and which gave it its meaning?

---

47. The Bishop's prayer is in *Apostolic Tradition*, xxii. 1. Dom Gregory Dix, in his edition, reads it as a prayer for the Spirit and for grace. Burton Scott Easton, in his edition, reads it as a prayer for grace for service, the Spirit having been given in Baptism. Dom Bernard Botte in his succession of authoritative editions of *Apostolic Tradition* has changed his mind on this point. The textual evidence and the issues are discussed in Lampe, G.W.H., *The Seal of the Spirit*, Longmans, London: 1951, pp. 136-142.

(2) The second ingredient in traditional Anglican Confirmation, the ratification of baptismal vows, comes from Reformation sources. The Reformers were mistaken when they supposed that their kind of confirmation rite followed early precedent.[48] They might have been well advised to forget historical argument and to defend their catechetical practice on pragmatic, pastoral grounds. The Reformation was trying to cope with the problem of catechesis and personal faith in a "second generation" Christian community — a matter in which the New Testament and the early Church (both of them characteristically "first generation") gave no direct help, and in which Medieval practice was thought to have been gravely defective.

A sympathetic grasp of the Reformers' intentions requires a consideration of the theology of faith. It is at this point, rather than in ritual continuity, that their work has enduring importance. They sought to recover an essential note of the believing community, the Christian life, and sacramental theology.

Faith, in the biblical sense, reaches towards utterance. Service of the "lips" without participation by the "heart" was condemned by the prophets.[49] The Bible speaks of man as a unity of "heart" and "lips" — albeit a unity which is broken by sin, so that the heart and the lips too often speak different things. Faith knits up that broken unity and restores wholeness, so that our words are ourselves. Thus, belief that remains unexpressed, that does not reorder life around an articulate center, could hardly be called belief at all in biblical terms. Salvation, according to St. Paul, comes when one confesses with his mouth "Jesus is Lord" and believes in his heart that God has raised him from the dead.[50]

The early Church retained much of this vital sense of faith. Initiation was a conscious, adult event, a sacrament of conversion. It was preceded by instruction and examination. It called for explicit renunciation of evil and confession of the rule of faith. It was followed by responsible moral discipline. A.D. Nock summarized the matter: "Judaism and Christianity demanded rentmciation and a new start. They demanded not merely acceptance of a rite, but the adhesion of the will to a theology, in a word faith, a new life in a new people."[51] Lapse from such commitments might require public repentance. Inward experience was taken seriously by the fathers as a constituent of sacramental reality. In a famous

---

48. Calvin made such a claim in *Institutes*, 1543 ed., IV.19.4. This claim that Reformed confirmation practice followed early church precedent was often repeated over the next century and half by apologists of the continental Reformed and Anglican churches. They were probably following Calvin, who usually cited the fathers reliably; but in this matter his reconstruction was entirely fanciful.

49. "This people ... honor me with their lips, while their hearts are far from me," Isa. 29:13, cited by Jesus in Mark 7:6f.

50. Romans 10:8-10. Cf. the Pauline emphasis on the Body of Christ as built up through the understandable, intelligible word.

51. Nock, A. D., *Conversion: The Old and the New in Religion from Alexander the Great to Augustine of Hippo*, Oxford, 1961 ed., p. 14.

sermon, Gregory of Nazianzus urged those who have postponed Baptism to "run to the Gift" while they are still master of their thoughts. Old age or the approach of death might make them unaware of what was signified. Only a body would be washed for burial. It was important to be baptized "while the grace can reach the depth of your soul."[52]

This conscious element had been eclipsed as infant baptism became normative in both East and West. No equivalent devices had been introduced in the medieval Church to demand personal commitment. The supportive introduction into the Christian myth, community, and life, which the social environment itself provided were regarded as sufficient.[53] The Reformers rejected the idea that faith could be merely "implicit." A faith which did only what the Church did, without serious thought or decision, was scorned by John Calvin as "ignorance tempered by humility."[54] The Reformers rejected just as emphatically an intellectualistic account of faith. True faith was not consent to authoritative teachings about God. Yet it could be described as a kind of knowledge—knowing God in his mercy, his gracious will. "Faith consists in the knowledge of God and Christ." Calvin was wise enough to see the mystery and dimness at the heart of religious knowledge. "Most things are now implicit for us." Some "implicitness" belongs to the very nature of faith. Moreover, the implicit level might be a needed preparation for faith, but it was not a place to stop. Faith should reach towards explicitness.

Valuable as this emphasis on explicitness is, it carries with it serious problems. It was certain to raise difficulty for infant Baptism — a rite defended on the basis of God's promise, but a rite in which the person baptized was incapable of personally confessing his faith. The search for explicit faith doubtless contributed to the verbal, intellectualist character of the Protestant scholasticisms of the seventeenth and eighteenth centuries. (All traditions, however, developed scholastic styles in the same period—as well as pietistic reactions. It was in the cultural climate.) The effort to make explicit faith normative in a large and varied Christian community, is likely to lead to schematization, to putting words into children's mouths, and to compelling what ought to be a free, inward, personal response.

Even though it is not easy to handle this dimension of Christian experience wisely, it will not do to dismiss the matter. In our self-conscious, critical, modern world, a faith that is true to its own potential must grip persons deeply and press for authentic expression.

In our own time, the acceptance of explicit faith as a theological necessity is no longer a Protestant emphasis exclusively. Vigorous catechetical and

---

52. Gregory of Nazianzus, Sermon 40, par. 11.

53. A brief summary of the strengths and weaknesses of medieval catechesis is given in Jungmann, J.A., *Handing on the Faith*, Herder and Herder, New York: 1959, pp. 11-19.

54. *Institutes*, lll.2.2-5. See the wise comments on religious consciousness in Quick, O.C., *Catholic and Protestant Elements in Christianity* Longmans,London: 1924, esp. chap. III.

biblical revivals have accompanied the liturgical renaissance in the Roman Catholic Church. The ideal of conscious, instructed, articulate participation in the Church's life and worship has been declared to be the right of every baptized person.[55] There is widespread ecumenical agreement today that faith ought to have as much explicitness as possible. There is also dissatisfaction with the measures now being taken to attain that goal and little pride in past accomplishment.

Some of this sense of the meaning of faith informed Anglican thinking about the function of Confirmation. A form of initiation in which the initiate was entirely passive was inappropriate to the nature of the Gospel, of faith, and of the Church's task. It was incomplete; something more was required.

In Anglicanism, the conscious, informed response was combined with the ancient rite of the Bishop's laying-on of hands. The now detached Bishop's part of Christian initiation was thus given greater pastoral significance than it had had in the late Middle Ages. And catechetical work was given a sacramental completion not possible for those churches with no Bishops and no equivalent historic rite. In a typically Anglican stroke, the old and the new were combined in a way that seemed likely to benefit both. In theory this was not a bad combination; and it has demonstrated some strengths. For the Church, the retention of infant baptism has moderated tendencies to sectarianism, but the combination with personal ratification has kept within the Church the ideal of a committed Church with committed adult members. For the individual born within the faith community, the two-stage rite expresses the interdependence between one's inheritance at birth and what one does about it later. The Anglican pattern has had a certain credibility. It has doubtless worked at moments. Much has been built up around it: theological definitions, priestly and episcopal role definitions, personal expectations and pastoral and parental duties.

Yet the combination may be rather fragile. Do the two elements in Anglican Confirmation, each with an integrity of its own, benefit by being combined? Do these two observances have any inherent connection with one another, or has their association been imposed?[56] One is part of a once-for-all rite of initiation. The other signifies a long process of growing up in the Christian life. Does not their combination overload the rite of laying-on of hands and cause theological confusion? The endless Anglican quarrels about the Holy Spirit in Baptism and in Confirmation suggest that it does. And does not the same combination

---

55. "The Constitution on the Sacred Liturgy," par. 14. In Ernest Koenker's study, *The Liturgical Renaissance in the Roman Catholic Church*, Univ. of Chicago, 1954, the author speaks of concern for active participation in and comprehension of the liturgy as "the fundamental interest of the liturgical Apostolate wherever it is found." (p. 45). See also Jungmann, J.A. "Christianity - Conscious or Unconscious?" in *Pastoral Liturgy*, Herder and Herder, New York: 1962, pp. 325-334.

56. Thirty years ago Cyril Richardson called attention to the disparate functions that this one rite was asked to serve. See his article "What Is Confirmation?", The *Anglican Theological Review* 23, 1941, pp. 223-230.

oversimplify the reality and expression of one's personal response to God? The inconclusive discussion of "the right age" suggests that it does.

The two rites — each from a different context of meaning — were combined at a past moment by an intentional act of responsible men. If in a changed situation the combination seems to have developed interior stresses, it canfbe responsibly altered, as long as its demonstrated values are recognized and kept.

B. Theological Confusion

In the early Church a great complex of meaning came to focus in Baptism. The whole reality of the Christian revelation—redemptive, Christocentric, eschatological, ethical, trinitarian—was signified in one simple rite. It could not be otherwise. The meanings were not separable. In dynamic, biblical terms, there could be no forgiveness without the positive new relation to Christ and his people; there could be no relation to Christ without the Holy Spirit as the reality of the age to come. God in his working is not divisible.

But we cannot apprehend or state this meaning all at once. Thus, it is understandable that as the rites of Christian initiation came to be used for Gentile converts and grew more complex, they underwent a kind of stretching-out of actions and significances. This stretching-out seems to have moved in both directions from the central Christian washing. In addition to the pre-baptismal catechesis, there were frequent exorcisms, signifying, along with the fasting, late in the preparatory period, an emptying, an expulsion of evil powers. After the Baptism, the anointing, doubtless thought of as a completion of the washing, came, on the basis of biblical imagery, to be specifically associated with the gift and seal of the Holy Spirit. The baptismal eucharist expressed the incorporation into the Christian community. Hippolytus speaks of a special chalice of milk and honey, carrying the eschatological meaning of fulfillment and entering upon the promises of God.

As long as these rites were observed in one continuous sequence, their meanings were understandable as parts of a great unity. Each event had its identity only within the rich totality. Together, they expressed the one fundamental Paschal Mystery—the redemptive reality in which sacramental life participates.

However, as, in the West, the ritual of Christian initiation became fragmented, it led to asking what one part might mean in isolation from the rest. The fragmentation of the unified rite led to a fragmentation of the unified meaning of which it spoke. The entire Western Christian community has been struggling with this inherited confusion.

For Anglicanism the problem has come to its most sharp focus in trying to specify the role of the Holy Spirit in Baptism and in Confirmation. Anglican formularies have used many phrases expressing the agency of the Holy Spirit in Baptism: "regenerate of water and the Holy Ghost," "baptized with water and the

Holy Ghost," "Give thy Holy Spirit to this child," "to sanctify him with the Holy Ghost," "that all things belonging to the Spirit may live and grow in him." It would be difficult to say more. Yet Confirmation has clearly been spoken of as "strengthening with the Holy Spirit," "increasing in the Holy Spirit;" the Bishop prays for the gifts of the Spirit; and the traditional lesson cites "receiving" the Spirit.

This duplication of themes is certain to suggest questions: Why are there two sacramental occasions, commonly separated by several years, in which the relation with the Holy Spirit is specified? Do we meet him twice? If so, was there something defective about the first meeting? Do we meet him in different ways at different times? If so, how do the two times differ? Is one more important than the other?

Such questions as these have provoked an extensive literature in which two general positions have been articulated:

1) The Anglican view at the Reformation, expressed in official formularies and maintained by many since, was that Baptism is complete Christian Initiation.[57] Entry into Christ and his Church and the gift of the Holy Spirit belong to water Baptism. Confirmation is desirable as an occasion for those who are baptized as infants to ratify the promises for themselves; it confers additional gifts of the Spirit belonging to adult responsibilities; and it introduces one to the Lord's Table.

In favor of this position is the explicit claim for the completeness of Baptism in the liturgical and theological tradition. In the New Testament, the laying-on of hands cannot be shown to be regular or essential as a completion of initiation. It is often a designation for ministry. Further, this view recognizes as a sign of Christian unity all trinitarian baptism; there is no necessity, on doctrinal grounds, of finding any essential inadequacy in the Christian initiation of groups which do not practice episcopal Confirmation. In an ecumenical era, the self-evidencing fruit of the Spirit in all Christian groups is part of the data for theology.

The principal difficulty of this view is that Confirmation is left somewhat problematic. If the public ratification of baptismal promises is pastorally desirable, why is it associated with this episcopal ministry? Why is it done only once? If the Holy Spirit is fully given at Baptism, what is the specific additional role of

---

57. Representing this point of view, although not with complete agreement among themselves, see:

Wirgman, A.T., *The Doctrine of Confirmation*, Longmans, London: 1897.

Stone, Darwell, *Holy Baptism*, Longmans, London: 1899.

Rawlinson, A.E.J., *Christian Initiation*, S.P.C.K., London: 1947.

Archbishops' Theological Commission Report "The Theology of Christian Initiation," S.P.C.K., London: 1948.

Lampe, G.W.H., *The Seal of the Spirit*, Longmans, London: 1951.

the Spirit at Confirmation? If Baptism is really complete, a duplication of one of its major themes after the passage of a few years does not seem to say so.

2) Another view, anticipated by Anglican writers from the sixteenth through the nineteenth centuries, but stated most vigorously within the last eighty years, is that Baptism represents the washing from sin and incorporation into the Body of Christ, but the Holy Spirit is associated specifically with Confirmation.[58] In favor of this view is the Lukan account of the apostles' visit to bring the Holy Spirit to the Christian community of Samaria which had received Baptism only. Some other New Testament passages, notably the model of Jesus' baptism, suggest that Baptism for washing, together with anointing for the Holy Spirit, form a sequence of distinguishable steps. The liturgical tradition soon became quite explicit about the gift of the Holy Spirit being the specific grace of Confirmation.

But there are serious questions about this view. It tends to reduce water Baptism to a negative, almost a pre-Christian rite. The division it introduces between Christ and the Holy Spirit is theologically intolerable; what God does, all of God does. Some expositors of this view have introduced distinctions in ways in which one may be related to the Spirit: "externally" at Baptism, but "internally" in Confirmation, for instance. But few people can attach specific meaning to such metaphoric terms for a personal, indivisible activity.

These two general positions—with many ways of defending and stating each—have defined the Anglican dispute over Confirmation for several generations. The terms of the debate have not been productive. In the present state of Anglican practice, disputants seem to have to plead for the primacy of either Baptism or Confirmation at the expense of the other. This static debate can divert attention from some of the more urgent questions concerning the Holy Spirit in Christian initiation. It is possible to ask when, and by what act, and by what minister the Holy Spirit is given, as though it were perfectly clear What the giving of the Spirit means. What does the Church mean by its claim to minister the Spirit of God in its own initiatory rite? Is this idiom of the Spirit being "given" or not "given" compatible with the gracious, personal character of God's relation with man? How does the gift of the Spirit relate to one's basic humanity? Does the Creator Spirit encounter a person for the first time only when he is sacramentally "given?"

---

58. Representing this point of view, again without complete agreement, see: Puller, F.W., *What is a Distinctive Grace of Confirmation?* Rivingtons, London: 1880. Mason, A.J., *The Relation of Confirmation to Baptism*, Dutton, New York: 1891. Dix, G., *The Theology of Confirmation in Relation to Baptism*, A. and C. Black, London: 1946. Thornton, L.S., *Confirmation: Its Place in the Baptismal Mystery*, A. and C. Black, London: 1954. Pocknee, C.E., *Water and the Spirit*, Darton, Longmans and Todd, London: 1967.

The terminology of "giving" and "receiving" the Holy Spirit is, in the New Testament, characteristic of St. Luke. In Acts, the gift of the Spirit was a power with unmistakable marks. It was so specific that one misguided person supposed it could be bought. The Spirit might come suddenly upon people, with or without tactual mediation. This is the biblical idiom that most specifically underlies the discussion of when the Spirit is sacramentally given. Yet in the same Book of Acts, the Spirit is depicted as sovereign over the Church—leading the apostles, taking them by surprise, and frustrating their plans for purposes of his own. If there is a tendency for Anglican discussion of the Holy Spirit in Christian initiation to make the Lukan idiom, or, indeed, only part of the total Lukan idiom, normative,-the tendency should not go unquestioned.

Other New Testament writers develop their conceptions of the Holy Spirit in ways that give no comparable place to his coming upon people in ecstatic signs or his being given by official ministers. St. Paul identifies the Holy Spirit primarily by ethical characteristics. The Spirit is the one by whom "the love of God is shed abroad in our hearts." The fruit of the Spirit, according to Paul, is love, joy, peace, patience, kindness, goodness, faithfulness, gentleness, and self-control. Moreover, the Spirit, for Paul, is not separable from being "in Christ." Paul loads the rite of Baptism with all the reality of the redemptive Mystery, and he speaks of no further ceremony. A writer comments: "Paul not only fails to mention the imposition of hands, but his theology definitely excludes it."[59] If Anglican theology of Christian initiation were to take its governing ideas rigorously from. St. Paul, some of the issues would have to be recast.

The Holy Spirit moves in human affairs as "God in action." He represents the presence of fresh possibility within the human condition. He fundamentally ministers himself. "In ordinary affairs a gift may be distributed apart from the giver, but the Gift of the Spirit is his personal relationship with us, and the Gift cannot be detached from the Giver."[60] He ministers himself through the Church. Part of his work is to bring into being the community of human response, a fellowship so united with him that he can work through it to further his purposes. Within the Church, he uses the sacraments as foci of his activity—shaping the community, renewing it, and bringing individuals into living relation with it and its Lord. In all his ways, he works to establish personal relationships with himself. In those relationships, he engages the depths of the personal life he himself has given to us. He affirms and dignifies our humanity, and he draws us in love to the intention of the Creator as shown in Christ. The Spirit is not divisible from the whole love, work, and presence of God, nor from the whole

---

59. Lee, E. Kenneth "The Holy Spirit in Relation to Baptism and Confirmation," in *The Modern Churchman* XII (1970), p. 317.

60. *ibid.* p. 318. See the similar comments in Davies, J.G., *The Spirit, the Church and the Sacraments*, Faith Press, London: 1954, pp. 7ff.

renewal of man. The Holy Spirit, in personal action, cannot be measured in separate moments, or divided qualitatively.

Any theology of Christian initiation which has led the Church to define two incursions of the Holy Spirit and to play off one against the other, has obviously moved in a mistaken direction. The Holy Spirit, in New Testament terms, represents the presence now of the age to come. He is given in Christ, but he represents that which is coming to be. A Christian's end is given in his beginning. Even though the Holy Spirit works patiently for a lifetime and more to accomplish his intentions within us, he does nothing that is not pledged from the start. The liturgies and theologies of "the first sacrament" should say at the start all that can be said.

C. Pastoral Problems

Confirmation has served as a rite of coming of age within the Church. For many years, pastors, educators, bishops, parents, and more recently young adults themselves, have complained that it has not worked as it ought.

A rite of entry on adult status is deeply rooted in culture and world religions. The parent religion of Christianity, Judaism, has long had a ceremony by which a boy (traditionally it has been restricted to males) becomes a "son of the Law." Such rites support an important transition, a moment at which a person leaves childhood and assumes adult prerogatives. They are often associated with learning the lore of the group. Following this ceremony, the person can think of himself as adult, because the community now treats him as such.

To be significant and life-supporting, such a rite of passage must correspond with the actual dynamics of growing up. It must express, shape, and interpret an experienced crisis.

The conditions of modern society are raising the question: *Is there a moment which can sustain believably the meaning of growing into adulthood in today's world?* Past designations of the "age of reason" were made without developmental studies and insights. Yet the time may have been chosen well, and the rites may have stood for a significant transition. But modern society presents us with a complicated situation, for which past experience provides no adequate precedent. In a technological culture (and not all the world is yet technological), persons do not pass quickly from the relative dependence of childhood to the relative independence of adulthood. We move through many stages in the process of growing up, stages having specific problems and specific qualities. We perceive ourselves and our world differently as we grow; the logic, thought forms, and moral judgments of one stage are not those of the next. The developmental studies of Erikson, Piaget and others, have helped to identify the dynamics of growth.

It is not just that such investigators have analyzed the stages by which infants naturally grow into adults; rather, modern conditions have called new stages into being. The pioneer work on adolescence was done by G. Stanley Hall in 1904. He was probably documenting a change which had only recently come in human development. Once he had named and analyzed it, one could observe that some individuals in previous eras had also had a period of adolescence; but as a mass pattern of development, it seems to belong to the industrial West beginning not long before the end of the nineteenth century.

The forces which began the extension of the growing-up process have continued their shaping influence. One social analyst identifies a new stage of life, still transitional, but having characteristicss unlike adolescence. He terms it "youth", and locates it between late adolescence and adulthood.[61] In general it can be observed that the passage from childhood begins earlier and earlier, while entry on adulthood is later and later. Children take on sophistication and physical maturity and they begin separating themselves from their parents at measurably earlier ages. Yet the society is not prepared to consider persons as adults until their middle twenties. Thus, growing to adulthood in the modern world carries one through a long, varied period of change, stress, quest, and reversal.

The question that past practices of Confirmation have asked is: What point within this process can gather up and express its meaning for the relation to God and membership in the Church?

Since a practical answer must be given, most of the congregations of the Episcopal Church have answered: about the age of twelve.[62] However, the age for Confirmation has extended in both directions from that age by five or six years. Those who put Confirmation very early cannot intend that it signify adulthood; rather they mean for it to introduce a child to the practice of full sacramental life in the Church at an early age. Those who put Confirmation late can stress its adult, voluntary character, but the later age leaves a baptized member of the Church without participation in the Eucharist through important years of his developing experience, a practice difficult to defend. It is often argued that the age of twelve years, the point at which most confirming has been done, combines the disadvantages of both extremes without taking much advantage of the strengths of either. The conclusion seems inescapable that in this long, often turbulent transition to adulthood, so many stages are passed through, that any single moment for Confirmation is too early to capture some important possible meanings of the process, or too late to express others.

There has been widespread ecumenical discussion among liturgiologists, Christian educators, theologians, and pastors about the best age for "a confession

---

61. Kenniston, Kenneth "Youth as a Stage of Life," in *Youth and Dissent*, Harcourt Brace Jovanovich, New York: 1971, pp. 3-21. Kenniston's essay has influenced this section of the present study quite heavily.

62. Weld, Edric A. "The Church Report on Confirmation Instruction," *Findings*, Oct. 1960, p. 10 f.; an article based on a survey for the Department of Christian Education.

of faith."[63] But little consensus has emerged. Important authorities with weighty arguments support divergent solutions.

Perhaps it is not premature to propose that for our moment in history, the wrong question has been asked. In the conditions of modern society, no single point can represent the meaning of growing into adulthood. Growth is a process—long and complex. Confirmation, insofar as it is part of Christian initiation, is an unrepeatable event. Are the two things compatible? Can one observance—whether located early or located middle or late—sum up the personal meaning of a difficult process that may last more than fifteen years?

The wisest way to come to terms with this question may be to observe that Christianity—in the New Testament, the early Church, the Eastern churches, and the medieval West—has not had a puberty rite. In the modern world, most Western churches have tried to observe such a rite. When it has been functional, a rite of coming of age in the Church has probably been useful. One need not question its value in our own or anyone else's past. But neither must we feel that any such rite, useful though it may have been at one time, is essential to Christian initiation and to Christian existence.

Becoming a mature Christian is always a demand, a challenge, and an opportunity. But the process of entering on maturity is always within a specific situation, the situation of the church-in-its-society. When that situation changes, the ritual and catechetical measures that may have signified maturation in the past, may, rather abruptly, seem inappropriate. The same worthy ends that were served by one means in the past may have to be served by other means suited to an altered condition.

That is not to say that now that adolescence and youth have become more prolonged and difficult, the Church would be pastorally responsible to withdraw the involvement, interpretation, and help it has provided for these years in the past. The problem is that the help does not seem to help very much; the interpretation tends to obscure. Truly sensitive involvement of the Church needs to consider such basic questions as these: Can a long process of personal development be met effectively by a single rite at any point within the process? If it can, should any two persons find the same point suitable for themselves? Might not the dynamics of coming-of-age be met better by a flexible response—a rite corresponding with moments of need or recognition and repeated as such moments recur? And most important of all, if the spoken ratification of baptismal vows is an important action of a person of faith, why must that action be associated normally with childhood? We never stop in our encounter with developmental stages and their tasks. We make a lifelong response to the baptismal reality. The privilege of bearing witness to that response ought not to end as though it were a childish thing to be put away.

---

63. See the symposium "The Proper Age for a Declaration of Faith," in *Religious Education*, LVIII, 1963, pp. 411-442.

Where Questions are Being Felt: (3) First Communion

The classic initiatory rites of the Christian community formed a sequence which ended in the Eucharist. This sequence cannot be shown to have been Christian practice from the start; the earliest New Testament accounts do not connect Baptism with the Eucharist. Yet once this succession of rites emerged in the second century, it proved to be coherent, expressive, and durable.[64]

In the early Church's understanding, Baptism was for the forgiveness of sins. It was an unrepeated, once-for-all rite, signifying a basic cleansing and the entry on a new condition. It sealed the relation in which a Christian stands with God. The baptismal rite led up to the Communion - the meal by which the baptismal fellowship was sustained. The Eucharist, too, was for the forgiveness of sins. But it was often repeated, signifying renewed absolution and the restoration of the baptismal condition.

There is, anciently and now, an impressive mutuality between the two Gospel sacraments. The experience of redemption calls for both of them. Christian faith brings one into a relationship with God in Christ which endures through every circumstance and every lapse from the new life, for it is rooted in God's character and promise. That is the reality for which Baptism stands. But, for our part, we are careless and neglectful; we need the meaning of that constant relationship to be gathered up and expressed freshly. We often act as though Christ were not Lord, as though God's Name were not written upon us. We need a renewal of the awareness of the favor of God. That is the reality for which the Eucharist stands. As an English theologian put it: "In Christian Baptism the whole course of the believer's life is summed up in one moment to be realized in all that follows, and this actualization is achieved primarily through the Eucharist."[65]

Persons born within the Western Christian tradition have had little opportunity to grasp the relation between Baptism and Communion. They usually know Baptism with little connection with Eucharist, and Eucharist with little express relation with Baptism. The Easter Vigil, of course, provides a yearly expression of the Paschal Mystery in its fulness. This great festival of the Church Year dramatizes the relation between Baptism and the Eucharist and expresses the participation of both Gospel sacraments in the redemptive history of Christ. It gives an occasion of renewal in the central, saving reality which can inform the other baptisms and eucharists throughout the year. This ritual observance is increasingly used and understood. Yet many persons, it may be supposed, think of the Church's sacramental occasions as separate from one another, for that is the way they experience them.

---

64. Bouyer, L., *Liturgical Piety*, University of Notre Dame, 1955 "According to the mind of the ancient Church, Baptism and Confirmation had no meaning except as milestones on the way to the Eucharist," p. 164.

65. Davies, *op. cit.*, p. 124.

The usual initiatory pattern in the Episcopal Church allows a dozen years to elapse between Baptism and the beginning of its renewal in Holy Communion. This separation of the rites is certain to cloud the unity of their meaning. The anomaly of baptized but non-communicant Christians has become so familiar that it goes unchallenged and unanalyzed. Why, if Baptism is full Christian initiation, does it not lead at once to communicant status? There is a widespread feeling that reception of Holy Communion should belong to a later stage of experience and be conditional upon some understanding of the rite and the faith of which it speaks. It is difficult to say just how much understanding is thought to be necessary, or why such tests should be imposed on children but not on adults. Similarly, it is difficult to see why the two Gospel sacraments are treated differently. If understanding is required for receiving the Communion, why is it not required for Baptism? If infancy does not exclude a person from one of the sacraments of initiation, why should it exclude him from the other? Any argument against admitting children to the Eucharist argues equally against baptizing them.

If the Eucharist were to be re-associated with Baptism, and if, as appropriate, children began coming to Communion at a much earlier age than has been customary, some revision of the emphases of eucharistic piety would be involved. Admission to Communion would no longer belong to a second stage of initiation, corresponding to new opportunities and demands of teenage years. It would belong instead to childhood, corresponding perhaps to sitting at dinner with parents and guests. It, like infant Baptism, would be a witness to God's love for us prior to our ability to comprehend. The eucharistic life would not be begun when a certain level of understanding had been attained; rather, understanding would grow within the experience of a practicing communicant. A child might well grow up not remembering a time when he was not receiving, with his family, at the Lord's Table.[66]

In the nineteenth century, the Roman Catholic Church began a practice which altered the sequence of the rites of initiation. Baptism was administered to

---

66. See:

Holmes, Urban T., *Young Children and the Eucharist*, Seabury Press, New York: 1972.

Bretscher, Paul G., "First Things First: A Question of Infant Communion," *Una Sancta*, Vol. 24, 1963, pp. 34-50.

Crawford, Charles "Infant Communion: Past Tradition and Present Practice," *Theological Studies* 31, 1970, pp. 523-536.

Dalby, J.M.M. "The End of Infant Communion," *Church Quarterly Review*, Vol. 167, 1966, pp. 59-71.

Fisher, J.D.C., *Christian Initiation: Baptism in the Medieval West*, ch. 6 "The Separation of Communion from Initiation."

Senn, Frank C. "Confirmation and First Communion: A Reappraisal", *Lutheran Quarterly*, Vol. 23, 1971, pp. 178-191.

Prayer Book Studies 18: Holy Baptism With The Laying-on-of Hands, The Church Pension Fund, New York: 1970.

infants by local pastors. Children made their first Communion, normally prepared for by first confession, at the age of six or seven. This first Communion traditionally became an important occasion for the parish and for each child. Confirmation came at an episcopal visitation when children had reached twelve years or so.

The integrity of the traditional sequence, which this practice violates, is regarded by some Roman Catholic scholars as a matter of importance.[67] The primitive sequence, they argue, provided part of the significance of the rites, and hence is an element of the sacramental sign. The modern alteration of the sequence makes the sacraments of initiation less coherent.

Some changes are taking place in the practice of this Roman Catholic pattern. First Communion is being made at earlier ages and at parents' discretion in some jurisdictions. There is some movement towards confirming at a very late age and on the initiative of the confirmed. This change would make Confirmation unambiguously adult in character. It is supposed that if this practice were widely adopted, only a portion of the baptized and communicating members would seek Confirmation; but if that step involved serious study and commitment, the confirmed members would bring vitality to the Church out of proportion to their numbers.

Changes in traditional practice have begun in Anglicanism as well. At the Lambeth Conference of 1968, the Bishops reported:

"We commend the following alternatives as possible lines of experiment:

"(a) Admission to Holy Communion and Confirmation would be separated. When a baptized child is of appropriate age, he or she would be admitted to Holy Communion after an adequate course of instruction. Confirmation would be deferred to an age when a young man or woman shows adult responsibility and wishes to be commissioned and confirmed for his or her task of being a Christian in society.

"(b) Infant Baptism and Confirmation would be administered together, followed by admission to Holy Communion at an early age after appropriate instruction. In due course, the Bishop would commission the person for service when he or she is capable of making a responsible commitment."[68]

The two directions which it was suggested that Anglican practice might take indicate the lack of consensus in the Church on Christian initiation. The

---

67. Fransen, Piet "The Oikonomia and the Age of Confirmation," in *Intelligent Theology*, Vol. ll, Franciscan Herald Press, Chicago: 1969, pp. 25 f.; and

Kavanagh, Aidan "Initiation: Baptism and Confirmation," *Worship*, Vol. 47, 1972, p. 262 and f.

Fr. Kavanagh remarks "The sequence of Baptism-Confirmation-Eucharist is with almost no exceptions regarded as intrinsic both to the nature of the initiation process and to the intelligibility of it for catechetical purposes," p. 271.

68. *The Lambeth Conference 1968*, Seabury Press, New York: 1968, p. 99.

two are dissimilar—perhaps even contradictory. Yet both are defensible, and both are being tried.

Yet, either of the recommendations of Lambeth would have the effect of associating Communion more closely with Baptism.[69] This may be a productive line for further thinking. For generations Anglicans have debated the separation of Baptism and Confirmation; the paths of argument are well-worn. It has not always been brought into the discussion that when Confirmation is separated from Baptism, and the classic sequence remains intact, Communion is also separated from Baptism. This division of Communion from Baptism is a separable question and deserves consideration on its own merits.

It is true that a baptized person who is not yet admitted to Communion is a member of the Body of Christ and is not cut off from the Holy Spirit or the redemptive life of the Church. But the question seems now to be: why, if Baptism is full Christian initiation, does it not admit one into the full sacramental practice of the Christian life? If the Eucharist is a meal of a caring, supporting community—a meal which speaks of Jesus sharing himself in the life of his people—its reality can impart itself to a child before he can think out its meaning or reduce it to words. When he does begin to think, his experience will have given him something to think about.

When considering first Communion, it is not only the case that allowing Communion to be association with Baptism as a rite of Christian childhood has something to be said for it; it is also the case that the conventional association of Communion with Confirmation as a rite of adolescence has had some undesirable (and possibly seldom-admitted) consequences.

The educational processes of the Episcopal Church seem to have been ordered very largely for the task of preparing children for Confirmation and for communicant status. There have been and are important exceptions. But all too often Christian education of children, despite devoted work by many people, has not been significant. A spurt of overambitious, content-centered, teaching leads up to Confirmation and first Communion. After that, involvement in learning processes declines rapidly. This pattern tends to say that educational work exists for the purpose of making communicants in the Church. Catechesis is connected with a natural completion (confirmation by a Bishop) and a new status (communicant). Such a thrust seems introverted and ecclesiastical at a time in history when the processes of the Church dare not turn in upon themselves. The aim of Christian education ought to be the making of servants of Christ (of whatever age) for his work *in the world*.[70] The redemptive reality signified by Baptism is

---

69. As the Lambeth statement itself recognized and commended, *ibid*.

70. For an attempt to describe this kind of Christian Education, see Hunter, David R., *Christian Education as Engagement*, Seabury Press, New York: 1963; and Russell, Letty M., *Christian Education in Mission*, Westminster Press, Philadelphia: 1967.

a reality for-the-world. The administration of Christian initiation ought not to appear to bring children to a new ecclesiastical status and then to have nothing more for them. Yet something rather like that has established itself as the general pattern. The adolescent rite has seemed too much like an end, an achievement. Nothing sustains it inevitably afterward. Thus the rite of Confirmation has come to be, in practice, what one eminent Roman Catholic theologian termed "the sacrament of exit from the Church."[71]

The Dynamics of Becoming

Christian Initiation in the modern West has been, generally speaking, unwilling to settle for a rite that provides a sacramental standing for infants. A one-stage rite for an infant has been felt to be incomplete. (A multi-stage rite for an adult has, to cite the other side, often been questioned. It risks psychological redundancy and theological confusion.) At a time when Christian life seems likely to call for serious decision—not only at the "age of discretion," but repeatedly, over a lifetime—this characteristic intuition of the West cannot be disregarded.

A. The Dynamism of Western Culture

Ever since the Renaissance and most intensely since the Romantic movement, the Western mind has been fascinated with the individual person and his development. The inner propulsions, the conflicts, frustrations, and satisfactions of personal growth have been recurrent themes of literature, psychology, and philosophy. Montaigne, Goethe, Kierkegaard, Dickens, Freud, Jung, and Joyce, will perhaps suggest the dominance of such interests. The passage from innocence to experience, the ordering of self-awareness in spiritual autobiography, the generational conflict, coming to terms with authority and life's "givens," the personal quest, the sense in experience of stages—of beginnings, middle, and end—in these are the materials of novel, drama, personality theory, and of modern self-definition. Modern man is *homo viator*.

Persons grow, as natural things grow. But consciousness, with its pain and glory, means that persons can refuse to grow, or they can grow in distorted ways. In their persistent quest for themselves, they may mistake the mark. For human beings growth is not something that happens; it is a problem, a responsibility, a venture, and a fulfillment.

With such preoccupations as these having dominated the experience of the West for many generations, it is understandable that rites of Christian initiation which take no account of process, of the movement towards maturity, seem

---

71. Fransen, Piet, *op. cit.*, p.34.

to leave something out. The Church needs to be a place for children, as well as adults, and initiatory liturgy ought to say so. But the Church needs also to be a place in which children grow up. Should not liturgy be expected to say this too? "Becoming a Christian" dare not settle for a childhood stage only. To do so risks settling for arrested development. The real problem of the Christian community in a post-Christian society is not "How can we make more children ritually complete Christians?" The more urgent question is "Why are there not more effective adult Christians?" The discussion of Christian Initiation cannot leave out the process that must follow any infancy rite. How does one get from the desired beginning to the desired end?

B. The Prophetic Christian Message

The Christian message presents itself to us as a Word with which we must come to terms. That Word holds the redemption and the judgement of every institution and person which bears it. The Christian Gospel is given primarily as a history, an event, a Good News which is not invented out of our needs and insights. The central event—the life, death and resurrection of Jesus Christ—is set in the midst of two communities, their histories and their faith. Thus the Christian message has an inescapable reference to geography, to time, to names. The significance of "under Pontius Pilate" in the Creed is often noted. The long and complex history has its unity through the constant activity of God redeeming, imparting himself, and calling, and men believing, and obeying—or else not.

But, for those born under Christian influence, God does not first meet us in terms of past and distant events. He meets us here and now in birth, growth, parents, community, play, and work—in the love of those near us and in the discovery of an order into which to grow. If ultimately we must encounter him on his terms, he begins by presenting himself to us on ours. In every situation of our experience God stands in confrontation and grace, offering us an opportunity for reaching out into the future to which he calls—or else for drawing back in unfaith.

But God cannot be adequately apprehended in terms of processes of personal and social life. A God who could be so discerned would be the immanent God of nature, tribe, family, and custom. The God of biblical faith is the God of history, not of natural cycles. He is Lord over all nations. If he calls a family, it is for the sake of all families. He is the God of surprise, rather than the predictable God of tradition. The God who meets us in the midst of our existence is the God and Father of our Lord Jesus Christ. He has declared himself to us as truly as in the Son, who "bears the very stamp of his nature." He asks us to meet him as he is, not as we might prefer him to be. The God of the prophets is not a God we can expect to ratify prevailing concepts of home, nation, or personal development. God in Christ transcends every vehicle. by which he is met. He introduces himself into our experience by parents, family, and congregation. But the prophetic note of the biblical message implies that he may teach us to differ constructively with parents, family, and congregation. He calls us by local, personal experience to serve universal ends. We are creatures of time and space, and the awareness of God reaches us through the particular relationships and structures which inform and order our existence. Yet the God who so reaches us can call us to bring about change in the only social and religious structures we have ever known.

The Church ought to provide for the recognition, in celebration or commitment, of such things as membership, growth, crisis, and vocation, whenever they come in Christian experience. But the liturgical provision for such occasions must set them in the context of God in redemptive, judging, sovereign love. Ritual in the Christian community is not just to acknowledge the presence of God in our developmental crises. It is for the recognition of God in his own Gospel. The Church's rites of passage do not center primarily on babyhood, parenthood, or coming of age. Rather, they set all of the generations of the Church—youth and age—in the context of the fullest expression of word and sacrament. The persons involved are not dealing with a moment of personal transition alone, but with the living God whose self-revelation reaches into the depths of life to shatter and rebuild. Such moments of passage ought all to be either the introduction to, or a significant ratification of, the baptismal reality and commitment. They ought to represent renewed dealings with the Gospel of which Baptism speaks.

C. The Generations and Rites of Passage

Liturgical provision for becoming a Christian and for recognizing growth in Christian life is governed not only by the specific character of the Christian message which such ritual occasions serve. It is governed also by the generational situation of our time.

As long as Christendom prevailed, rites of passage could be seen as moments at which a young person moved into patterns of life, which, in most essentials, had been determined by, and were represented in, the style of an older generation. The adults tended to look on with satisfaction as this socialization process took each fresh step. But such assumptions hardly apply to the complex relationship between generations in today's society.

Ours is not a time in which the old teach the young, or in which "becoming" is a demand that falls to youth alone. Probably all serious learning is mutual; we are able to teach others at the level at which we are meeting and dealing with our own questions; the effort to teach always confronts the sensitive teacher with the need to repossess what he has. Teaching and learning are parts of a single process which takes place within both instructors and students.

Part of growing up in our time is that children are forced rapidly into a body of perceptions and ways which separate the young from the old, and often make them critical of the life patterns into which they seem to be expected to grow up.

Part of adult experience in our time is that we come to recognize that, despite ourselves, we learn significantly from the young. Roles are mixed. The young reject much of the older generation's ways and wisdom, but often on the basis of ideals professed by that older generation. The adults feel threatened by the young, yet ultimately many adults have been liberated and changed by them. Each generation needs the other; each has difficulty understanding the other; each has been the teacher of the other.[72]

In this complex situation, rites of passage within the Church dare not appear to be carefully controlled ritualizations, by which an older generation seeks to impose its idea of what is good for a younger generation. The facts of the present time are that where Christian community is vital, both old and young are assisting one another in greater awareness of God, redemption, community, and obedience. The process of "ratifying" in life the meaning of Baptism is not one in which the adults can appear to have dealt with the matter and to wait for youth to do what they have done. The only authority an adult has for seeking a response to Baptism on the part of someone else is the authority of one who asks of others no more than he is asking freshly of himself. "Confirmation," as an expression of Christian response, is a lifelong demand and joy. Ritual ought to provide for saying so.

The Proposed Rite: Some Principles

The foregoing sections of this essay have surveyed some of the problems and points of view that are now part of the ecumenical conversation about Christian initiation. It should be apparent that many serious questions are in the air. Yet new possibilities and new insights are also present.

No liturgical change can by itself solve all of the problems or utilize all of the fresh possibilities. Choices which must be made will assign priorities and reject some lines of development.

Two further factors may be noted which define the present context of liturgical change:

First, no church's practice of Christian initiation is ever entirely a matter of liturgical rites. No baptismal text has ever stood alone. It is always supported, and in some respects limited, by teachings and practices which particularize and fill out its meaning, perhaps in partially different ways. Such factors as theologies (in Anglicanism, none of them official or definitive), popular understandings, preaching, catechetical practices, hymns, ceremonial, art, role expectations of

---

72. Mead, Margaret, *Culture and Commitment: A Study in the Generation Gap*, Doubleday, New York: 1970; esp. ch. 1.

clergy, parents and congregations all shape the process of becoming a Christian. Any rite, as it is lived, is a combination of the rite itself and the things that are read into it.

Ritual expresses and gives form to an inner life which it does not create. Where the faith that gives Baptism its reality is weak, liturgies in themselves will not renew it. A crisis in Christian initiation is a crisis in the Church's understanding of itself as it lives under God and in relation to the society in which it is set. Official liturgical texts in themselves can give only limited direction. Processes of change in baptismal understanding and practice are under way. We have departed from the rather uniform Anglican pattern of the past, but, unless a consensus is taking shape now, there is little agreement about what direction to take. Powerful forces—only partly understood—are at work. Liturgical changes can do only a few things. They can loosen uniform regulations which have come to seem arbitrary and restrictive. They can open new possibilities where there is widespread dissatisfaction with old practice. They can preserve, in the midst of change, the essential action and meaning of the sacraments of initiation. That is a great deal, but it is not everything.

Second, we are in a pluralistic society, a pluralistic Church, and a pluralistic church-society relationship. The Episcopal Church probably must expect, allow for, and learn to enjoy living with differences in baptismal practice. It is unlikely that any one pattern will be equally applicable everywhere. Factors such as coming of age, family structure, child rearing, employment, the relation of generations, and provincial religious traditions—all matters which influence Christian Initiation—vary so much throughout the United States that local, diverse experiment will be called for. New styles of life, thought and community are coming into being. As the forces and trends that shape our society are felt widely, the varieties of baptismal understanding and practice that have represented differences between churches will probably come to be included *within* most churches.

Pastors, parents, and children who are at home with certain initiatory practices may have to learn to coexist charitably within a single congregation with those who have come to live happily and responsibly under other practices. The society is mobile, and people accustomed to one practice can quickly find themselves in an area where another practice predominates. But this is not some remote, painful possibility; it is the condition now. Confirmation practice has varied widely in recent years. The lines of experiment commended by Lambeth and the varied courses allowed in the General Convention action on *Prayer Book Studies* 18 all have tended to break down uniformity. Nothing seems likely to reverse the trend towards diversity. If it is caused by a realistic Christian response to a diverse situation, it may represent a direction in which the Church is being called to change and learn.

The Shape of the Proposed Rite

The simplest way in which to express the distinctive feature of the rites set forth here may be to say that they separate the functions that have been combined in Confirmation as it has been known in the Episcopal Church. Some of the historical, theological, and practical considerations which make this s seem like a desirable change at this time have been indicated in the foregoing sections of this essay.

The post-baptismal blessing, as has been described earlier, is a detached portion of the early Church's baptismal liturgy. As such, it is inherently a rite of a moment, done once in a lifetime. The learning and growing—and forgetting and starting again—which is a Christian response to the grace of Baptism, is a lifelong process. It requires a ritual expression appropriate to its specific character. The combination of these two significantly different functions in one rite seems to detract from each. We look for one expressive moment for ratifying baptismal promises (one part of what has been known as Confirmation), and in our time there is no such moment. We seek, at the time of ratifying the baptismal promises, a divine gift which has its own reality, but which is definably distinct from Baptism (another part of what has been known as Confirmation), but we seek it in a rite which, in its origin, had no identity except within the completeness of the initiatory sacrament.

The rites now being proposed make a different combination of functions. Water baptism is followed immediately by the signing with the cross ("consignation"). This unified sacramental rite confers full Christian standing and should, in principle, reach its completion in the baptized person's first Communion and entry on full life in the Christian community. That aspect of Confirmation which has been catechetical, voluntary, and responsive is made a separate service, to be used at the Bishop's visitation, and to be used when occasion warrants. It is a way of relating the growth, the restorations, and the new departures of Christian experience to the unrepeated starting point in Holy Baptism.

The vindication of this division of the functions of traditional Confirmation must be found in the rites themselves, as they are read and discussed in the Church, and as they may be tested in the practice of the living Christian fellowship. But a few further comments can be made about the implication of this reshaping.

Baptism as the One Rite of Initiation

The rites given in *Prayer Book Studies* 26 do not have the two-stage structure that has been the common Anglican use. The two rites are differently related to one another. No norm of infant Baptism and adolescent Confirmation is stated or implied, and no adult who is baptized will have to ratify his already adult vows in order to enter on the full rights of a Christian. This simple change may help clarify what Baptism is. Christian initiation is not a birth rite. No part of it is by nature an adolescent rite. Nor is Christian initiation a specifically adult rite. It is basically a rite of being joined to Christ and his people. As such, it is appropriate to any life-stage when proper pastoral conditions are met. At any life-stage, it is irresponsible when proper conditions are not met.

At whatever stage of life a person is baptized, the rite used would be essentially the same, and in every case sacramentally complete. The one Baptism unites persons who come to faith by many routes. Various experience patterns can inform one another; none is normative; the liturgy of Baptism is not written for one pattern, so that other patterns seem exceptional. The Church ought to be a fellowship in which the twice-born and the once-born coexist in the new life. Each needs the other. One keeps the Church from being a community of the unconverted—surely a deplorable condition. The other keeps the Church from being a community of the converted—a condition ahnost as bad. The single, uniform, complete rite of Baptism is a sign that membership in Christ and his people is not bound to any single model of personal experience.

The unified rite of baptism, consignation, and eucharist is here set forth as the standard. Whenever the rite is administered (except in emergency conditions) and to whomever, all of it should be administered. It is not liturgically fragmented or theologically ambiguous. The prayer for the gift of the Spirit is restored to the rite of Baptism, not because it supplies something otherwise lacking in Baptism, but because it expresses something that is part of the meaning of Baptism, but whichseems to be less clear if left implicit. There should be no question. In Christian initiation, all of God is linked with all of a person. All that is pledged for the future is signified at the start.

It is not just the redemptive meanings—forgiveness, Christ, Church, the Spirit—that are included in Baptism; it is also the commitments of Christian life. Baptism is—or ought to be understood as being—a commissioning for rministry; it is strength for spiritual combat; it is the ordination of the laity; it is the sacrament of childhood and of maturity. It sets one within the people of God, the holy priesthood; it brings one into the eucharistic fellowship. There is nothing left over that must be said at a later stage because it was not said at Baptism.

Being and Becoming

However complete Baptism may be sacramentally, it must always be considered the beginning of a process of response. It is apparent in the case of infant Baptism that the demonstration of the meaning of the rite must come after it. The child is set within the new order and life. Momentous things are declared in his or her behalf by others. But any conscious difference it will make to the child will come later, if it comes at all. It may not be equally clear that most of the same factors apply in the case of adult Baptism. An adult convert, to be sure, brings articulate faith of his own at the time of baptism. But faith is not a momentary experience.

It is a deeply held orientation of all of life. The faith that underlies the baptismal event can at best be only the start of the faith which, from that point on, must underlie the baptismal life. Momentous things are declared by the one baptized at the moment of baptism, but the validation of those declarations will come later, if it comes at all. No Baptism, adult or infant, ought to be carried out without care for antecedent conditions that make it a responsible act. But every Baptism is also an act of expectation and promise; it looks to what comes after it.

In the terminology of the New Testament and the early Church, anyone baptized was spoken of as newly born. The categories of infancy and age which were characteristically used of baptized persons were not terms of chronological age, but of salvation. They spoke of a life begun.[73]

The motivation of Christian life is often expressed as "become what you are." The baptism rite should say as much as possible about "what you are." It is a summation at the start, of that which can only be fully apprehended at the end. But from the start, the "becoming" develops from the "is." To say much about "what you are" at the beginning, does not remove the urgency from the "becoming." Rather, it sets the process in perspective. From Baptism on, all of life is a response to the total, loving self-giving of God signified by Baptism. The demand for response is total and absolute. The actuality of response is limited and partial. At any moment, as much of a baptized Christian as he can commit, ought to respond as fully as he can, to as much of the love and will of God as he knows. Response to God moves in individual ways, gradual or impulsive, with crises, struggle, lapses, and restorations. The baptismal life begins at the font and never ends.

The ritual of the Church ought to provide expressions for this life of response. The sacramental system is concerned about the process of "becoming" as well as about the declaration of what "is." They are together parts of the "now" and the "not yet" of life in Christ.

Response to Baptism involves the whole texture of life: inward, unsharable depths; thought and imagination; relation with others; work, play, citizenship, and a thousand things. Ritual simply provides moments which gather up, express, inform, or reorient—routinely, or in moments of personal concentration—the meaning of that constant response.

Three moments of liturgical response seem particularly focal:

One is the frequent participation in the Eucharist as the repeated renewal of the community in the redemptive life. Little specific connection is made in the communion liturgies with the baptismal starting point. However, as had been commented, the Easter Vigil is a rich and powerful dramatization of the unity of the

---

73. See the brilliant article, Morrison, Clinton "Baptism and Maturity," in *Interpretation*, XVII, 1963, pp. 387-401.

Gospel sacraments. But for those who sense the relationship, Baptism, the sign of redemption once given, and Communion, the sign of redemption ever renewed, have an eloquent complementarity.

Another occasion of renewal of Baptism is the participation. in the baptism of others. Here the already baptized community makes its own promises of the one baptized. It is reminded of the gift in which its own life is constituted. In a deep identification, another's "no" to sin and "yes" to God is said again for oneself. One's own past and future are made present Both of these liturgical rites can say much for us, if there is much within us needing to be said. But in our time, some personalization of this infinitely varied life of response seems desirable. Confirmation has done something like this in the past, but it has only allowed for it to be done once, and the moment for doing it usually seemed abritrarily chosen.

The proposed "Form for the Affirmation of Baptismal Vows with the Laying-on of Hands by the Bishop, also called Confirmation" is a specific occasion, at the Bishop's visitation, for a public renewal in the gift, and commitment to the responsibilities of Baptism. It is not intended to be the completion of Baptism; Baptism is not incomplete. But it represents the solemn renewal of the baptismal covenant. It is therefore especially_ ppropriate for those who come to a new and deeper understanding of the meaning of their Baptism and wish to rededicate themselves to the Church's mission, for those who return to the life of the Church after a period away from it, or for those who enter the Episcopal Church from another. The Bishop's laying-on of hands is the traditional and appropriate climax of this rite. The minister of this rite is thus the chief pastor, through whom the life of the Church most obviously widens into the historical and the present day world-wide Christian fellowship.

This provision for personal response and affirmation may have the flexibility which will let it fit the various circumstances of our changing experience. This renewal of baptismal promises made before the Bishop is not associated with any one designated moment of life; it can be used at any age; and it can be used more than once. No special status or privilege attaches to it; thus it should not create an elite within the fellowship. It imposes little and allows for much.

The Proposed Rite: A Commentary

The rites of *Prayer Book Studies* 26 will be found to contain a mixture of the familiar and the unfamiliar. Some comments on their specific features may be helpful.

The text contains two services:

The service of Holy Baptism (pages 133-141) contains all of the essential material which has formed the Prayer Book baptismal order, plus the post-baptismal blessing which has been in the past one part of Confirmation. The parts of this service comprise a liturgical unity, and they are performed by the Minister of Baptism. This service would, of course, be used only once in the life of any Christian person. It contains the actions which give full sacramental standing within the people of Christ and entry into the eucharistic life. It represents the gracious acceptance which God does not retract and whose sign is not repeated.

The "Form for the Affirmation of Baptismal Vows with the Laying-on of Hands by the Bishop also called Confirmation" (pages 142-146) seeks to develop more explicitly the adult ratification of baptismal promises—the catechetical function of Confirmation. For any individual Christian this service would not be part of a once-for-all rite of becoming a Christian. Baptism in its completeness is that. Neither is it meant to be associated specifically with a moment of coming of age. It is not a ritual admission to communicant status. Rather, it represents the unpredictable reality of the human response to grace. It provides a ritual opportunity within the Christian community for the expression, publicly and before the Bishop, of some of the moments of restoration, recognition, and new beginning which mark the stir of life.

These two rites are so designed that they may conveniently be used together. The promises which are renewed in the affirmation service are those said in the baptism service which will usually have immediately preceded it. The Eucharist beginning with the Intercession or the Offertory ordinarily would follow. When the Bishop is present, he is the presiding minister of the entire sequence of rites, assisted by such other ministers as he may appoint.

When these services are used together, the Bishop presiding, the sequence of actions is as follows: the service opens; lessons are read; and the Word of God is preached. The candidates for Baptism are presented; they make their renunciations and promises, either speaking for themselves or else godparents speaking for them; the water and the chrism, if it is used, are blessed; the candidates are baptized and sealed with the sign of the cross (made with chrism, if desired); they are greeted and received by the congregation. Those who are to make special affirmations of their baptismal vows are presented. (Attention has been called to them before the saying of the Creed in the order of Baptism.) These persons renew before the Bishop, their commitment to the call of God signified in their Baptism; the Bishop prays for them and lays his hand on them; all exchange the peace. The service continues with the Offertory of the Eucharist. A simple alternative ending has been provided, when the Eucharist does not follow.

This sequence of events is fairly straightforward. The printed form of these rites, however, must allow for exceptional conditions in which they must sometimes be used. There may be baptisms but no affirmations of baptismal vows, either because the bishop is not present or because no persons are, prepared for this special observance. There may be persons prepared to affirm their baptismal vows when the Bishop is present, but when no one is baptized. In that case, the vows are not said in the baptismal order; they are supplied as a part of the affirmation service. It is hoped that the rubrics make clear how these rites combine in the various possible ways. A table on page 209 may further clarify the structure and relation of these services

A. Holy Baptism

Opening versicles, collect, lessons, sermon:

> The baptismal rite opens with a doxology and dialogue, and proceeds to a service of the Word like that which stands asthe first part of the Communion order. This practice is a link with the early Church in which initiatory rites took place within the Eucharist. But beyond historical precedent, Baptism is not a service which ordinarily stands alone, nor is it properly a rite which interrupts the progress of some other liturgical observance. It is the start of a unified sequence of initiatory acts whose completion is in the Eucharist itself. Moreover, the rite of Baptism is a response to the Word. Prior to the act of Christian initiation stands the Gospel, its proclamation and its hearing. The readings and preaching at Baptism set this sacrament within the context of God's redemptive work and the total faith and mission of the Church. Baptism is something the Church does for an individual, but on the basis of something God has done for mankind.

Presentation of the candidates:

> The custom that persons coming to an initiatory rite be presented by someone who sponsors them in their steps of entry traces to the early Church. Different meanings have been placed on this sponsorship at different times. But the practice remains 'valuable. The sponsor personalizes the concern of the Christian community for the individual initiate, before, during, and following his baptism.

Those candidates who can answer for themselves indicate, by their response to a question addressed specifically to them, that Christian Baptism is something they willingly seek.

Those who cannot make the baptismal commitments for themselves will be dependent on the communication of the love and support of God to them through others. Their own growing life of trust, love, and obedience will begin by being imparted by older Christians. The Godparents therefore commit themselves to the

Christian nurture of the one they present. The Godparents, however, are representatives of the adult generation which will share in the responsibility for a child being baptized. Thus the pledge to support the newly baptized is said by the entire congregation.

Renunciations:

A part of every initiatory rite is a separation from a former loyalty or condition. In the early Church, the renunciations had specific reference to pagan religions which were regarded as manifestations of the rule of the Evil One. But in any cultural and religious situation, adherence to God implies rejection of his rivals. Idolatry is a problem not of religious affiliation, but of human nature gone wrong. But evil is perceived differently in different ages. The three renunciations in this service correspond roughly to the traditional rejections of the devil, the world, and the flesh. But the phrasing is meant to relate the heart of the persistent human distortion of God's purpose to the terms of our modern experience. The first refers to a basic unmanageability in history. A discreative power is at work. Even with good intentions, destructive things are done, and we all consent in that perversion of life. The second refers to the ordering of human affairs, on large and small scales, in ways that oppress and demean persons and misuse God's creation. The third refers to that within us which mistakes our own priorities, finds evil attractive, and assigns final allegiance to something less than God.

Profession of Faith and Commitment:

The categorical "no" to loyalties which rival God is answered by a categorical "yes" to Cod himself. The promises are made first by the candidates in three brief affirmations. Then all join in making, or, in the case of the already baptized, in renewing, the baptismal profession of faith in the words of the Apostles' Creed. This formula grew up in the very early Christian generations as a summary of the Church's central message. It was the rule of faith, the tradition of what is to be believed. The Creed was the statement of the faith to which a new A Christian committed himself in the decisive step of Baptism. This credal formulary has thus been associated specifically with Baptism since early times. The Prayer Books of the Episcopal Church, unlike those of England, and unlike most other liturgies, have merely asked for belief in "all the articles of the Christian faith as contained in the Apostles' Creed" without using the full text. This rite uses the Creed in the question and answer form of the early Church. Persons who are already baptized use the Creed as an opportunity to renew the fundamental orientation of life to the realities witnessed in this ancient rule. Before the Creed is said, if there are those who will make special affirmations of their baptismal vows later in the service, the Bishop calls attention to their presence. The Creed, and the promises which follow it, will have special importance for what they are to do at a later point.

After the Creed, four promises are made. They pledge the candidate to faithfulness in the Christian fellowship, to the duty and joy of apostolate, to a relation in Christian love with other persons, and to the use of social structures for the common good. These promises identify some of the principal commitments that are inherent in the baptismal life.

Following the Creed and the promises, a short litany expresses the prayer of the congregation for those entering on Christian faith and life.

Blessing of the Water:

Introducing the action by a call to give thanks, the Bishop, or in his absence the priest, blesses the water of the font. This prayer of consecration draws on the rich biblical imagery of water. In the story of creation, in the account of the Exodus, and in the event of Jesus' baptism by John the Baptist, the Church has found symbols for the interpretation of its own rite. Centrally, however, Christian Baptism is understood by the Pauline teaching of a death and resurrection with Christ. This prayer also contains an allusion to the baptismal commission from the end of St. Matthew.

[*Blessing of the Chrism*: Anointing has not been a specified part of the baptismal services of the Prayer Books after 1549. However, there does not seem to have been strong feeling against it, and its use has become fairly widespread.[74] This rite makes explicit allowance for it, but does not require it. When the Bishop presides, he may bless Chrism for his own use at this service. Chrism so blessed may be used by the priest when he administers Baptism at other times.[75] The prayer refers to Christ as himself the Anointed One. The very term "Christ" means "the anointed", as does the derivative "Christian." In Luke 4:18, Jesus' ministry is spoken of as carried out by the promised anointing of the Spirit of the Lord, and Acts 10:38 speaks of Jesus as anointed with the Holy Spirit. Generally, anointing was used to set apart persons as kings or priests; it was a sign of an honor given by God himself. This prayer follows Acts 4:27 in specifying Jesus as anointed to be "servant", thus drawing attention to the evangelical paradox of the servant-king.

---

74. A great deal of historical information on this subject has been gathered in Mitchell, L. L., *op. cit.* Appendix I "Anglican Use of Baptismal Oil," pp. 177-187.

75. A rubric on page 146 permits the Bishop to use this prayer to bless Chrism for use at subsequent baptisms in the parish even when there are no persons to be baptized at this service.

This striking imagery of anointing, like the imagery of water, links the Christian initiatory rite with Christ and his redemptive significance.]

The Baptism:

At this central action of the rite, the text follows the traditional directions to the minister, and it uses the ancient trinitarian formula. The candidate's name is used, identifying and dignifying him in his personal uniqueness. The solemn trinitarian wording expresses the link of each baptized person with the fulness of God's own life. The congregation's "Amen" is a token of its participation in this act of Christ through his Church.

The prayer following the baptisms contains a revision of the old petition for "the seven-fold gift of the Spirit." A prayer along these lines has time-hallowed associations as a post-baptismal intercession. In the Prayer Book tradition, it has appeared in the Confirmation service. But its origin can be traced to a post-baptismal prayer, which in the patristic period accompanied the signing with the Cross. The list of seven gifts of the Spirit, as it has come through the sacramentaries and the Prayer Books, is repetitive. It was based on Isaiah 11:2 which describes the characteristics of a wise and peace-loving king. The Hebrew text cites six gifts; the list of seven depends on the Greek version of the Old Testament. The Christian use of this text to describe Jesus and Christian character is very old. The present prayer is a fresh paraphrase of the sources. In the first of the phrases used, it recalls Solomon's prayer, and it seeks to give greater precision and variety in this list of the gifts and graces of the Spirit.

The "sealing" is done by the Bishop if he is present, whether he administers Baptism personally or not, or, if the Bishop is not present, by the priest. It is done by the minister placing his hand on the recipient's head and marking a cross on his forehead. He may use the Chrism to mark the cross. This signing with the cross, technically known as "consignation," represented a restoration by Archbishop Cranmer of an early and catholic but non-Roman practice. It has been a continuous part of Anglican baptismal practice since the Prayer Book of 1552.

"Sealing" is not a word with a history in the official liturgical terminology of Anglicanism. But it is a useful identification for that portion of the confirmation action, as it has been known, which now becomes part of the total baptismal rite.[76] The "seal" suggests a picture of branding or stamping something, so that it can be identified as belonging to its rightful owner. From very early times, being a Christian was thought of as being sealed by the Holy Spirit. It was a mark

---

76. The term "Confirmation" is assigned now to the Affirmation service, and it would be confusing if it were also used to designate the part of the baptism rite now under consideration.

of God's possession, and a pledge of a bond with him that would endure, until he finally claimed all who were his at the day of redemption. This figure is not extensively developed in the New Testament.[77] However, in later generations, it became a common expression for the meaning of the rites of Christian initiation.

Throughout the early Church, whatever initiatory rites were observed were carried out as a continuous unity. The term "seal" could apply to the entire sequence, but so could the term "Baptism." In the course of time, in many parts of the Church, the gift of the Spirit—the "seal"—became specifically associated with one moment in the initiatory ceremonies, the post-baptismal anointing or laying-on of hands. In the West, the post-baptismal ceremonies became detached and grew into an independent rite.[78] To specify the gift of the Spirit as belonging to one point in the rite seems like an over-definition in the light of the varied practice and theological imprecision of the early centuries.

Yet the post-baptismal sealing is an appropriate feature of Christian initiation. It is part of the enacted *kerygma* of the initiatory sacrament. Anointing or signing with the cross are gestures of interpersonal physical contact which express some of the meanings of Christian membership and life. But it is highly desirable that these post-baptismal rites, once again, be as close as possible to Baptism, so that it may be clear that they explicate parts of the rich, unified meaning of becoming a Christian.

The newly baptized are greeted and presented to the congregation. The congregation and the minister together receive the new members into Christ's Church and encourage them to continue in his service.

If the Form for the Affirmation of Baptismal Vows is not to follow, the rubrics on page 139 give instructions for passing at once to the Eucharist.

Affirmation of Baptismal Vows:

> If the service of Affirmation of Baptismal Vows is to follow, those who wish to make such affirmations, "and have been duly prepared", are presented to the Bishop as soon as the newly baptized have been received. After the presentation to the Bishop, the service continues with the Dedication to Mission on page 145. The persons affirming their baptismal vows have already taken part, with the congregation, in a baptismal service in which vows have been taken or renewed by all. These persons are distinct in that some special meaning attaches for them to these

---

77. But see Ezek. 9:4-6; II Cor. 1:21-22; Eph. 1:13 and 4:30; and Rev. 7:3ff., 9:4, and 14:1. Valuable material on this image can be found in Lampe, G.W.H., *The Seal of the Spirit*, Longmans, London: 1951, and Danielou, J., *The Bible and the Liturgy*, Univ. of Notre Dame: 1956, ch.III, "The Sphragis."

78. See pp. 16 ff. of the present Supplement, especially Section D pp. 25 ff.

common words of pledge and commitment. Something has happened or is going to happen in their own experience which requires public expression, and which is appropriately related to the fundamental realities of believing existence expressed in Baptism. Thus the service of Affirmation of Baptismal Vows uses what has already taken place in the rite of Holy Baptism. It repeats none of it, but goes at once to that portion of the Affirmation service which looks ahead to life and mission.

Alternative ending:

If for any reason the rite of Holy Baptism is being observed apart from the eucharistic setting, the rubrics and prayers on pages 139 and 140 suggest ways of bringing the service to an adequate conclusion.

B. Affirmation of Baptismal Vows

In Baptism God declares what he has done, is doing, and will do for a person he has made and loves. He draws his child into a gracious, personal, articulate relation with himself, a relation that promises life abundant and everlasting.

Most persons, at Baptism, make the fullest response to God they are capable of making at the time. Godparents and adult converts earnestly try to enter into what the Church means by Baptism, insofar as they grasp it.

But the response to Baptism, which begins at once and permeates the whole texture of life, is never simple. Children have a lifetime in which the relation with God, declared on their behalf in infancy, is a factor in the tumultuous business of growing into responsible adulthood, facing education, marriage, and vocation, and assuming an authentic life-stance. The conscious relation with God may not survive as a creative, governing force in life. The adult who is baptized probably brings to his Baptism, along with much trust and idealism, many serious misunderstandings about what is involved. The life of faith on which he enters with enthusiasm will have surprises and difficulties, and will require constant death and resurrection. Faith sometimes lapses, at times to revive. Christian experience is inconstant at best. But the awareness of God sometimes grows in sudden accesses of insight and clarity - the recognition of a deeper relationship and new obligations and the acceptance of new disciplines.

The Form for the Affirmation of Baptismal Vows provides for, and encourages, the liturgical expression of some of the deep joy and serious rededication that is taking place in every vital congregation. Just what is done with this service depends on whether or not it meets an actual need, and meets it better than the once-for-all puberty rite which Confirmation tended to become, and whether pastoral imagination can develop its possibilities. The preparation for this service will take place in behind-the-scenes pastoral work, much of which will not be expressed at the service itself. Persons returning to Christian faith and fellowship, persons making a public affirmation of their faith and commitment to the responsibilities of Baptism, persons coming to a new church home—all of these, and perhaps more as experience may suggest, are persons who may well desire to relate their present experience to their Baptism and to articulate freshly their present level of response to God. The results of the counseling and soul-searching that may lie behind this service should show in a liturgy of celebration and joy. The rite is brief, especially when it is part of the baptism service. It provides a basic liturgical and theological structure which can help interpretritually some of the significant moments in Christian experience.

Versicles. Collect, Lessons, Sermon, Presentation, Creed and Promises:

All of this material duplicates that in the baptismal rite and is used only when there is no Baptism. When it is used, the collect and choice of lessons are changed from those in the baptismal rite to accord more closely with the function of this service. But the promises are identical with those made at Baptism.

Dedication to Mission:

The Bishop addresses those who have been presented to him. He cites the renewal of baptismal vows and the recognition of Christian calling which all have just made. The Bishop then asks these particular persons if they will renew their individual commitment to Christian life and work. The reply uses the language from the Prayer Book confirmation promise to follow Jesus Christ as Savior and Lord and from the Office of Instruction concerning "my bounden duty as a member of Christ's Church."

The Bishop's three-fold prayer draws first on themes of the redemptive work of Christ and the calling, in him, of the whole Church. The individual is a called person within a called people. But the call and the covenant are often renewed. The Creator recreates. He extends his summons freshly in new situations.[79] Within the faithfulness of God and the givenness of redemption in Christ, old patterns of life are broken to be replaced by new. The first part of the Bishop's prayer sets the restorations and new departures on which this service centers in the context of constancy and new beginnings of life under God.

Next, the Bishop lays his hand on each one individually, and, addressing him by name, commissions him. The prayer is concluded when the Bishop once again prays over the entire group of those who have renewed their vows and committed

---

79. Among many instances of this pattern in the Old Testament, see II Kings 23 [Josiah]; Nehemiah 8-10 [Ezra]. The setting of covenant renewal is often strongly liturgical.

themselves freshly to obedience and mission. The words of this last part are the familiar "Defend, O Lord," from the Prayer Book confirmation rite. It asks God to support these persons in all that they now enter upon. The people respond with a single *Amen* to the Bishop's three-fold prayer. The Peace is then exchanged.

The rubrics provide for the continuation of the service with the Eucharist or for a brief alternative ending.

The material headed "Concerning the Service" and "Additional Directions and Suggestions" on pages 132, and 141-143, should be self-explanatory. A few additional observations, however, may be useful.

The directions which precede the service of Holy Baptism, page 132-133, emphasize the role of the Bishop in Christian initiation. The rubrics of the service itself are written from the standpoint of baptisms at which he presides. Certain ministries are specifically his and are exercised only when he is present. Some ministries which the bishop performs when he is present may be done by others in his absence. When he presides, he may appoint others to assist him. The universal and historically continuous Church is the society to which a person is admitted at every Baptism. However, the scope of the baptizing community is most clearly indicated when it is represented visibly by a congregation gathered around a Bishop. Thus, even though full Baptism may be observed when the Bishop is not present (as valid Baptism may be performed with no clergyman of any order participating), all baptisms will takesome of their significance from their obvious derivation from the more complete observance which takes place when the Father in God presides.

The directions on page 141 recommend that Christian initiation be associated with certain specified times in the Christian Year. In the early Church, Baptism took place, except in emergency situations, at Easter and Pentecost. In the Middle Ages this association of Baptism with appropriate times broke down. The rubrics of the Anglican Prayer Books made no effort to specify times for baptisms. (Times for ordinations were recommended, though frequently not observed.) Most baptisms have been governed by the times when a child was born and Godparents could be conveniently assembled. The rubric suggests that the location of Baptism within the Christian Year can say something valuable about both Baptism and the Church's expressive use of time.

The rites of Christian initiation are basically actions. Important things are done. The acts in progress are articulated and interpreted by words. But the actions are basic. The rite now presented continues the elemental actions and meanings of the sacramental tradition. But certain new wordings are given; some new actions are included; and new sequences of basic movements are made possible. Ministers are reminded that the effectiveness of these rites in practice depends, to a great extent, not on how they read on paper, but on how they are enacted in use. Planning and practice will help these partially unfamiliar actions and wordings to go smoothly and coherently as they are actually used in bringing new members into the fellowship of Christ.

A chart showing the structure of the rites.

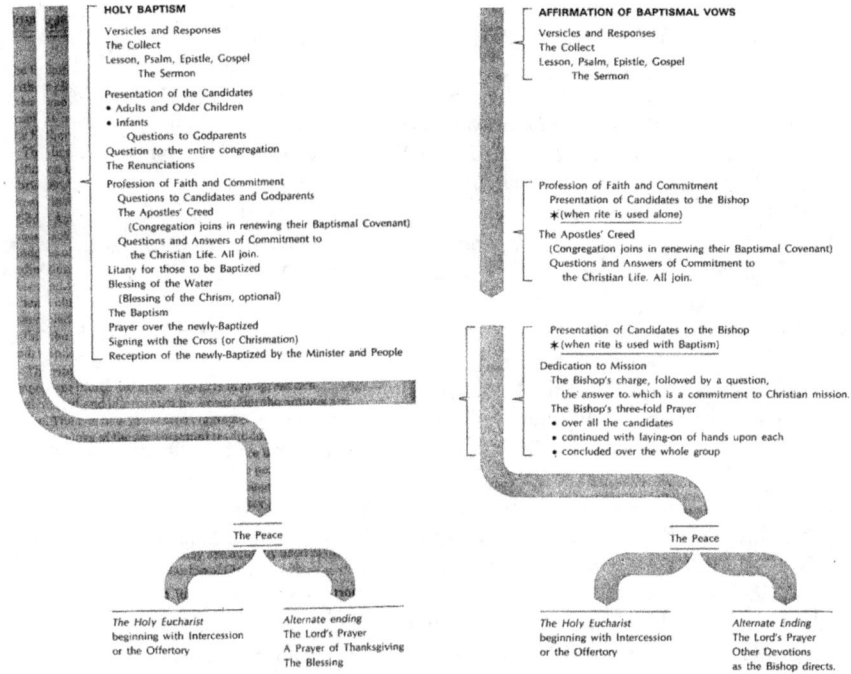

Bibliography

Books[80]

Akeley, T.C., *Christian Initiation in Spain c. 300-1100*, London: Darton, Longman and Todd, 1967.
Aland, K., *Did the Early Church Baptize Infants?*, Philadelphia: Westminster Press, 1963.
Arndt, E.J.F., *The Font and the Table*, Richmond: John Knox Press, 1967.
Bailey, D.S., *Sponsors at Baptism and Confirmation*, London: S.P.C.K., 1952.
Baillie, J., *Baptism and Conversion*, New York: Scribners, 1963.
Baptism and Confirmation, Standing Liturgical Commission, (*Prayer Book Studies I*), New York: Church Pension Fund, 1950.

---

80. For general works on Liturgy and Sacramentalism, see the Select Bibliography in *Prayer Book Studies* XVII Vol. 4, pp. 275-282, in *Prayer Book Studies* 18, Vol. 5, pp. 15-16, and *Prayer Book Studies* 21, Vol. 6, p. 31.

Baptism and Confirmation (Report of the Church of England Liturgical Commission), London: S.P.C.K., 1959.
Baptism and Confirmation Today (Report of the Joint Committees on Baptism, Confirmation and the Holy Communion of the Convocations of Canterbury and York), London: S.P.C.K., 1955.
Barth, K., *The Teaching of the Church Regarding Baptism*, London: S.C.M. Press, 1948.
Beasley-Murray, G.R., *Baptism in the New Testament*, London: Macmillan, 1963.
────── *Baptism Today and Tomorrow*, New York: St. Martin's Press, 1966.
Bohen, M., *The Mystery of Confirmation*, New York: Herder and Herder, 1963.
Bouyer, L., *Christian Initiation*, London: Burns and Oates, 1960.
Bromiley, G.W., *Baptism and the Anglican Reformers*, London: Lutterworth Press, 1953.
Carr, W., *Baptism: Conscience and Clue for the Church*, New York: Holt, Rinehart and Winston, 1964.
Christian Initiation: Birth and Growth in the Christian Society, Church of England Board of Education, London, 1971.
Commission on Education of the Lutheran World Federation, *Confirmation: A Study Document*, Minneapolis: Augsburg Publishing House, 1964.
Confirmation: or the Laying On Of Hands (Volume 1: Historical and Doctrinal), London: S.P.C.K., 1926.
Confirmation Crisis, New York: Seabury Press, 1968.
Crehan, J., *Early Christian Baptism and the Creed*, Westminster, Md.: Newman Press, 1950.
Cully, K.B. (ed.), *Confirmation: History, Doctrine, and Practice*, New York: Seabury Press, 1962.
Cullmann, O., *Baptism in the New Testament*, London: S.C.M. Press, 1950.
Davies, J.G., *The Architectural Setting of Baptism*, London: Barrie and Rockliffe, 1962.
Davis, C., *Sacraments of Initiation: Baptism and Confirmation*, New York: Sheed and Ward, 1964.
Dix, G., *Confirmation, or Laying on of Hands?* London: S.C.M. Press, 1950.
────── *The Theology of Confirmation in Relation to Baptism*, Westminster: Dacre Press, 1946.
Eliade, M., *Rites and Symbols of Initiation*, New York: Harper Torchbooks, 1965 (published by Harper in 1958 under the title *Birth and Rebirth*).
Every, G., *The Baptismal Sacrifice*, London: S.C.M. Press, 1959.
Fisher, J.D.C., *Christian Initiation: Baptism in the Medieval West*, London: S.P.C.K., 1965.
────── *Christian Initiation: The Reformation Period*, London: S.P.C.K., 1970.
Flemington, W.F., *The New Testament Doctrine of Baptism*, London: S.P.C.K., 1948.
Gilbert, W.K. (ed.), *Confirmation and Education*, Philadelphia: Fortress Press, 1969.
Gilmore, A., *Baptism and Christian Unity*, Philadelphia: Judson Press, 1966.
Gilmore, A. (ed.), *Christian Baptism: A Fresh Attempt to Understand the Rite in Terms of Scripture, History and Theology*, Philadelphia: Judson Press, 1959.
George, A. et al., *Baptism in the New Testament*, Baltimore: Helicon, 1964.
Greenslade, S.L., *Shepherding the Flock: Problems of Pastoral Discipline in the Early Church and in the Younger Churches Today*, London: S.C.M. Press, 1967.
Hamman, A. (ed.), *Baptism: Ancient Liturgies and Patristic Texts*, Staten Island: Alba House, 1967.
────── *The Paschal Mystery: Ancient Liturgies and Patristic Texts*, Staten Island: Alba House, 1969.

Holy Baptism with the Laying-on-of-Hands, (*Prayer Book Studies* 18) Standing Liturgical Commission, New York: The Church Hymnal Corporation, 1970.
Jagger, P., *Christian initiation: 1552-1969*, London: S.P.C.K., 1970.
Jeremias, J., *Infant Baptism in the First Four Centuries*, Philadelphia: Westminster Press, 1962.
────── *The Origins of Infant Baptism*, London: S.C.M. Press, 1963.
Lampe, G.W.H., *The Seal of the Spirit* (2nd ed.), London: S.P.C.K., 1967.
Marsh, H.G., *The Origin and Significance of the New Testament Baptism*, Manchester: Manchester Univ. Press, 1941.
Marty, M.E., *Baptism*, Philadelphia: Fortress Press, 1962.
Mason, A.J., *The Relation of Confirmation to Baptism*, London: Longmans, Green and Co., 1891.
Minchin, B. (ed.), *Becoming a Christian*, London: Faith Press, 1954.
Mitchell, L.L., *Baptismal Anointing*, London: S.P.C.K., 1966.
Modern Liturgical Texts, London: S.P.C.K., 1968.
Moody, D., *Baptism: Foundation for Christian Unity*, Philadelphia: Westminster Press, 1967.
Moss, B.S. (ed.), *Crisis for Baptism*, London: S.C.M. Press, 1965.
Neunheuser, B., *Baptism and Confirmation*, New York: Herder and Herder, 1964.
Pocknee, C.E., *Infant Baptism Yesterday and Today*, London: Mowbray, 1966.
────── *The Rites of Christian Initiation*, London: Mowbray, 1962.
────── *Water and the Spirit*, London: Darton, Longman and Todd, 1967.
One Lord One Baptism (Faith and Order Report), Minneapolis: Augsburg Publishing House, 1960.
Repp, A.C., *Confirmation in the Lutheran Church*, St. Louis: Concordia, 1964.
Schlink, E., *The Doctrine of Baptism*, St. Louis: Concordia, 1972.
Schnackenburg, R., *Baptism in the Thought of St. Paul*, New York: Herder and Herder, 1964.
The Theology of Christian Initiation (Report of a Theological Commission appointed by the Archbishops of Canterbury and York), London: S.P.C.K., 1949.
Thornton, L.S., *Confirmation: Its Place in the Baptismal Mystery*, Westminster: Dacre Press, 1954.
Thurian, M., *Consecration of the Layman: New Approaches to the Sacrament of Confirmation*, Baltimore: Helicon Press, 1963.
Wagner, G., *Pauline Baptism and the Pagan Mysteries*, Edinburgh: Oliver and Boyd, 1967.
Wagner, J. (ed.), *Adult Baptism and the Catechumenate*, New York: Paulist Press, 1967.
Wainwright, G., *Christian Initiation*, Richmond: John Knox Press, 1969.
Whitaker, E.C., *The Baptismal Liturgy*, London: Faith Press, 1965.
────── *Documents of the Baptismal Liturgy* (2nd ed., rev. and suppl.), London: S.P.C.K., 1970.
White, R.E.O., *The Biblical Doctrine of Initiation*, Grand Rapids: Eerdmans, 1960.
Wirgman, A.T., *The Doctrine of Confirmation*, London: Longmans, Green and Co., 1897.
Yarnold, E., *The Awe-Inspiring Rites of Initiation: Baptismal Homilies of the Fourth Century*, Slough: St. Paul Publications, 1971.

Selected Articles in English

"Baptism, Confirmation and the Eucharist," (Report on a Faith and Order Study), In *Studia Liturgica* 8 (1971-2), pp. 81-97.

Clark, Neville, "Christian Initiation," in *Studia Liturgica* 4 (1965), pp. 156-165.
"Documentation and Reflection: Confirmation Today," in *Anglican Theological Review* 54 (1972), pp. 106-119.
Finn, Thomas M. "Baptismal Death and Resurrection: A Study in Fourth Century Eastern Baptismal Thought," in *Worship* 43 (1969), pp. 175-179.
Goodson, Mercer L., "What About Confirmation By Priest?" in *The St. Luke's Journal* 16 (1972), pp. 72-80.
Guerette, R.H. "Ecclesiology and infant Baptism," *Worship* 44 (1970), pp. 433-437.
Jagger, Peter J. "The Anglican Rite of Infant Baptism: A Decade of Revision," in *Worship* 45 (1971), pp. 22-36.
Kavanagh, Aidan "Initiation: Baptism and Confirmation," in *Worship* 46 (1972), pp. 262-276.
Lee, E. Kenneth, "The Holy Spirit in Relation to Baptism and Confirmation," in *The Modern Churchman* 12 (1970), pp. 316-325.
Marsh, T., "Confirmation in its Relation to Baptism," in *The Irish Theological Quarterly* 27 (1960), pp. 259-293.
——— "The History and Significance of the Post-Baptismal Rites," in *The Irish Theological Quarterly* 29 (1962), pp. 175-206.
Mitchell, L.L., "The 'Shape' of the Baptismal Liturgy," in *Anglican Theological Review* 47 (1965), pp. 410-419.
——— "What Is Confirmation?" in *Anglican Theological Review* 55 (1973), pp. 201-212.
Morrison, Clinton, "Baptism and Maturity," in *Interpretation* 17 (1963), pp. 387-401.
Powers, Joseph M., "Confirmation, The Problem of Meaning," in *Worship* 46 (1972), pp. 22-29.
Shepherd, M.H. "Confirmation: The Early Church," in *Worship* 46 (1972), pp. 15-21.
Stanley, David M. "The New Testament Doctrine of Baptism: An Essay in Biblical Theology," in *Theological Studies* 18 (1957), pp. 169-215.
Stevick, Daniel B. "Confirmation for Today: Reflections on the Rite Proposed for the Episcopal Church," in *Worship* 44 (1970), pp. 541-560.
——— "Types of Baptismal Spirituality," in *Worship* 47 (1973), pp. 11-26.
Turner, H.E.W., et al. "One Baptism for the Remission of Sins" (a symposium), in *Theology* No. 544, Oct. 1965, pp. 455-479.
Wilburn, Ralph G. "The One Baptism and the Many Baptisms," in *Theology Today* (1965), pp. 59-83.
Wiles, M.F., "One Baptism for the Remission of Sins," in *Church Quarterly Review* 165 (1964), pp. 59-66.

www.ingramcontent.com/pod-product-compliance
Lightning Source LLC
Chambersburg PA
CBHW061348300426
44116CB00011B/2031